Facebook® Application Development

FOR

DUMMIES®

Facebook® Application Development

FOR

DUMMIES®

by Jesse Stay

WILEY

Wiley Publishing, Inc.

Facebook® Application Development For Dummies®

Published by
Wiley Publishing, Inc.
111 River Street
Hoboken, NJ 07030-5774

www.wiley.com

For general information on our other products and services, please contact our Customer Care Department within the U.S. at 877-762-2974, outside the U.S. at 317-572-3993, or fax 317-572-4002.

For technical support, please visit www.wiley.com/techsupport.

Wiley also publishes its books in a variety of electronic formats. Some content that appears in print may not be available in electronic books.

Library of Congress Control Number: 2011926323

ISBN: 978-0-470-76873-0

Manufactured in the United States of America

10 9 8 7 6 5 4 3 2 1

WILEY

About the Author

Jesse Stay began his career at age 10 as a developer writing BASIC programs in his spare time. He would frequently be found copying programs from the back of *3-2-1 Contact* magazines and reading ahead, way ahead, in the books of his computer programming classes in high school. In third grade, Stay won third place in his elementary school computer fair, going against the likes of kids several years older than he was. For his Boy Scout Eagle Scout project, Stay wrote a computer program in Pascal to help track the blood types of those in his local church congregation.

At the same time, as an avid entrepreneur, Stay was always looking for the next way to make money — from the lemonade stands as a kid, to selling T-shirts from the artwork of others in his high school art class, to his own lawn-mowing business. He always had a knack for making money "grow on trees," something his parents always told him wasn't possible.

Later on in life, Stay worked under the direction of the VP of marketing at CWDKids.com. It was there that he was put in charge of helping with the affiliate marketing and search engine marketing programs for the company. He built many scripts in both Perl and VBA to help in this effort. Later, at Media General (a publishing company, owner of many news organizations throughout the Southeast), Stay worked to make print classifieds profitable online by developing creative techniques to help customers find what they were looking for. He took that knowledge to BackCountry.com, where he built an innovative ad management platform to build and buy thousands of ads, saving the company thousands while increasing sales.

It was the combination of his background in SEM, affiliate, and classified ad tools and management; his entrepreneurial spirit; and his passion for programming that drove Stay to realize the power of social networking APIs and Facebook Platform. Stay quickly realized that with social networking, his software could sell itself.

In 2007, Stay left his full-time job to start his own consulting company. Since then, Stay has written three books on Facebook and Facebook development; consulted for some of the most successful brands in social media; opened his own startup, SocialToo.com, which Stay still runs today; and built a successful blog with thousands of followers. Stay has also written developer documentation online for Facebook itself as a contractor. Even today, Stay believes in making money "grow on trees" through entrepreneurship and savvy business techniques.

Stay maintains and administers numerous Facebook Pages with fans numbered in the hundreds of thousands and Twitter accounts with followers in the tens of thousands, and he has written for some of the top blogs on the Internet. Three of those include InsideFacebook.com, AllFacebook.com, and LouisGray.com.

Stay has been named by Mashable.com as one of 20 developers to follow on Twitter and one of 10 entrepreneurs to follow on Twitter. Stay was also named by *Entrepreneur* magazine as one of 20 developers to follow on Twitter by Mashable's Ben Parr.

Stay currently works (he calls it service) as social media architect and manager of social strategy and solutions for The Church of Jesus Christ of Latter-day Saints (the Mormons). In his current position, Stay gets to help build relationships and social technologies for some of the largest humanitarian organizations in the world. In addition to that, Stay works with the Mormon Tabernacle Choir on its social strategy, as well as FamilySearch.org, which has the world's largest database of linked individuals (Stay proudly calls it the world's largest social network). Stay believes firmly in using "social" technologies to build fruitful relationships that have a strong effect on the world.

Stay has keynoted for major conferences and has spoken all over the United States. He has spoken at some of the largest Facebook conferences in the world, and he loves to share with others how they can learn just a "little more" to gain that extra edge on Facebook strategy. Stay has spoken and continues to speak for both business professionals and marketers, and developers, and has a knack for making both audiences come out enlightened.

In his spare time, Stay likes to play trumpet, work in his garden, hike, mountain bike, and travel the world. Stay speaks fluent Thai and loves international culture. Stay has five kids and a beautiful wife and, most of all, enjoys spending time at home with his family.

Dedication

To Rebecca, Elizabeth, Thomas, Joseph, Jesse III, and Baby on the way. Without them, this couldn't have been possible. I'm especially grateful to my wife, who has shown great patience in allowing me to spend almost a year writing this, all while I was working a full-time job, running a company on the side, speaking, and consulting, along with everything else I do. She keeps me going, and she continually amazes me how she's able to support me in everything I do. It is she who inspires me to keep on pushing harder. She made this possible.

Author's Acknowledgments

If you're not included here, I've probably thanked you in person already. If not, I apologize, because it's impossible to include everyone who made this possible. Thanks to my family for supporting me along the way. Thanks to my boss, and those who work with me, for being flexible enough to allow me to finish this while working a full-time job (and running a company on the side!).

A special thank-you to each and every blog or news organization that has ever covered me or my companies and books over the years: Mashable, TechCrunch, ReadWriteWeb, TheNextWeb, Venturebeat, *New York Times,* to name a few — I'm very grateful. I've tried to say thank you back by including each and every one under http://delicious.com/jessestay/ coverage.

Thanks to some of my dearest advisors and mentors over the years. I truly look up to them, and they have made much of what I do possible through their advice and shared knowledge — they are all dear friends: Guy Kawasaki, Jason Alba, Louis Gray, Rodney Rumford, and Jeremiah Owyang, to name a few. I treasure each chance I get with them to learn something new.

Thanks to Stephan Heilner and Ray Hunter for their contributions to the mobile chapter. They are two of the best mobile developers I know, and they were invaluable in helping to make that chapter interesting.

Thanks to Katie Feltman, Christopher Morris, and the entire team at Wiley for being so patient with me as I wrote this. The Wiley team has been one of the most pleasant publishers to date to work with, and I've thoroughly enjoyed my experience with them thus far. A special thanks to Allan Carroll, one of the best Facebook developers I know, who graciously was willing to help with the tech edits. Be sure to try out his new service, Piick.com, if you get a chance.

Lastly, thank you to my mother and father. They brought me into this world, and I've treasured the advice they've given me over the years to make me the person who I am. You are two of the smartest individuals I know.

Publisher's Acknowledgments

We're proud of this book; please send us your comments at http://dummies.custhelp.com. For other comments, please contact our Customer Care Department within the U.S. at 877-762-2974, outside the U.S. at 317-572-3993, or fax 317-572-4002.

Some of the people who helped bring this book to market include the following:

Acquisitions, Editorial, and Media Development

Sr. Project Editors: Christopher Morris, Kelly Ewing

Acquisitions Editor: Katie Feltman

Copy Editor: John Edwards

Technical Editor: Allan Carroll

Editorial Manager: Kevin Kirschner

Media Development Project Manager: Laura Moss-Hollister

Media Development Assistant Project Manager: Jenny Swisher

Media Development Associate Producers: Josh Frank, Marilyn Hummel, Douglas Kuhn, and Shawn Patrick

Editorial Assistant: Amanda Graham

Sr. Editorial Assistant: Cherie Case

Cartoons: Rich Tennant (www.the5thwave.com)

Composition Services

Project Coordinator: Kristie Rees

Layout and Graphics: Joyce Haughey, Julie Trippetti

Proofreader: Debbye Butler

Indexer: Ty Koontz

Publishing and Editorial for Technology Dummies

Richard Swadley, Vice President and Executive Group Publisher

Andy Cummings, Vice President and Publisher

Mary Bednarek, Executive Acquisitions Director

Mary C. Corder, Editorial Director

Publishing for Consumer Dummies

Diane Graves Steele, Vice President and Publisher

Composition Services

Debbie Stailey, Director of Composition Services

Contents at a Glance

Table of Contents

Introduction

It's like a scene out of the movie *West Side Story.* You're on either one side or the other. On one side, you have the developers, who like to spend the wee hours of the night coding, Mountain Dew flowing through their veins. They like dark rooms. Vi (an editor for hard-core programmers) is either a curse word or the place that every piece of output that comes from their brains flows from. They don't sleep much and speak in Big O Notation (a mathematical notation for summarizing computer algorithms). They're either a Mac or a PC, an Android or an iPhone, and if they ever have to develop the other they do so unwillingly!

On the other side, you have the marketers, who think in terms of clicks and visitors and conversions. Dollar signs are above their heads, and they love it when people know about them and their products. *Brand, market, user, demographic,* and *retention* are common words off the tips of their tongues. Advertising, SEO, and affiliate programs are all tools in their arsenal.

For some reason, both sides have always had a difficult time talking with each other — neither wants to be on the other's turf. Programmers have a difficult time worrying about the business side and often don't do well in knowing how to increase visitors to a Web site or increase sales or anything that deals with working with people.

At the same time, marketers often don't care as much about knowing how the sites they're promoting actually work, or the technicalities or algorithms behind the products they're selling. A marketer's job is to get his brand into as many hands as possible, not to write the things he's promoting. They don't understand why one would want to learn to code. Up until now, they didn't need to.

Up until now, marketers and developers have had no need to coexist. Technology made the products, and marketing sold the products. However, with Facebook and the launch of Facebook Platform in 2007, that all changed. All of the sudden, technology sold itself, and developers could now also become marketers, just by writing code. Marketers need to take note!

About This Book

I wrote this book as a middle ground so that marketers and developers could come together. I've found in the last few years in my speaking and other engagements that I've started to have more and more marketers coming to me to ask how to properly set up a Facebook tab or to integrate Facebook into their Web sites. I've had many developers come to me to ask how they can properly promote their products. This book is intended to be an answer to all those questions.

The truth is, if you're a marketer or a developer, this book should show you something. Even if you don't want to read it from start to finish, you should be able to pick and choose the elements that look interesting to you, and discover something from them.

Marketers and developers, by reading this book, may come to understand each other's world, at least a little. At the very least, they'll each feel a little more inclined to find out about each other's field, because in an era where marketing has completely merged with technology, both fields have to learn a little about each other!

The fact is that Facebook has finally made it possible for developers to promote their technologies without the need of marketing expertise. In this book, I show you how.

At the same time, Facebook has made it really easy for marketers to use technology without any coding expertise. In this book, I show you how.

In every case, I try to explain in simple terms how to develop Facebook applications in a manner so simple that someone with very little coding expertise can pick it up. In most cases, just some simple HTML and maybe JavaScript knowledge should be sufficient. If you're a marketer, I strongly suggest that you spend some time getting familiar with both of these, but even if you don't, this book can help you get your hands dirty with Facebook Platform. This book should be very easy for both audiences to read.

Facebook is a constantly changing environment. This is especially true with Facebook Platform. For this reason, I try to remind you in every place possible where you can go to get the latest information. If you ever have any questions, just ask them in this book's Facebook group at `stay.am/dummiesgroup`.

Conventions Used in This Book

If you've read a *For Dummies* book before, you're probably pretty familiar with the conventions I use in this book. It's pretty simple: I use italics to identify and define new terms. I also put search terms and keywords in italics. Whenever you have to type something, I put the stuff you need to type in **bold** type so it's easy to see. And for code snippets and HTML, as well as URLs, I use a monospaced font like this:

```
www.staynalive.com/dummiesbook
```

Foolish Assumptions

Of course, I'm assuming that this book is just for developers and marketers. This book could work well for anyone really. The book is for all those people who want to know a little more than they should about Facebook. It's for those who want to be able to cause a little trouble with what they know. It's for those who like to just get things done and not worry about seeing whether others can get it done for them. I've argued back and forth with my editor on the possibility of just calling this book *Hacking Facebook For Dummies.* The truth is, this book is all about hacking Facebook.

If you visit Facebook, the company, you'll see little stamped "HACK" artwork on the walls all throughout the company. "Hacking" permeates the culture of Facebook, from its developers to its marketers to the executives. Mark Zuckerberg himself, at least I hear, tells his employees to go out and break things. They have regular "hackathons," where employees spend all night getting cool things done and building cool products. To be a hacker just means that you want to get things done and that you'll use all the tools in your arsenal to make that happen. I assume that you're one of these people, and I'd like to extend that hack culture to everyone in my audience.

In many cases, I do assume that you at least have a little HTML, and in some cases, JavaScript knowledge to understand what I'm talking about. If you don't, I suggest that you spend some time trying to at least understand what I'm talking about. You can find other *For Dummies* books for those topics. Of course, you can always ask in this book's Facebook group if you ever have any questions (`stay.am/dummiesgroup`).

How This Book Is Organized

I try to take you through all the different parts of Facebook development in this book. I try to cover it all. You'll find that I start out very simple. Toward the end, I get into a lot more of what you can do with Facebook Platform and describe how you can integrate it into an application or Web site. You can pick and choose any section to get what you want — skim it or read it — you're bound to find something you can benefit from.

Part 1: Understanding the Basics of a Facebook Application

Baby steps, right? I take you through the very basics of what makes a Facebook application. I show you how to set up your first application and discuss how to find documentation. I show you how to create test accounts and describe the different pieces of a Facebook application.

Part II: Integrating with the Facebook.com Environment

I call this "fishing where the fish are." Actually, it's a common term in marketing, which means that you go out and put your message where those you want to target are already located. In this case, that's Facebook.

I show you all the places in the `Facebook.com` environment that you can integrate with, and I describe what types of things you can do on `Facebook.com`. You discover how to "hack" Facebook, from within `Facebook.com` itself.

Part III: From Fishers to Farmers — Building Facebook on Your Own Site

After you're able to hack `Facebook.com`, I show you how to go from the fish to the farm, bringing Facebook Platform onto your own Web site or application. With just some simple HTML, and the capability to copy and paste, you find out how to, at a minimum, build a social environment right on your own Web site. You discover how to truly build relationships on your Web site using technology.

Part IV: Delving into APIs

Want to really get your hands dirty? This is a part you can't miss. I show you all the different things that you can do with Facebook Platform on Facebook.com itself, or on your own Web site. I introduce you to Graph API and show you how making a simple request in your browser can reveal information about a user.

If you really want to get your hands dirty, I give you examples of how you can access this information using JavaScript and even PHP. Or, maybe you don't want to understand those things. Even so, this part will be interesting for you to find out what is possible with Facebook Platform.

Part V: Turning Your Facebook Application into a Legitimate Business

This is the part that can make developers uncomfortable, but I really think they'll like this section. I show you how to leverage ads, Facebook Pages, credits, and more to turn your application into a legitimate business.

As a marketer, you'll want to read this section to discover what is possible, and maybe you'll even find out a few ways to build this stuff yourself, and see why this is important.

Part VI: The Part of Tens

This is really my favorite section. Here, in each chapter, I give you ten things that you can discover about specific subjects.

Icons Used in This Book

Where necessary, you see little icons of information that you can either ignore or pay attention to in order to discover a little bit more about the subject matter. If anything, it gives you some cute little pictures to look at instead of just seeing the text.

Wherever you see this cute little Dummies Man head, I leave a little tip that can make you just one step more knowledgeable about the subject matter. These are the places you'll probably find yourself saying, "Hmm, I didn't realize that!"

I promise not to bore you by becoming too repetitive, but if I ever have to remind you of something, this is where I put it. If it's here, you should probably pay attention. These are the things that I want to be so ingrained in your head that you'll be able to recite them by memory when you're done with the book.

Anywhere you see this, pay attention. This means that you should beware of something, and I don't want you to learn a lesson the hard way like I probably have.

If you're a marketer, you can probably ignore this stuff, but if you really want to understand what makes these things tick, you'll want to read it. This is where I really get into the meat of what I'm talking about.

Where to Go from Here

The first thing I recommend that everyone do is set up a Facebook Page. I go through this in detail in Chapter 5. If you have any sort of brand, you'll need to at least do this.

If you're a developer, you'll probably want to get started immediately in Chapter 1. If you're a marketer, you'll find Chapter 5 and onward pretty interesting, and you'll want to skim over Part IV.

There's that Remember icon again. Always, always check the Facebook documentation to see what's changed since I originally wrote this. At the time this book went to print, it was the most up-to-date book of its kind. I guarantee that won't always be the case, but what's most important is that you know where to go to get information.

Facebook Platform is a living, breathing platform. It changes frequently. You should always check back to developers.facebook.com, look on this book's Facebook Page at facebook.com/dummiesbook, reference the book's Web site at staynalive.com/dummiesbook, or ask a question in the book's Facebook group at stay.am/dummiesgroup if you are ever in doubt. You can access all the code in this book at this book's companion Web site at www.wiley.com/go/facebookappdev.

Part I

Understanding the Basics of a Facebook Application

The 5th Wave
By Rich Tennant

"Jim and I do a lot of business together on Facebook. By the way, Jim, did you get the sales spreadsheet and little blue pony I sent you?"

In this part . . .

You're probably excited to get going, or maybe you're a little hesitant at this new world of Facebook development. I start by showing you the foundations. Here are the basics you need to get started. All audiences should be comfortable in this part.

I start by showing you what a Facebook application is and how you can get acclimated in the Facebook environment. I show you how to build your first Facebook application, and where you can find help. I even show you all the elements you need to know to set up your application.

Chapter 1

Getting Acquainted with Facebook Application Development

In This Chapter

▶ Knowing where to build your application

▶ Understanding Facebook applications

▶ Getting to know the tools

▶ Finding help through documentation

So you're ready to build a Facebook application! Whether you want to build a simple HTML Facebook tab to welcome visitors to your Facebook Page or a full-blown, fully integrated Web site that enables visitors to log in with their Facebook profile and see their friends, there's no doubt that Facebook is a powerful platform that improves just about any brand it touches. Whether you're a marketer looking to just find out what's possible with Facebook and maybe get your feet a little wet, or an already-experienced developer looking to expand the possibilities of your development experience, in this chapter I show you how Facebook apps can help you achieve your goals.

What's a Facebook Application?

If you keep reading, you'll quickly become acclimated to what a Facebook application is and why you might want to consider using such a thing. However, there may be a good chance you've never even touched Facebook Platform before and you want to find out why so many other developers and businesses are interested in Facebook.

Facebook applications basically come in two forms:

  ▶ **Facebook hosted.** This is typically what most people mean when they say "Facebook application." Facebook allows developers, companies, and brands to build their own Web sites right on Facebook.com, which includes Facebook's own headers and footers. When you build a

Facebook-hosted application you are in essence making an extension of Facebook itself. Users of your Facebook-hosted application never have to leave Facebook to use your Web site or application.

✔ **Hosted on your own Web site.** You can integrate Facebook features right into your own Web site. For instance, you can authenticate users through their Facebook accounts right on your own site. You can get a list of the user's friends and list them on your site. You can pull almost any type of data about users and their friends and apply it to your own Web site's content.

In this book I show you how to implement the two methods, but I also show you some simple ways you can integrate in both environments with very little effort. In most cases, it involves a little HTML knowledge, and the capability to copy and paste. Even marketers should pay attention to this stuff, as you'll have that one step ahead of the competition.

Understanding the Facebook Application Development Process

Anyone can create a Facebook application, and the great thing about it is there is no approval process to get up and going! To develop a good application, you just need to follow the rules Facebook has set up (I cover those in Chapter 15), know how to set up your application (I cover that a little later in this Chapter and in Chapter 2), and then start getting people to use it. For the most part, there are no crazy application processes like Apple App store or Android Marketplace. You create it and it's live.

Social applications aren't exactly like typical programs you would typically write. When you work with Social APIs, you have to consider that your code will naturally promote itself. The code you're writing enables people to share information quickly and effectively. In essence, writing social apps makes you both a programmer and a marketer, because your code is now selling your product. So what things do you need to consider?

✔ **Expect you'll need to scale.** Although this is no longer the gold rush of 2007 when simple Facebook applications would go from one to two million users in just two days, there is still a good chance your Web site or application could grow very quickly. All it takes is for someone with hundreds of thousands of fans to talk about your application or Web site and soon you are getting slammed with new users. Use a hosting facility that can handle your scaling quickly. Hosting services like Amazon EC2 and Slicehost or Rackspace or Fibernet all have great services for this. I cover this more later.

✔ **Never build on just one network.** You're building in a very volatile environment. Social APIs ebb and flow. They change with the wind. You'll find entire feature sets get removed during your development process. Policies change. So relying entirely on a single network could end up completely killing your product. It's a huge risk! I recommend you diversify. Not only that, but come up with ideas that have your own foundation. Build something that works well on its own without social networks, and then use social networks to complement the product you're building. If you keep that attitude you'll never have a problem if a social network kills a feature or changes its policy. Stay self-reliant.

After you've thought of what you want to build, or how you want to integrate Facebook Platform into your Web site, you can start to build it. Getting started is really easy — here are a few things you should know:

✔ **You can host anywhere you want.** At a minimum, you need only a place you can render HTML files. Any hosting provider can do this. If you're doing something that simple, pick something cheap.

✔ **There is no approval process to launch an application.** Although Facebook does have an application directory, it is nowhere near as prominent as it used to be. Any application can still launch without being included in the Facebook application directory.

✔ **You can write in any language you like.** There are libraries for just about every language out there. Pick your favorite, then go. PHP is always good because that's what Facebook develops internally, but you can really use anything! I share a few of the various libraries later in this chapter.

✔ **To get going immediately, just go to `http://facebook.com/developers`.** That's it! You can go through the steps in Chapter 2 to learn details of what you need to enter, and what you need to do, but this will at least get you started. The docs are all at `http://developers.facebook.com` if you prefer to get the latest and greatest information right away.

Thinking socially

As you're planning your application or Web site, think "social." I'm not just talking about the capability to allow your users to chat with each other, either. A great social application builds relationships between users. You should look over your Web site and application and consider how you can use social technologies and APIs to build relationships between your users and customers.

Are you organizing your data categorically, or by the content your users' friends are liking and sharing? Are you giving them easy ways to share your data with their close friends and family? Do your layout and application facilitate easier sharing between individuals? All these will help make a successful use of Facebook API within your application or Web site. Always ask yourself this, and you'll come up with a great application.

A basic Facebook application hosted on Facebook will be hosted on your own servers somewhere, and will get rendered through an iFrame in your browser. On your Web site, you either include *Social Plugins,* simple pieces of HTML you can copy and paste into your Web site, or you can make simple requests to Facebook to get and render information about your users that are also on Facebook. I cover all that in detail later.

Picking a Platform That Works Right for You

You have two ways of developing on Facebook. Each of these ways makes for a different platform of development. The term *Facebook Platform* in general just means accessing Facebook's APIs to access these two methods, but as you're developing, you'll first want to decide within Facebook Platform which path you want to take.

What you build on Facebook all depends on your strategy, your goals, and the time frame available to you. Over the course of building your application, there's a good chance you'll choose a number of different strategies. I share just a few strategies that I think you should consider as you're planning your application. In this section, I dive a little deeper into what you can do with these different Facebook Platforms.

Fishing where the fish are

A generally accepted principle in marketing is what marketers call "fishing where the fish are." The idea is that as a marketer (or developer trying to market your application), in essence, you're fishing for those potential customers and users you want to bring into your application or Web site. It really makes no sense to go fishing and just wait for the fish to come to you. The most effective means for you to find new customers and users is to go out where they are and "fish where the fish are."

In the early days of the Web, this was difficult to do. Marketers and Web site builders were stuck building Web sites and having to come up with their own means to advertise and bring users and customers to their brands. They would try to "fish where the fish are" by placing their Web site name on their products and alongside their TV commercials, but all that was doing was letting people know where they were. There was no way to get into the conversations of people and to enable those conversations to happen.

Along came social media and social networks like Myspace, Ning, and Facebook. Companies could create Myspace profiles and Facebook Pages and have a presence right on the networks and places on the Web where people were talking with each other. Instead of people coming to your Web site, you were able to bring your Web site to the people, reducing the steps it would normally take for an individual to find your brand.

Soon, social networks were providing as many ways as possible to enable your brand to get in front of its users and to get into the conversations of those people passionate about your brand. Facebook was one of the first, and in 2007, it opened its massive database of close friends and families for brands, companies, and Web sites to build things right on top of Facebook.com, where the users were already participating.

This global movement toward Facebook.com for brands was compared to a "gold rush" of sorts, with applications seeing millions of users in just days, and it is something you can still embrace today. Here are some simple ways you can "fish where the fish are" on Facebook:

✔ **Facebook Pages:** Consider a Facebook Page (that's with a Capital "P," not to be confused with a user's personal profile) your brand's profile on Facebook. Because profiles must be occupied by real people, Facebook has provided a place, Pages, for brands to build community and discussion around their brand.

   With a Facebook Page, people interested and passionate about your brand are able to "like" the Page by clicking the Like button on the left side (or sometimes top) of the page (see Figure 1-1). When they like your Page, your Page appears in their list of interests on their profile and the act of liking appears on that user's wall in his or her profile. Other people have the opportunity to see that and like your Page, and it naturally promotes itself.

   In addition, as a Page administrator, you can post updates to your Facebook Page. Each update you post appears in the news feed of users who have liked your Page. They have the opportunity to comment on and like these posts, and their friends can see them and might also want to comment and like those posts. You have just enabled something for them to talk about, and they are now talking about your brand!

✔ **Facebook applications:** Perhaps you have seen your friends throwing sheep, or maybe they just planted a new vegetable in their virtual garden. Each of these actions is happening as a result of some "application" providing a means for their users to share their activities on Facebook.

   You can build your own applications on Facebook. In fact, that's one of the first things I cover in Chapter 2. As a business, developer, or brand, you can build out your own version of your Web site right on Facebook. com, and users never have to leave the site.

In addition, you're given "integration points" (covered in Chapter 4), where you can interrupt the process of users who are using your application to enable custom publishers (that's the box where you enter your status updates), custom tabs, automated posts to the news feed, and more. It's good you understand what you can do with an application on Facebook — it enables you to truly dive down and actually swim with the fish.

✔ **"Share to Facebook" links:** At a minimum, you should have some means on your own Web site to allow your users to share with their friends on Facebook.com (see how Mashable does this in Figure 1-2). You can use a site called ShareThis.com to provide simple share links, or you can use simple social plugins that Facebook provides to enable a "Like button," where users can like things on your site and share those with their friends on Facebook.

The Like button

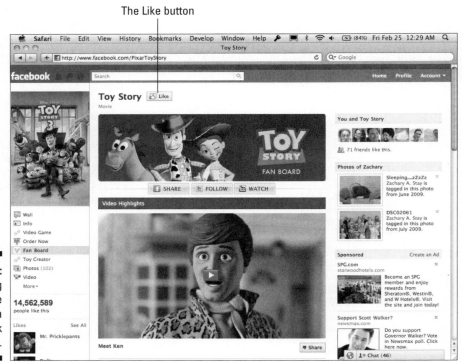

Figure 1-1:
Clicking
the Like
button on a
Facebook
Page.

Figure 1-2:
Notice how
Mashable
encourages
users to
share their
articles to
Facebook.

✔ **Facebook tabs (or custom links):** Facebook tabs (now custom links, as Facebook has removed what were previously tabbed links at the top of the page in exchange for a list of links on the left, below your Page's profile picture) give you a customized theme for your own Facebook Page by allowing you to create your own customized experiences within the Page. This can be a promotion, encouraging users to like the Page in exchange for something free, or maybe just a welcome message, greeting users to the Page. I cover this more in Chapter 4.

✔ **Facebook advertising:** This is a powerful one. Go, right now, to `http://facebook.com/ads` and set up a simple ad (see Figure 1-3). You don't have to publish it, but at least familiarize yourself with the process.

You'll notice immediately that Facebook gives you very granular controls over who sees that ad. You can type in specific interests, genders, age ranges, and locales, and Facebook tells you the exact number of people who will see that ad. You can then set a budget regarding how much you want to spend on that ad per day.

Or, you can target the friends of all the fans of your Facebook Page and make it an even more personalized and familiar experience. Facebook ads are a very powerful tool in your arsenal to "fish where the fish are" if used right.

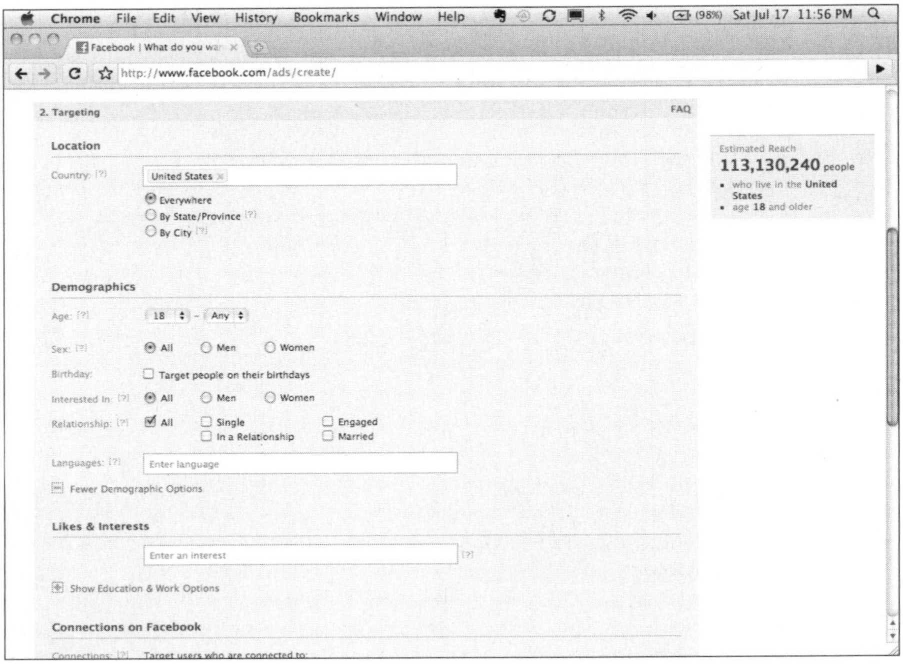

Figure 1-3:
Setting up
an ad on
Facebook.

From fishers to farmers

I talked about Facebook enabling brands to go out and be where their users and customers are using applications, advertising, and Pages. Fishing is critical to the success of your company if you want to stay ahead.

Throughout history, civilizations of fishers and hunters always turned to farming eventually as the more effective means of bringing food to the table. In fact, even today, the most thriving nations in the world have all learned to farm. Farming is, in essence, the process of confining the prey to your own turf such that the prey can be easily harvested at the least cost.

Thus it is with brands and companies. You too will be more effective when you can bring the "hunt" to your own turf and go from "fishing" to the farm. As a brand, you should know how to farm, and Facebook makes this possible as well (and no, I'm not talking about FarmVille!).

Facebook provides several means to allow you to bring customers to your own turf through simple HTML and coding on your part. You can take any of these methods and apply them to your own Web site, in essence cultivating your own "farm" in the process. Here are some of the tools Facebook provides to cultivate your farm:

✔ **Facebook Graph API:** Facebook has provided a simple application programming interface (API) that, with a little JavaScript knowledge (at a minimum), you can access on your Web site and bring users' friends, likes, comments, and news streams right to your own Web site. Facebook Graph API is for those who want to have the full flexibility of customizing the Facebook experience right on their own turf. I cover this in more detail in Chapter 7.

✔ **Social Plugins:** If JavaScript is a little too complex for your expertise or needs, you should definitely consider Social Plugins. Social Plugins are basically just pieces of HTML that you can place on your own Web site and immediately include functionality such as Like buttons, widgets that include streams of the latest activity (likes, shares to Facebook, for instance) from Facebook users who visit your site, as well as widgets that display the most popular pages on your site based on the number of Facebook users who have liked and shared those pages. Facebook provides a simple tool, at `http://developers.facebook.com/plugins`, that you can preview your plugins and copy and paste code right into your Web site. With Social Plugins, all you need to know is how to copy and paste, and you'll be farming with the pros!

✔ **Open Graph Protocol:** Did you know that your own Web site could be a Facebook Page of its own? That's right — by adding some simple meta tags, called Open Graph Protocol, and a Social Plugin or two, you can set your site so that when someone likes your Web site (using the Social Plugins I mention previously), Facebook recognizes that Web site as a Page on its network. You can now post updates to those who liked your Web site and track analytics surrounding Facebook users who visit your site, and your site will appear in users' Facebook search results and in their interests for their profile. Open Graph Protocol is how you build the foundations for your farm using Facebook. I cover Social Plugins and Open Graph Protocol in Chapter 6.

✔ **Facebook Credits:** At the time of this writing, these are only in very limited beta. However, in the future, these will (sometimes literally!) be the currency of your farm. Facebook is enabling a credits-type system, where, with simply your Facebook credentials, you can purchase anything on the Web with a prefilled credits account you will have set up. Facebook Credits are powerful for you as a farmer, because they enable a very simple and convenient way for customers to purchase your products with as few steps as possible, in a manner that is already familiar to them. I talk about Credits more in Chapter 15 — you'll want to read that one.

Releasing your application to the building block Web

After you create your farm, you can take it one step further and allow other people to access your farm. You do this by enabling APIs and pieces of data you release to other developers to use on their own Web sites (or farms). I call this "the building block Web."

In the early days of the Web (back in those days, they versioned it Web 1.0), Web site owners built their own sites. These sites were built entirely for readers to find, come back frequently, and read or purchase items from. You couldn't extract the data from those sites, nor could you know when new data existed. All users had was a browser, something like Netscape Navigator or Internet Explorer, which they used to view the Web. These browsers were users' only peek into those Web sites. In those days, the browser was "the platform" and was what Web developers would use to organize and share their data with users.

Shortly afterward, developers began to build simple access points into their data. Really Simple Syndication (RSS) came about, enabling programs to know when new data existed for a Web site and enabling readers to easily recognize and parse that data. XML-RPC, SOAP, and REST all came about, giving developers even more access to data from those Web sites. Very soon, Web 2.0 emerged, making the Web itself "the platform."

I see a new platform emerging with technologies such as Facebook. This one focuses on the very platforms themselves. Now every Web site is expected to provide its own API and its own access points. Each Web site is providing its own little component that developers can take from and build their own much larger products as a whole. Although Facebook may provide a user's friends and family connections for an application, Google may provide search for that application. At the same time, Flickr may provide the photos, and YouTube the videos. Each Web site has its own piece of the puzzle to contribute.

You should be thinking of how you can contribute as you consider your application. What core strength do you offer? Your application should be simply another building block in the new Web, and you should make that as accessible as possible to others so that they can incorporate it into their own farms on the Web.

Understanding How Your Application Will Access Facebook

Now that you understand the general philosophies and paradigms of Facebook development and hopefully have a good idea of where you want to start and what your strategy is, it's time to start understanding the depths of the Facebook application environment. Depending on whether you're fishing or farming, your application will access Facebook's APIs entirely differently, and your users will interact with your application in a different way. I start with how an application on the Facebook.com environment is set up.

The Facebook.com environment

You certainly want to read Chapters 2 and 3 to get more details on this, but I give you a summary here. When you host an application on Facebook, you are not really "hosting" it, per se, but instead you are using Facebook as a proxy between you and Facebook users.

A typical Facebook application works like this:

1. Users go to `http://apps.facebook.com/`*yourapplicationname*.

2. Facebook makes a call to your servers (through an iFrame HTML tag).

3. Your servers look at what was called and format data accordingly. During this time, your servers may also make calls back to Facebook's API to retrieve additional information (such as friends, profile information, and so on) before returning that data to the user.

4. Your server then returns the formatted data to Facebook.com in an iFrame (note that sometimes this can just be a redirect message sending the user to authenticate or authorize your application).

5. Facebook.com parses (reads) that data and formats it further by adding the Facebook header. Read more about this in Chapter 2 and even more thoroughly in Chapter 4.

6. Facebook returns the entire formatted page to the user.

   See Figure 1-4 to further understand the flow of a typical application in the Facebook.com environment.

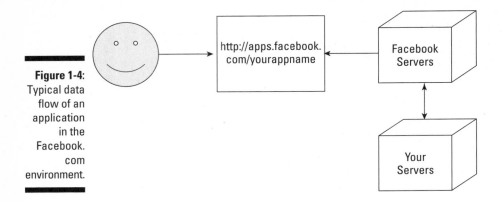

Accessing Facebook from your own Web site

The architecture of an application built on your own Web site will be a little different from that of a Facebook.com-wrapped application. The difference is that instead of Facebook.com proxying and controlling your application, your own Web site will have 100 percent control over the rendering of your application. The user might possibly never see the Facebook.com header and footer, and you can basically render the data however you like. Here's how the flow of an application built on your own Web site works:

1. The user visits your Web site.

2. Your Web site renders simple JavaScript and HTML-like tags (called XFBML) as part of your normal HTML back to the user.

3. The user's browser runs the JavaScript, which makes calls back to Facebook (note that this can also happen back on your server before rendering the HTML back to the user). Facebook returns data such as authentication information, user profile information, information about the user's friends, and more.

4. The browser renders that data back to the user in a dynamic, personalized manner that includes his or her Facebook profile information and friends.

   Figure 1-5 shows the flow of a Facebook application rendered through your own Web site.

Figure 1-5:
Architecture
of a simple
application
hosted on
your own
Web site.

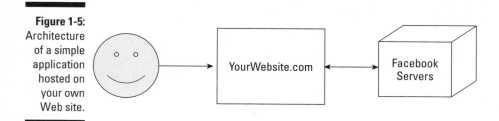

Selecting a Development Language

Now it's time to figure out what you're going to build this thing with! If you're already a developer, you probably have a preferred language you like to write in. If you're a marketer or a business owner, you probably don't really care to do much development, but you're reading this book to hopefully get your hands at least a little bit dirty. That's okay. Facebook has solutions for both types.

Facebook either provides, or has developers who have provided libraries for just about every programming language. I cover a few of those in the following sections.

The Facebook JavaScript SDK

The Facebook JavaScript SDK is Facebook's default and easiest-to-use library, and it's the focus of most of the new examples in Facebook's documentation at the time of this writing. Including the software development kit (SDK) is simply a matter of calling the library and then initializing it using some simple JavaScript code. I show you how to do this in Chapter 3.

You can find out more about the SDK under the developer documentation. At the time of this writing, you could find it here: `http://developers.facebook.com/docs/reference/javascript`. All information, API method calls, and references can be found on the developer documentation site.

The Facebook JavaScript SDK is open source! Although most of its calls are just making requests to Facebook's Graph API, you can get access to all the underlying code that makes those calls on its GitHub repository. If you have some coding skills, this might be a great opportunity for you to contribute and give back to the other developers who may be experiencing similar needs as you. This also gives you, the developer, the added advantage of being able to sift through the code and debug on your own if you encounter any difficulty.

The Facebook PHP and Python SDKs

Facebook's official server-side SDKs are PHP and, even more recently, Python. Facebook has made these libraries as simple as requiring the library code, instantiating a new Facebook object (usually passing in your App ID and API secret), and then simply passing in the path to the Graph API method call that you want to make to the Facebook object you just created.

The Facebook PHP and Python SDKs are also completely open source. You can check out the source code to the PHP SDK on GitHub at http://github.com/facebook/php-sdk. You can check out the source code to the Python SDK on GitHub at http://github.com/facebook/python-sdk. On each GitHub page, you can find valuable readme documents, code updates, Wikis, and more. You can also report issues with your given library and converse with those who wrote it. If you ever experience an issue with the PHP or Python libraries for Facebook, you should report your problems and ask your questions here before going to the Facebook Developer Forum (which I talk about in Chapter 2).

The iPhone and Android SDKs

Facebook isn't just for the Web! At the time of this writing, Facebook has provided two official mobile SDKs for development on mobile phones. They have provided an iPhone SDK, and more recently, an Android SDK for mobile application developers to integrate into their iPhone and Android applications.

Each mobile SDK is available on GitHub just like the other Facebook SDKs. I cover this in detail in Chapter 13, and walk you through the process. You can also get all the details for this at http://github.com/facebook/facebook-iphone-sdk.

For Android, read http://github.com/facebook/facebook-android-sdk to get all the details. Android involves loading the libraries into Eclipse and adding those into your project. Also see Chapter 13 for more details on Android integration. I walk you through setting up an entire application in Android there.

Other "nonofficial" SDKs

If Python, PHP, or JavaScript doesn't suit your fancy, someone has probably created an API for your language of choice. Here are a few of the more popular ones, but you can always use Google Search to find more:

- ✔ **Perl:** WWW::Facebook::API is probably the most thorough Perl SDK at the time of this writing. You can find it by search on CPAN or by going to `http://search.cpan.org/~unobe/WWW-Facebook-API-0.4.18/lib/WWW/Facebook/API.pm`. The `cpan WWW::Facebook::API` command should also install it for you via the command-line cpan shell.

- ✔ **Ruby:** Many Ruby libraries are available for the Facebook API. rfacebook (`http://rfacebook.rubyforge.org`), the OpenGraph Ruby library (`http://github.com/intridea/opengraph`), and the MiniFB Ruby library (`http://github.com/appoxy/mini_fb`) all came up in my search on Ruby Facebook libraries when I wrote this.

- ✔ **Java:** Common libraries include RestFB (`http://restfb.com`), Facebook-Java-API (`http://code.google.com/p/facebook-java-api`), fb4j (`http://fb4j.sourceforge.net`), and the Facebook Java Web App (`http://code.google.com/p/facebook-java-webapp`).

- ✔ **.Net:** Although you find many forks and even some smaller initiatives in the .Net world, the two main libraries for .Net are Facebook.NET (`www.nikhilk.net/FacebookNET.aspx`) and the Facebook Developer Toolkit (`www.codeplex.com/FacebookToolkit`). Look at each and decide which one works best for your needs. Also, be sure to look at the latest commit dates for each to see how active the community is behind it.

Referring to the Facebook Documentation

When in doubt, look it up! Facebook has amazing references online to all its API materials. Whether simple API lookups or more in-depth library calls, Facebook provides documentation to take you every step of the way through the development process.

Perusing Developers.facebook.com for information

Developers.facebook.com (see Figure 1-6) should be your start for any information you want to find about Facebook APIs, tools, and libraries. Especially considering that Facebook changes this documentation frequently, this is a good place to start, because what may be the documentation today may be in a different location by the time you read this. Search around and get to know this place and what is available to you — and check back frequently.

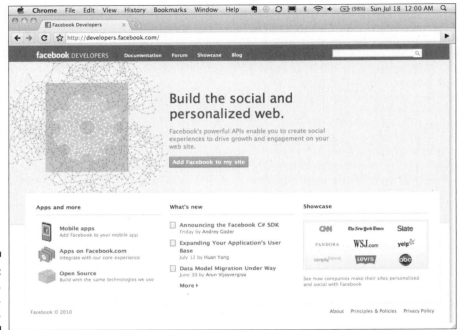

The Facebook documentation Web site

At the time of this writing, you could find all developer documentation for Facebook APIs, tools, and libraries at `http://developers.facebook.com/docs`. This may or may not be the correct URL by the time you read this, so be sure to search around if that's not the case. (I'll try to post new locations on my blog as well as my own Facebook page and this book's Facebook Page if things change. You can find the book's Facebook Page at `http://facebook.com/dummiesbook`.)

The Facebook Documentation page on Developers.facebook.com (see Fig-ure 1-7) serves as a single location for you to find all you need to get started and continue going in Facebook development. This is where you can find a reference of every API call, helpful tutorials, how-tos, and wizards to take you through the process of creating, understanding, and continuing to develop your application.

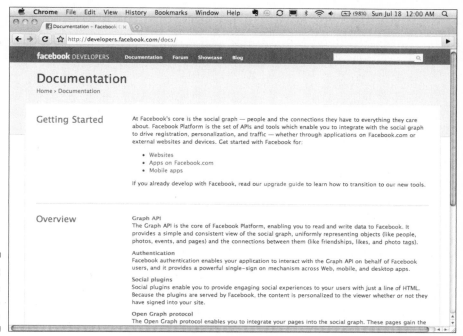

Figure 1-7:
Developers.
facebook.
com.

The documentation page consists of a few major sections that cover pretty much the entire Facebook API. Starting with a few getting-started sections, you can then move on to gain a general sense of each component of the Facebook API, such as the following:

- **Graph API:** In Facebook's simple, URL-based API into the Facebook social graph, you find out all about how to use it and how it can be powerful to you in learning about the people who visit your Web site or application. See Part IV for a more thorough explanation and walk-through of this.

- **Authentication:** Facebook uses OAuth 2.0 to authenticate users. Find out what that means and see how to use it in your application to identify users and incorporate their Facebook profiles into your application. I cover this in Chapter 9.

- **Social Plugins:** In Facebook's most simple way of integrating its API into a Web site or application, a simple copy and paste puts simple Like buttons and stream widgets into your application or Web site. Chapter 6 also covers these.

✔ **Open Graph Protocol:** This is an open standard Facebook set up to identify pages and things on the Web. Simply place a few meta tags and you're set. This overview covers what that is, why it's important, and how you can implement it on your Web site. I go into more detail about this in Chapter 6.

After you acclimate yourself, you can then delve a little deeper and use the references to find out more about each API call or tag that you need to place in your HTML or code. You can discover the following:

✔ **Core APIs:** Get every single Graph API call and Social Plugin available, and get a description of how each can work.

✔ **Developer SDKs:** From PHP to Python, from the iPhone to Android, discover what you can do and how to use your preferred language and programming environment to write Facebook applications.

✔ **FQL (Facebook Query Language):** Facebook is gradually making this less necessary with its Graph API. However, at times, you may need to retrieve specific data that Graph API just cannot provide. FQL enables a custom-ized solution to retrieve granular data from Facebook in an SQL-like format. This section of the documentation shows every table available on Facebook and demonstrates how to access data from those tables.

✔ **XFBML (Facebook Markup Language for Web sites):** With Facebook's tag language, you can access every single tag, see examples, and know what it can do on your Web site.

✔ **Old APIs and client libraries:** Facebook hasn't always supported the same API formats. For deprecated APIs, you can still look up information about those APIs and find out how to use them through this documen-tation. Sometimes you can find a few things by using these APIs that haven't yet been migrated to the new formats. It might help reading through these as well.

Documentation is important! Get to know what you can and can't do with it. If you can't understand JavaScript or programming concepts, study the XFBML and overview sections. Find out as much as you can about what you can do with the API, and your app will be much richer and much more powerful to you in the long run.

OpenGraphProtocol.org

Facebook created the Open Graph Protocol so that it could easily identify content that users were sharing and liking on the Web (see Chapter 6). However, it wanted to open the standard so that anyone who wanted to duplicate it or use it for his own Web site could do so without worry of copy-right or patent infringement, or repercussions from Facebook. So Facebook released it under a special, commonly known license called the Open Web Foundation License and gave it its own Web site independent of Facebook for people to read and study from.

OpenGraphProtocol.org is your source for everything Open Graph Protocol. (See Figure 1-8.) It covers the standard and what it is, along with examples of how to implement it. It's a basic, one-page site, so it's good for you to read it and understand it if you can. If it isn't enough, you can always go back to the Facebook developer documentation and find out more about the Open Graph Protocol there as well.

GitHub

Facebook hosts most of its official development SDKs (PHP, Python, JavaScript, iPhone, and Android) on GitHub as open source (see Figure 1-9). GitHub is an open source repository of code that anyone can sign up for and post code for others to use (according to the code's licensing terms, of course). The great thing about GitHub is that it enables any developer to take a piece of source code and "fork" it into the developer's own repository on the site. The developer can then safely develop his or her own instance of the code without worrying about the code interfering with the main branch of code it was forked from. Then, if the maintainer of that code likes what the person who forked the code has done, he or she can then reincorporate that code into his or her main branch.

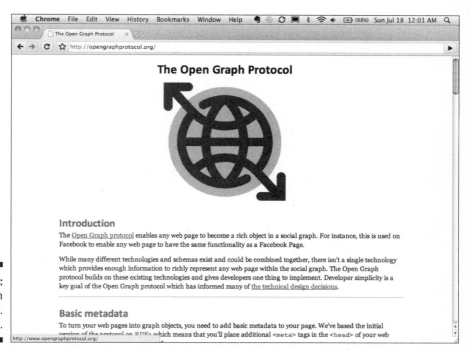

Figure 1-8: OpenGraph Protocol. org.

Another major feature of GitHub is that it provides a great place to store documentation surrounding the code that is being stored. Documentation for all the Facebook SDKs is found there, including setup instructions and code examples. I encourage you to check it out and study what is available so that you can discover how to implement your preferred SDK. Maybe if you're feeling particularly savvy, you can even contribute a little back to the code base and help the overall ecosystem on Facebook thrive.

GitHub's a little hard to explain in such a short amount of space. If you're looking for a greater tutorial on how to use GitHub and what steps you need to take to get started, I recommend the great walk-through at `http://learn.github.com/p/intro.html`. Also, see the `github.com` links I share in the SDKs section above to get an idea of what it looks like and where some of the Facebook code lies.

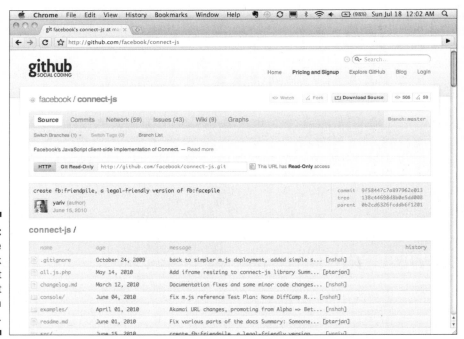

Figure 1-9:
The Facebook JavaScript client libraries on GitHub.

Chapter 2

Building Your First Application

*W*riting a Facebook application is actually quite simple. Three steps are all you need to know and you'll be hacking like a pro on Facebook. The first step (the hardest one) is filling out the right forms during the application setup. In the second step, you can write some simple HTML or API calls that display information for the user, and for the last step, you can go to your application on Facebook.com to view and test what you just wrote!

If any of these steps sound scary, don't worry. In this chapter, I walk you through the process of getting your development environment set up and creating a simple Facebook application. And I promise that it will all seem much less scary when you're done.

Understanding the Development Process

Before embarking on Facebook application development, understanding the development process grounds you and adds a feeling of security. You start the cycle by getting your tools and development environment in place. You need the following:

✔ **A text editor to write and edit code:** For example, I'm a hardcore *vim* geek myself. (vim is a text editor from the early days of the Internet that has some different styles of editing and creating text than you may be used to in a traditional editor. If you're new to programming or aren't sure what it is, you may get along better with one of the more traditional text editors, such as BBEdit or Eclipse.) But you can try BBEdit, Textmate, Eclipse, or even Notepad on your PC. The goal is to just have a place where you can write, write, write!

✔ **A server location to host your applications:** You can find all kinds of Web hosting services. I recommend the following:

- MediaTemple (`http://mediatemple.com`) for its simple setup and configuration interface

- Slicehost (`http://slicehost.com`) for the hard core because it gives you a full dedicated server you can work with

- Fibernet (`http://fiber.net`), which is what I use currently because their pricing and offerings work great for me (they are also local to where I live, but they have remote options).

- Bluehost (`http://bluehost.com`) if you aren't looking to do too much

Also, watch my service SocialToo.com for some simple options for Facebook custom Page options that you can code and customize.

✔ **A language (or languages) that you use to code your application:** For example, you can use HTML (HyperText Markup Language) to create an `index.html` file that simply displays a static page for users to read and view. Of course, you can also use PHP, Perl, Ruby, Java, or whatever language floats your boat if you really want to get down and dirty (that is, add more functionality, such as detecting a user's Facebook friends or reading information about the users who visit your Facebook application). You can also get down and dirty by using HTML and just throwing some JavaScript on top.

✔ **The Facebook Developer application:** You need to install the application that will soon become your portal into every app you develop. This application gives you the tools you need to set up, edit, and manage your applications. It also gives you important information about the status of Facebook Platform and other tools, such as new feature announcements and server outages.

After you have access to Facebook's development tools, you need to tell Facebook some basic information about the application you plan to develop. At a minimum, Facebook needs to know what to call your application and where you host it. That way, Facebook can give users the right direction when they want to visit your application. This part of the process provides Facebook with setup information for your application, and by using these settings, Facebook can then give you some information that you can use as you build your application. For example, when you're ready to develop, you will need to provide your application with an application ID and sometimes an API key and an API secret (I cover these later in the chapter). This is where you can retrieve those for use in your application.

To actually build the application, you create the code using the language you chose for your development environment and save the file to the server hosting location you just provided to Facebook. Then, you post and test your application by visiting the appropriate URL for your application that you set up in your application settings.

Setting Up Your Hosting Environment

Selecting the right hosting environment can be confusing and beyond the skill set of many reading this book. Not all of you are programmers, and even if you are, you may not have the server setup experience to do so. If you do have some experience, nothing is limiting you from selecting your own hosting provider. Here are some providers I really like that can help you get started:

- ✔ **Bluehost (`http://bluehost.com`):** This is the simplest of the bunch. With Bluehost, for as little as $6.95 a month, you get your own basic Web site and the capability to edit your own HTML files. Don't expect to get very advanced though. You have no root access, and dynamic options are limited in what you can do. Rumor has it that Bluehost also has issues if your application ever gets too much traffic, so be prepared to scale if this happens.

  Bluehost is a nice, simple option for getting a Web site up and running quickly, and for cheap. For something very simple, these guys are the ones to go with.

- ✔ **Fibernet (`http://fiber.net`):** This is the service I use. I am using a beta right now of a cloud-based service that allows you to scale very easily. Hopefully by the time you read this book, this service will be available to the general public. I chose Fibernet because of its great pricing and great service. Fibernet is a bit more for the advanced user, but it gives you the full flexibility you need.

- ✔ **MediaTemple (`http://mediatemple.com`):** MediaTemple can give you a few more options, and its plans vary depending on how much you want to scale. MediaTemple is built to scale, though, and can work well for a simple site that hopes to grow in the future.

  MediaTemple provides a virtual dedicated server option if you need full access to the file system and root access. However, you may find you will not have quite the flexibility you need if you have hard-core programmers or sysadmins working on your team.

- ✔ **GoDaddy (`http://godaddy.com`):** Like it or hate it, GoDaddy certainly knows how to make a statement, and it does so with cheap prices and easy setup as well.

  GoDaddy won't provide you with a dedicated server option, but it can handle just about everything else, from e-mail to domain setup and hosting to simple file hosting and storage. If you're looking for a simple, all-in-one solution, GoDaddy may be a good choice for you.

- ✔ **Joyent (`http://joyent.com`):** Joyent is one of the most Facebook-friendly hosting providers. It provides an option for Facebook developers that allows developers to host one application on its servers for free, for an entire year. Its premise is that it wants to get you off the ground and started so that you can focus on scaling later.

When it comes time to scale within that year, you still will have to upgrade, but if you never need that, Joyent turns out to be a cost-effective solution for Facebook server hosting. Its service requires a bit of setup and technical knowledge, but it does prove to be simpler than some of the more complex solutions, such as Rackspace and Amazon.

✔ **Slicehost (`http://slicehost.com`) and Rackspace (`http://rack space.com`):** Slicehost is one of my favorites because I like dedicated servers. Slicehost provides a cost-effective solution to building and managing virtual, dedicated servers for your application. You're given a full server in your preferred operating system, and you are responsible for the management and control of that server after that.

Rackspace does provide a nice management interface enabling backups and more, but you should have some knowledge in server hosting with the company. Rackspace also provides several cloud services and other dedicated hosting services you can choose from. It has some of the best support in the industry, and from my experience, I highly recommend Rackspace if your needs are similar to mine.

✔ **Amazon EC2 and S3 (`http://aws.amazon.com`):** Amazon EC2 is also a powerful option. Based 100 percent in the cloud, you have full flexibility to deploy entire dedicated servers on demand as you have the need to scale.

EC2 is not for the faint of heart. You will need a good amount of hosting knowledge and, in some cases, even a little software development knowledge to get some of its services off the ground. This can be a powerful solution though, and some services even complement some of the other services, such as Slicehost with an Amazon setup.

Just as I wrote this, Amazon released the capability to host an entire static Web site in its storage service, S3. If your Web site consists only of HTML files, with a little advanced knowledge you should be able to set up an S3 instance that points to your static HTML files and serves them on the Web. This is a great option if your entire site or application is in HTML and JavaScript.

✔ **Hire someone:** Of course, when all else fails, you can hire someone to help you. Run an ad on Craigslist, or post something in the Facebook Developer Forum. Or, you can post it on this book's Facebook Page or Group (`http://stay.am/dummiesgroup`); maybe someone there knows someone. There are also contractor sites like Elance (`http://elance.com`) for finding contractors that you could try if your budget allows for that option. When all else fails, get help!

After you have your hosting provider selected, you need to set it up so that a URL (something like `http://socialtoo.com`) points to a file somewhere on your server. You can usually do this in your server configuration. (This would be in your administration settings on services like Bluehost and MediaTemple. You may have to do a little hacking and have a little more knowledge to set this up on the other services.) You may just want to point it to a default file like `index.html`.

Understanding index.html

Each server can set a default file for each directory called on your Web site from a user's browser. Perhaps the user just calls `http://socialtoo.com`. My server knows that when `http://socialtoo.com` is called, it should look in the directory called `thisdirectory`. In `thisdirectory` is a file called `index.html`. I've configured my server to know that when no filename is specified (such as `thispage.html`), it calls `index.html` by default, and the browser returns the contents of my `index.html` file. Most Web servers default to this functionality. So, when I refer to the file `index.html` in this book, you now know why I use the name `index.html`.

What about my domain?

You've set up your server, and you have a file to point to. Now, where do you set up your domain to point to your server? First, you need to find a Domain Name System (DNS) service, which tells the Web that you own the domain and where to point the URL to know where your servers are. You can use a service like GoDaddy to do this.

Second, you need to set up *name servers,* which point your domain to an actual server on the Web. I like to use a service called ZoneEdit (`http://zoneedit.com`) to do this. GoDaddy also provides this service, as do many hosting providers. Your hosting provider might provide both services. With these services set up, the process for your browser knowing where to look to find your servers will look something like this (also see Figure 2-1):

1. The user visits yourdomain.com.

2. The user's browser asks its name servers, "Where can I find domain.com?"

3. The browser's name servers notice that zoneedit.com knows where domain.com is hosted. They ask zoneedit.com.

4. Zoneedit.com responds with an IP address location to where your servers are hosted.

5. The browser's name servers respond to the browser to look at the IP address returned by zoneedit.com.

6. Your servers look at the URL sent by the browser, and look in the assigned directory for the files needed to present the data to the user. Your servers return those files back to the browser.

7. The browser reads those files and presents them back to the user.

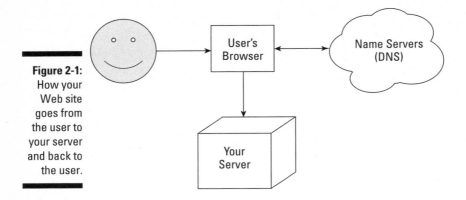

Figure 2-1:
How your
Web site
goes from
the user to
your server
and back to
the user.

Using existing content or servers

Because Facebook relies on iFrames, you can technically just import content
from another Web site you run. Of course, doing so may not preserve the
look and feel that Facebook provides and may not be as effective as just writing your content with a Facebook audience in mind, but it is a quick solution
to hosting in the Facebook environment. If you already run a Web site, keep
in mind that you can just import this Web site's URL into your application
settings that I talk about later in the chapter.

Or, if you already have your own Web site, it may be worth just piggybacking,
at least from the start, off your existing Web site setup and just adding a file
or two as I walk you through the Facebook setup. If your application is going
to be big, you may want to consider another solution. Nothing is wrong
with using an existing Web site's URL and hosting setup to host your
Facebook application.

Getting the Facebook Developer
Application Ready to Go

The Facebook Developer site, Developers.facebook.com, is the central
location for developers and application owners on Facebook. (If you aren't
a developer, don't be intimidated by this page — it's very friendly even to
marketers!) You can go to the Facebook Developer page to find out about
Facebook Platform.

To get you acclimated to the Facebook development environment, I encourage you to take a look around the Facebook Developer site. Knowing what's
available at http://developers.facebook.com and how you can use

it can really help you in the future — especially when Facebook decides to release a new feature, change existing features, or change the face of your code as you know it. (You can't say I didn't warn you; change happens, and you should be prepared.) Normally, Facebook gives you warnings on the Developer site (and the Developer application, which I show you next), so get in the habit of checking back there if you ever suspect that a feature isn't working or that a change has occurred.

On the Facebook Developer site, shown in Figure 2-2, you find the following sections:

- ✔ **Mobile Apps:** Facebook enables developers to fully integrate Facebook into the mobile experience. Facebook provides SDKs for the iPhone and Android to do this. According to Facebook, people spend more time on Facebook on their cell phone (via apps such as Facebook for the iPhone as well as text messaging notifications from Facebook) than on the rest of the site. Considering this information, this is a very important piece for Facebook! This section gives you a lot of the information you need to integrate into the mobile experience, and I cover this in more depth in Chapter 13.

- ✔ **Apps on Facebook.com:** This is where you'll want to spend most of your time for this chapter. As a developer, marketer, or brand, you need to decide whether you should develop on Facebook.com itself, integrate Facebook into your own Web site, or both. This section can help you make that decision and should give you all the information you need for developing applications on Facebook.com.

- ✔ **Open Source:** Facebook is passionate about open source! It has contributed a wealth of libraries, software, and platforms that it uses in-house for other developers to use, learn from, and contribute. Even its JavaScript SDK for accessing Facebook Platform is open source. You can find out about all the software Facebook has released as open source or contributed to in this section.

- ✔ **What's New:** This is where you can go to find out about all the new announcements, status updates, and more surrounding Facebook Platform. Click the More link, and you can even subscribe to the news via RSS. This is essentially Facebook's blog for developers.

- ✔ **Showcase:** As a marketer, you're really going to like this section. This shows all the different use cases and showcases examples of brands and organizations using Facebook Platform either on Facebook.com or integrating Facebook on their own Web sites. Study this section to get some great ideas on implementing Facebook Platform into your own brand and environment.

- ✔ **Add Facebook to My Site:** This button is where you start to integrate Facebook into your own Web site. I discuss this in Part III. Look around this section though, and see whether you start getting excited about what you can do beyond the Facebook.com environment.

✔ **Documentation:** This is the Bible for everything surrounding Facebook development. Go here and search for what you want to find out about. Look around and see whether you can discover something new!

✔ **Forum:** Have a question? Always ask here first. Millions of developers use this forum to ask and answer questions. This is your opportunity to ask your question and share the answer with the world. Be sure to search to see whether your question has already been answered though!

✔ **Status:** Not sure if Facebook is having server problems at the moment? There's a good chance it is, but before you blame Facebook, check here and see. If you still think it's having issues that haven't been reported, you can report them at `http://bugs.developers.facebook.com`.

The first thing you want to do when visiting the Facebook Developer site is to install a special application that enables you, as a developer, to have all the tools you need to set up an application. This application is called, quite fittingly, the Developer application.

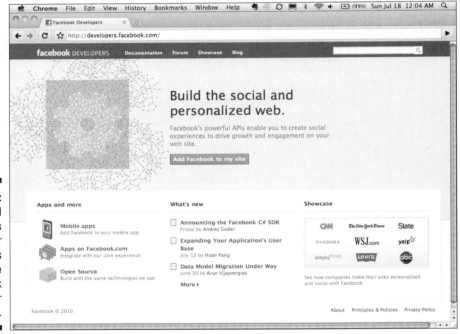

Figure 2-2:
Find instructions for developers on the Facebook Developer site.

Installing the tools you need

To add the Developer application to your Facebook account, follow these steps:

1. **Go to** www.facebook.com/developers.

   The Log in to Developer page appears.

2. **Click the Allow button.**

   If you click the Allow button, Facebook accesses information in your account, including who your friends are.

   You arrive at the Facebook Developer application, as shown in Figure 2-3.

That's it! You now have the Developer application associated with your account. From now on, when you type in **www.facebook.com/developers**, you see the Facebook Developer application.

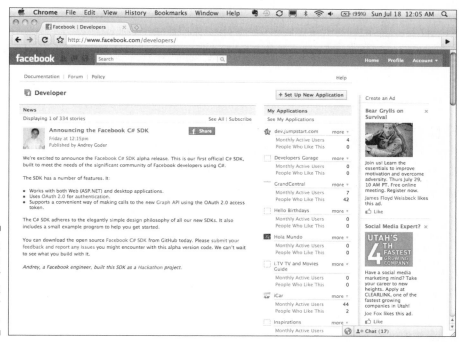

Figure 2-3:
The
sought-after
Facebook
Developer
application.

Looking around the Developer app

You'll find that any part of the Facebook interface changes its look and feel, terminology, and even functionality quite frequently. The Developer application is no exception, so if you see things different from what I describe here, be sure to check this book's Facebook Page or ask in the book's Facebook Group at `http://stay.am/dummiesgroup`. Be sure to click the Like button on my personal page (`http://facebook.com/stay`) or this book's Facebook Page (at the top of the page) so that you get regular updates about changes and updates in the Facebook Platform environment (and, on my personal page, updates about technology in general that I think you should know about!).

Here are some sections of the current Developer application that you should look for:

- **News:** This is where Facebook posts regular updates about news and announcements surrounding the platform. Remember, you need to pay attention to this — Facebook frequently adds new updates to its platform, and application owners who don't watch this section can get caught off guard.

    To ensure that you don't miss any updates, add this section to your favorite RSS reader by clicking, or copying the target URL to `Subscribe` in the upper-right corner. Don't do RSS? Check out the site `http://feedmyinbox.com`. It allows you to take any RSS feed and send it straight to your e-mail account, with no RSS reader necessary!

    What's an *RSS reader*? RSS readers are tools that read a common syntax called "RSS" (Really Simple Syndication), and present new updates to Web pages, blogs, and other types of sites when they occur. For instance, if you want to get all the updates on the News section of the Developer app, you would paste the subscribe URL into your favorite RSS reader and whenever a new post to that blog goes live, you'll see it in your reader, without ever having to go back to check the page. This simplifies the need to go back to all the pages you visit to see if there are updates. For a good RSS reader, I suggest signing up for Google Reader.

- **Status:** Is something broken in your code? Use this section for updates on the status of Facebook Platform. Facebook is still a young platform, growing rapidly, and it occasionally experiences growing pains! Although downtime doesn't occur frequently, you need to plan and expect such occurrences from time to time. The Status section tells you whether Facebook Platform is down.

- **My Applications:** If you're like I am, and after reading this book, go to town building application after application on Facebook Platform, this section can grow fairly long over the years. This is where every application you create goes. If you've created an application or two, they should appear here.

It is also here that you can go back and edit your application settings at any time after you create your application (I get to that part next). You can also get powerful analytics called Insights, information about your application such as your application ID and application key and secret, as well as easy ways to advertise or even set up translations for your application into multiple languages (I cover that in Chapter 14).

If you're in a hurry to get started, click the Set Up New Application button, shown in the upper-right corner of Figure 2-3, and skip to the next section in this chapter.

✔ **Documentation:** At the top of the page, you see a few links; these are resources for you, as a developer. Most of them take you back to `http://developers.facebook.com`. Documentation just takes you back to all the Facebook documentation that you need to write your application.

If you really want to code and get your hands dirty, you need to become familiar with this section. Here you can find a full reference of every call possible in the API, how to authenticate, what the rules are, examples, tips, tutorials, and more. This is a powerful section if you want to pick up where this book leaves off.

✔ **Forum:** Also in the links at the top of the page, this is where you go if you have a question. You can also get there by going to `http://forum.developers.facebook.com`. If you ever have a question, go here first and do a search for what you're looking for. If your question hasn't been answered yet, open a new topic and hopefully another Facebook developer like myself or others may be listening. Who knows? Occasionally even a Facebook employee or two will drop in and help answer your questions if you ask nicely!

If you find an answer to your question, it is always good etiquette to share that answer for others to find later. Something I like to do is to share the answer on my blog and then insert a link to the thread I created in the forum. You can also just post your full answer on the Developer Forum itself. By approaching it in this manner, you ensure that others don't have to repeat the same question you just found an answer to. Be a good citizen!

✔ **Policy:** Rules! Rules! Rules! I cover this in much more detail in the last part of the book, but to develop on Facebook Platform, you need to know the rules. Facebook has gotten less strict over the years, but you must follow certain rules to avoid getting banned by Facebook or losing your business model because you neglected to read the rules. Read this section thoroughly.

✔ **Help:** The Help section is where you can go to find help on commonly asked questions surrounding Facebook Platform. You may find that this section answers questions you were not able to answer in the Developer Forum. However, when in doubt and if you are unable to find the answer here, check the Developer Forum!

Creating Your Own Application in Five Minutes

Creating your first application is surprisingly easy, and you can have a simple app set up in the Facebook.com environment in just five minutes! If you follow along with the examples in this chapter, I show you how to create the basic foundations of an application that allows users to share, collect, and organize inspiring quotes with their friends. This enables your users to, more than just sharing on and reading your wall, organize and see the quotes by what their friends are sharing, rather than reading a static list of quotes like a traditional Web site provides. The power of Facebook Platform is that you have the capability to provide full relevance for the user surrounding his or her experience in your application. Rather than having to search for quotes, the user can immediately see what his friends are sharing, and choose from that rather than having to guess what he might like to see.

Minute 1: Set up your application

Follow these steps to name your app and add some simple settings — for example, telling Facebook what path to follow when people want to visit your application:

1. **On the Developer page, click the Set Up New App button.**

   You arrive at an Essential Information page that looks a lot like what is shown in Figure 2-4.

2. **Type a name for your application in the Application Name text box.**

   Your app name can be *almost* anything — it doesn't even have to be unique. But you probably want to pick something that describes your application well. In this example, I call the application *Inspirations*. You can do the same if you want to follow along.

   Facebook, like any company, has to protect its trademark. So, Facebook doesn't allow any applications that include the words *Face* or *Facebook* in the name. As a general rule of thumb, if the name you choose might in anyway confuse users into thinking Facebook wrote it, you should probably pick another name. That is, of course, unless you don't care whether Facebook disables your application later on.

3. **Click the Facebook Terms link, read the terms, and if you want to continue with your application, click the Agree option.**

4. **Click the Create App button.**

   This takes you to a screen that looks something like Figure 2-5, with the title Edit *Application Name*. See the nearby sidebar "Weird IDs, keys, and secrets" for a discussion about the crazy sets of numbers and letters that Facebook assigns to your new app (these will be visible after you save your application).

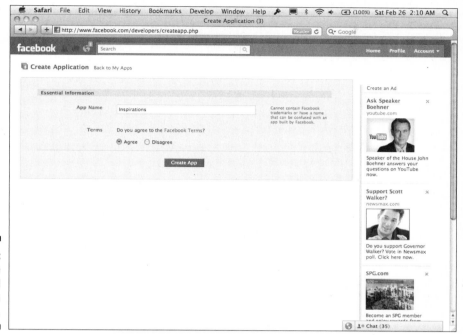

Figure 2-4:
The
Essential
Information
page.

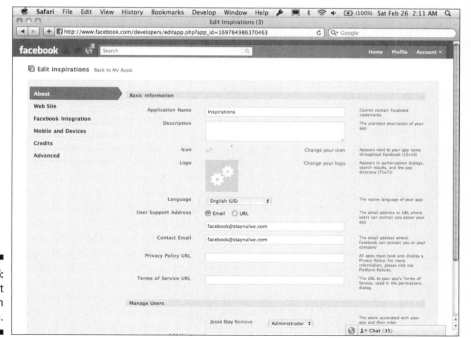

Figure 2-5:
The Edit
Application
screen.

5. Click the Facebook Integration link on the left.

You arrive at the page (see Figure 2-6) where you enter paths and settings for your application's *Canvas Page.* It's called that because it's your canvas, as a developer, on Facebook. Developers must follow certain guidelines on their Canvas Page (outlined in the Facebook terms), but for the most part, you have lots of freedom to do what you want.

6. Type a unique name in the Canvas Page text box; users will go to this path when they use your application on Facebook.

The path for your Canvas Page must be unique. In this example, I enter **inspirationsapp**.

7. Type the path that points to the `index.html` file that you set up on your server (see the section "Setting Up Your Hosting Environment," earlier in this chapter) in the Canvas URL text box.

I type **http://inspirations.staynalive.com/**, which points to a file called `index.html` on my Fibernet server.

To avoid getting an error message, your Canvas Callback URL must have a trailing forward slash (/) at the end.

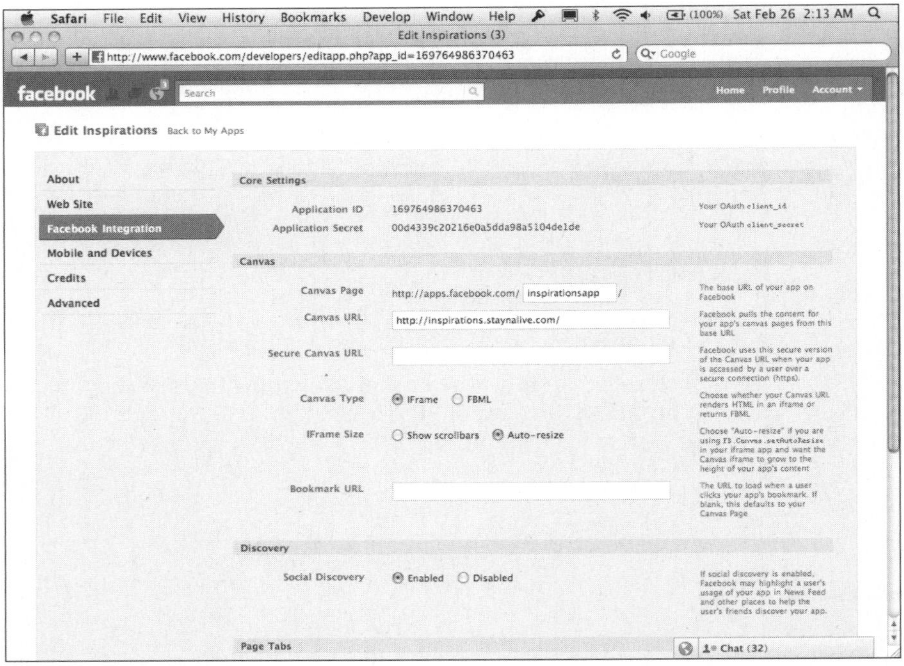

Figure 2-6:
The
Facebook
Integration
settings.

8. **Select any remaining options in the Canvas settings section.**

   For this example, select the iFrame Render Method option and leave all other settings at the default options. (When you set this up, there may not be a render method to choose from. This is because Facebook is deprecating the FBML render method as I write this. For now, focus on the iFrame render method if you have the option.)

9. **Click the Save Changes button.**

   Your application is set up, and you're ready to write some code!

Minutes 2–4: Write your application

In these steps, you take the file you created on your server earlier in the chapter and write some very simple HTML. Facebook will parse your HTML and render it back to the user in an iFrame on Facebook.com.

These steps should get you started:

1. **Open the HTML file (that you created earlier in the chapter) in your favorite editor.**

   This is where you insert your HTML. If you're creating this file for the first time, save it now so that you can reference it later.

   Writing code sounds scary. In this example, all you're doing is creating some simple HTML to put on your Canvas Page. Most people know a little HTML, so this should be simple. If not, I recommend *HTML 4 For Dummies, 5th Edition,* by Ed Tittel and Mary Burmeister. Here you can find out how to do some really cool stuff with HTML. After that, you might want to read *JavaScript For Dummies, 4th Edition,* by Emily A. Vander Veer (both published by Wiley) if you want to take your Facebook application even further.

2. **Copy and paste basic HTML into your file.**

   Because we're in a time crunch, I'm going to keep this nice and simple. In my HTML file, I wrote the following:

```
<html>
<body>
<h1>Inspirations</h1>
<div id="quote">
        "When I examine myself and my methods of thought, I come to the
        conclusion that the gift of fantasy has meant more to me than
        any talent for abstract, positive thinking." -Albert Einstein
</div>
</body>
</html>
```

3. **Add some HTML and JavaScript to show your profile picture and name.**

   Here, you add a dynamic picture of yourself, the application owner, and your name. This may sound a bit intimidating, but you can just copy what I did (replacing your application ID) and it should work. I cover what each of these sections of code does in later chapters.

4. **Add some initializing JavaScript right below the opening body tag.**

   Again, you can just copy and paste this. This tells Facebook what your app is, and that you want Facebook to be able to process XFBML on the Page:

```
<div id="fb-root"></div>
<script src="http://connect.facebook.net/en_US/all.js" charset="utf-8">
        </script>
<script>
    FB.init({appId: '169764986370463', status: true, cookie: true, xfbml:
        true});
</script>
```

What is *XFBML*? XFBML stands for "Facebook Markup Language for Web sites" (I know — I don't really understand where the X comes from either). It is a simple markup language invented by Facebook (actually, it was an internal set of libraries used inside Facebook, called "FBML" at the time before it was released to the public) to allow you to very easily create things like profile pictures in a Web site environment. Because your code is in an iFrame, Facebook treats your code similar to a Web site and XFBML will work. In reality, you could use JavaScript and HTML to do this as well, but that would take more time, wouldn't it?

5. **Add the following HTML below the opening** <div id="quote "> **tag (and before the Einstein quote) that you created in Step 2:**

```
<span id="facebook_stuff">
   <div id="profile_pic"><fb:profile-pic uid="683545112"></fb:profile-
        pic></div>
   <div id="profile_name"><fb:name uid="683545112" useyou="false">
        </fb:name>
</span>
```

If all goes well, you should now see my Facebook profile picture and my name below it to the left of the quote you just printed. Notice the funny <fb: tags — those are the XFBML I talked about. The string <fb:profile-pic uid="683545112"/> tells Facebook to replace that piece of text with my profile picture.

Weird IDs, keys, and secrets

On the Edit Application page, notice that Facebook assigns an application ID, an API key, and a secret to your application when you save your application settings for the first time. These IDs are important, and although you probably don't need to memorize them, you will use them frequently throughout your application if you ever decide to get your hands dirty with core elements of the Facebook API. This is what they mean:

✔ **Application ID:** This is the unique, numbered ID for your application. Facebook is in the process of migrating to this over the use of the API key (which I discuss next). When you initialize your API calls, you use this to identify it is your application making those calls. I cover this extensively in Part IV.

✔ **API key:** This string is used as an alternative way to identify your application to Facebook. You can still use it, but I encourage you to use your application ID whenever possible, because Facebook

appears to be moving in the direction of using the application ID for identification now. You may still need to use this in some of the language SDKs for Facebook that you use, though.

✔ **Secret:** Also known as the *secret key,* this can be considered your password for accessing ultrasensitive data on behalf of users. Never reveal this in your HTML or JavaScript, where users can read it!

Your secret key enables you to make calls on behalf of the user when the user is not actively logged in to Facebook. Users can grant your application "offline access" permissions. When a user has granted this permission, you can use the secret key along with your application ID or API key (both should work, at least at the time of this writing) to make calls on your server without the user needing to interact with your application. An example of this would be a script that reads through your application's users and checks for new updates about those users to store in your database.

The second tag, `<fb:name>`, prints the name of the specified user (in this case, me). The string `useyou="false"` tells Facebook to not display the text *you* if it is you who are visiting the Canvas Page and that user ID is your own.

Want to replace my name and profile picture with your own? You just need to find your Facebook ID. The easiest way to get your Facebook profile ID is to click your picture on your Facebook profile and then look at the URL. At the end of the URL, you can see `"id="`, followed by a long number. Just copy that number and replace it with yours for the uid in the example in the code sample above. Now your own profile picture and name should show up! You may want to write this ID down because you'll probably use it again.

Your HTML should now look something like the following:

```html
<html>
<body>
<div id="fb-root"></div>
<script src="http://connect.facebook.net/en_US/all.js" charset="utf-8"></script>
<script>
    FB.init({appId: 169764986370463', status: true, cookie: true, xfbml: true});
</script>
<h1>Inspirations</h1>
<div id="quote">
            <span id="facebook_stuff">
            <div id="profile_pic"><fb:profile-pic uid="683545112">
             </fb:profile-pic></div>
            <div id="profile_name"><fb:name uid="683545112" useyou="false">
             </fb:name>
            </span>
            "When I examine myself and my methods of thought, I come to the
            conclusion that the gift of fantasy has meant more to me than any
            talent for abstract, positive thinking." -Albert Einstein
</div>
</body>
</html>
```

Minute 5: View and test your application

Now you can view your application! Follow these steps:

1. **Go to** `http://apps.facebook.com/inspirationsapp` **(or the name of the app you just chose).**

   Because you can't choose mine, this will probably be something different!

   If everything went well, you should see something that looks like what is shown in Figure 2-7.

2. **If it doesn't look right, go back and look at your HTML to see what might be different from what you did in the previous steps.**

   If your app still doesn't work, be sure to ask on this book's Facebook Group or in the Facebook Developer Forum.

That's it! You just created your first Facebook application in only five minutes. (Okay, if you were doing it while reading this, it may have taken just a bit longer, but you get the idea of how simple this is.)

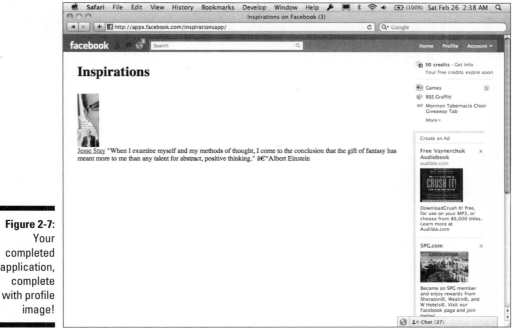

Figure 2-7:
Your
completed
application,
complete
with profile
image!

Chapter 3

Delving Deeper — Understanding Your Application and Navigating the Application Setup Process

In This Chapter

▶ Figuring out the structure of your application

▶ XFBML or JavaScript?

▶ Understanding your application's setup

*N*ow that you've written your first app, this chapter takes you a little further to help you understand a few of the things you just did. I take you through the application setup process, which should give you additional clarification about those fields that you filled out in Chapter 2. In addition, I cover a little more about using plain HTML and JavaScript versus integrating XFBML, and I describe why either one might appeal to you.

When to Use JavaScript and When to Use the Server to Access Facebook Platform

Among the toughest decisions my clients make when working on applications are issues like, "How much of the rendering should they control on the server side? How much should they handle on the client with JavaScript?" In reality, you can do just about everything with JavaScript, making calls back to the server as needed to get dynamic data from your database. You might also have times when you want to control everything from the server, making API calls back to Facebook using a library — like Facebook's native PHP or Python libraries — to make all the calls on behalf of the user. When do you access the API in JavaScript, and when should you do so on your server?

The short answer is, "It's up to you, and it all depends on your needs." It may be that JavaScript isn't your forte and that you prefer accessing the Facebook APIs in a language such as PHP. Or perhaps it's just the opposite, and you'd rather not touch a server-side language like PHP to make your calls to Facebook. The following sections describe the advantages that I see to using a JavaScript-controlled architecture as well as the advantages that you could gain from a server-side-controlled architecture.

Advantages to a JavaScript-controlled architecture

In some cases, you want to use a JavaScript-controlled architecture. Here are some advantages of doing so:

✔ **No server administration worries:** One advantage that you have to using JavaScript is that you have less need to worry about gaining access to a back-end server architecture. For instance, consider that you work in a large corporation and you find a lot of red tape to gaining access to the back end for your Web site architecture. You only have access to the front-end, HTML side of the code. In this case, it may be much easier to just consider JavaScript calls and then ask your infra-structure team to provide you with the appropriate API calls to get the data from your database using Ajax and page reloads.

Ajax is a style of JavaScript coding that stands for "Asynchronous JavaScript and XML." It allows you to make calls to a server somewhere from the user's browser without ever having to redirect the user to another site. The user can stay on the same page forever, and you can dynamically get new data from a server somewhere as the user interacts with that page.

✔ **Compatibility with other JavaScript APIs:** Another advantage that you have to using JavaScript may be that you are already using other JavaScript-controlled APIs. OpenSocial, for instance, is a very JavaScript-heavy API, and while it now has REST APIs that you can use, it was origi-nally built to run on the user's browser. Something like this would work much better with a JavaScript-controlled Facebook application than a server-side application — you would have less code to work with! If this part doesn't make much sense to you, don't worry — just know that if your application already uses OpenSocial or another JavaScript-heavy API, you may want to go the JavaScript route.

REST APIs are server-side APIs that, in short, allow any server to access the API in a standardized fashion. This is in contrast with a proprietary JavaScript API, where the specs for accessing the data on another server aren't published but are intended to be accessed through provided JavaScript SDKs only. With traditional REST APIs, any server, or any browser for that matter, can access the data on other servers in any way they like, with or without a provided SDK from the makers of the API.

✔ **Ease of coding:** Finally, JavaScript, at times, can just be easier! In the Inspirations example, for a simple application, it's simply a matter of copy and paste. If you need only to do a quick call to authenticate the user and pull its list of friends, it wouldn't be much more code than the example I share in Chapter 2, and if you ever have to transfer the application to another developer, he would probably have a little JavaScript knowledge. JavaScript has a *huge* advantage because of this!

Advantages to a server-side-controlled architecture

In other cases, you want to use a server-side-controlled architecture. Here are some reasons to do so:

✔ **It makes sense:** Sometimes it just makes sense to load the page and all the data from the server, requiring an entire page refresh. That's okay. Sometimes that's the easier thing to do. It's important that you don't get caught up in doing JavaScript just to do JavaScript when the server-side version may actually be faster.

✔ **Automated back-end calls:** The best times to use a server-side API call to Facebook Platform is when you need to make calls on behalf of a user without the user being actively logged in. When you need to use a secret key to access user data, and at times even a nonexpiring session key (given with `offline_access` permissions), that is the best time to make server-side API calls.

✔ **Compare and contrast:** Beyond that, my best suggestion for when to make a server-side versus a JavaScript call is to look at what is easier and what produces the fastest results. Sometimes the Facebook JavaScript SDK can be a bit slow to load. Here, doing a server-based call might make sense, where you can just load the page first and then wait for Facebook to do its stuff to produce anything related to Facebook. Or, perhaps you can do it in fewer lines of code in PHP, Java, or Ruby on Rails than you could in JavaScript. Perhaps development could be faster on the server. When these cases are true, don't hesitate to use the server to your advantage.

Using JavaScript: Deciding whether to use XFBML or pure JavaScript to access Facebook Platform

When you're looking to save time in your HTML, *XFBML* (Facebook Markup Language for Web sites) is your friend. *FBML,* the original name for this markup language, was originally developed by Facebook as an internal markup language to make internal development of its Web site easier. After launching Facebook Platform to developers in 2007, Facebook quickly realized that this markup language would be a big benefit to developers on Platform as well, so it released many of the tags it was using internally — and many others — to developers to speed the development process when simple, repetitive tasks were needed. Originally these were released in a non-iFrame format that is now being deprecated. Now they are made available as XFBML in an iFrame format, as well as for use on Web sites. In short, XFBML is a series of tags used to make your coding much easier.

XFBML can be a great tool in helping you mimic the `Facebook.com` environment without having to look up the code to do it. In general, users on `Facebook.com` do not like to leave the site when they are on it. Because of this, the more fluid you can make the experience to feel like the rest of their `Facebook.com` experience, the less likely they will be to leave your application. Using XFBML tags can ensure that you use Facebook's existing look, feel, and fluidity, while at the same time ensuring that if Facebook ever changes its user interface in the future, you will not be left rushing to alter your code to handle the new user interface. Ideally, it should all just adapt!

I won't spend much time on what XFBML tags are available. For more information, refer to Facebook's Developer documentation for the most up-to-date details on this markup language.

I strongly recommend looking over the Facebook documentation on XFBML for more information. Get to know the available tags because, especially if you're creating a custom Page link (formerly known as "tabs") application, you want to know how you can speed up the process.

Enabling XFBML in an iFrame environment

Facebook has made it easy to include Facebook Markup Language for Web sites (XFBML) on any Web site or iFrame Canvas Page. All you need is a little JavaScript knowledge (or even just the capability to copy and paste). To do this, you need to add a little bit of code to the bottom of your Web page. You can see how I did this in Chapter 2. I called the Facebook JavaScript SDK and called a basic `init` block, and then Facebook knew how to render XFBML tags on the page.

As a reminder, in the example in Chapter 2, you added some simple JavaScript that basically initialized your application and enabled your iFrame HTML file to be read. You started by adding an empty `div` with the ID `root`. This gave Facebook a place to put stuff later — no need to worry about what happens with this, other than that you need to have it somewhere on the page.

Next, you called Facebook's JavaScript Client SDK. This gave you access to all kinds of libraries that Facebook provides to access its API.

Next, you initialized your JavaScript with Facebook so that Facebook would know it is your application that is making the API calls (via the `FB.init` block in the `<script>` tags). You called `FB.init` and passed the ID of your application, which told Facebook that this is the application that will be making calls on behalf of the user.

The next parameter you passed to `FB.init` was `xfbml: true`. This stated that you wanted Facebook to parse any XFBML on the page and enabled the libraries for doing the parsing.

Now when you go to `http://apps.facebook.com/inspirationsapp` (or your equivalent app URL), you successfully see a Facebook profile image and your name (or mine if you didn't replace my code) right below it. All of this is being rendered in an iFrame HTML tag on `Facebook.com`.

Making traditional JavaScript calls to Facebook in an iFrame environment

Although XFBML makes things a lot easier, with a little more effort, you can make traditional JavaScript calls to get the same information. You can do this through the `FB.api` call, which I explain later in this book.

Taking the example from Chapter 2, here's how an example application using just JavaScript could work:

```html
<html>
<body>
<div id="fb-root"></div>
<script src="http://connect.facebook.net/en_US/all.js" charset="utf-8"></script>
<script>
    FB.init({appId: '169764986370463', status: true, cookie: true, xfbml: true});
</script>
<h1>Inspirations</h1>
<div id="quote">
            <span id="facebook_stuff">
            <div id="profile_pic"><img src="https://graph.facebook.
            com/683545112/picture" border="0" /></div>
            <div id="profile_name"></div>
            </span>
            "When I examine myself and my methods of thought, I come to the
             conclusion that the gift of fantasy has meant more to me than any
             talent for abstract, positive thinking." -Albert Einstein
</div>
<script>
     FB.api('/683545112', function(response) {
     document.getElementById('profile_name').innerHTML = response.name;
    });
</script>
</body>
</html>
```

In this example, all I do is replace the `<fb:profile-pic>` tag with a simple `<img>` HTML tag, calling a Facebook Graph API URL (which I explain later in this book). This renders the given user's profile image automatically. Then, to get the name, I make an `FB.api` call and return the results for the name into the `profile_name <div>` tags I set up (using JavaScript's `innerHTML` method). If this doesn't make much sense yet, that's okay. I explain what all this means in future chapters. What's most important is that you understand that you don't have to use XFBML to accomplish what XFBML does. XFBML just makes things a little simpler.

Using the server: Accessing Facebook's API from your server in an iFrame environment

Making Facebook API calls from your server-hosted environment — at least in an iFrame, `Facebook.com`-hosted application — can be a bit more tricky. If your coding skills aren't advanced, you may want to skip this section — again, you can still do all this in plain HTML and JavaScript! Facebook's own documentation isn't 100 percent clear on this. It actually isn't that difficult, though. I show you how to do this in PHP. The basic steps are as follows:

1. Install and call the Facebook PHP libraries.

2. Identify your application and get back a `$facebook` object.

3. Start making API calls with the `$facebook` object.

Here's how you do that in PHP. If you want to try it, you need to have PHP set up on your server, and your Web server needs to know how to recognize PHP files and execute them. This is the same block as shown previously, but in PHP (with one additional Login button if for any reason the user is not logged in):

```
<html>
<body>
<h1>Inspirations</h1>
<div id="quote">
            <span id="facebook_stuff">
            <div id="profile_pic"><img src="https://graph.facebook.
            com/683545112/picture" border="0" /></div>

<?php
require 'facebook.php';

// replace "SECRET_KEY_GOES_HERE" with appropriate values
$facebook = new Facebook(array(
 'appId' => '169764986370463',
 'secret' => 'SECRET_KEY_GOES_HERE',
```

```
 'cookie' => true,
));
$user = $facebook->api('/683545112');
?><div id="profile_name"><?php echo $user['name'] ?></div>
            </span>
            "When I examine myself and my methods of thought, I come to the
            conclusion that the gift of fantasy has meant more to me than any
            talent for abstract, positive thinking." -Albert Einstein
</div>
</body>
</html>
```

This example looks a lot like the JavaScript example earlier in the chapter. When you call $facebook->api() on the user object 683545112, it returns that user's public data, and you can then retrieve things like the user's name without anyone even needing to authenticate.

On the back end, PHP is doing some crazy things like parsing out an encrypted string (the signed token) and figuring out who the currently logged-in user to Facebook.com is. Because you're using a library, you don't have to worry about that stuff though. I explain more about what's going on behind the scenes later in the book, though, just in case you don't have PHP and need to replicate this in your own environment.

If you want to retrieve more information about the user, direct him through the authorization process. I go over that in detail in Chapter 9, so don't worry about that for now. If any of this seems too complicated, don't worry — I'm only show-ing this so that you can see that this works in PHP on the server side as well.

Understanding the Application Setup Process

Now you're ready to get your application set up by filling out the Application Setup form. In my consulting, this is the section where my clients have the most issues. Facebook often changes it, and you find very little documenta-tion on what each field does. I go through each field here so that you know exactly what you need to fill out. I list each field under each individual sec-tion. Although you may not have to read this now, you might want to book-mark this for reference later.

This section changes quite frequently. In fact, from the time I wrote this to the time I edited it, the section was almost entirely different. I suggest that you check back on this book's Facebook Group (http://stay.am/dummies group) if something doesn't look the same here and you want to find out more about what it does.

About

In this section, you fill out all the information about your application: What's its name? What does it do? Who are the contacts for your application? Who are the developers and admins of your application? At the time of this writing, this section looked like what is shown in Figure 3-1.

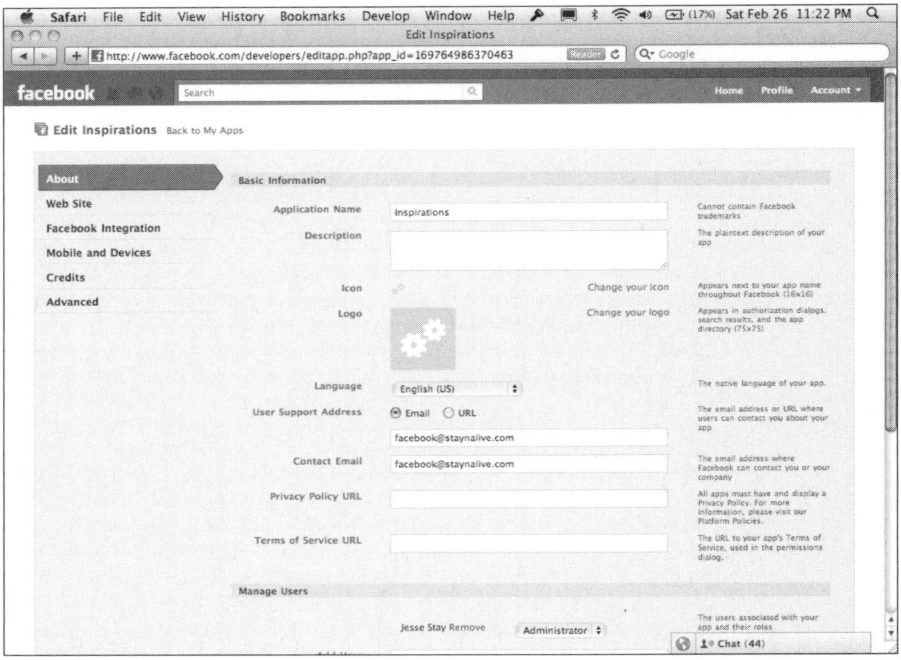

Figure 3-1:
The About section in application settings.

Settings on this page include the following:

✔ **Application Name:** This is the name of your application that appears on your application's page and in the Facebook Application Directory, and is also what the search engines index. It would be good to make sure that the name of your application here is tuned for search engine optimization (SEO) so that people can find it outside of Facebook as well as within. This field does not have to be unique.

✔ **Description:** Limited to 250 characters, this is what describes your application in the Facebook Application Directory. Make it something that describes your application in simple terms so that users want to click it and install it!

✔ **Icon:** This is a small, 16-x-16 representation of your logo. Keep it simple — this will appear next to updates in the user's news feed that your application makes on his or her behalf. It will be something by which users can recognize your application, so keep that in mind when you choose a graphic for this.

✔ **Logo:** This is a bigger representation of your application's logo. It has a maximum size of 75 x 75 pixels, and it appears next to your application in the Application Directory and elsewhere when Facebook has room to display a bigger version of your logo.

✔ **Language:** This is the default language for your application. This may come in handy if you are using any of the Facebook internationalization features (which I describe later in the book).

✔ **User Support Address:** This is visible to users and is where they can contact you if they need support for your application. You can choose either an e-mail address or a specific URL that takes them to either a contact form or a Web site with more information on how to contact you.

✔ **Contact E-mail:** This is the main e-mail address for Facebook communication to you. Facebook, on occasion, may send abuse reports and other information it receives to you through this e-mail address.

✔ **Privacy URL:** If you have a specific page where users can set specific privacy settings for your application, this is where users are taken to set the privacy settings for your application.

✔ **Terms of Service URL:** If you need your users to agree to your own terms of service, this is the URL that users are taken to during the authorization process.

✔ **Developers:** The people you list here will be able to edit the application and have access to the application when it's in Sandbox mode. (See the "Advanced" section, later in this chapter.) If you opt to do so, these users will also be displayed on the application's About page for the application, showing who created the application.

You can assign various roles to each user. You can add them as any of the following:

- *Administrators:* Administrators have full access.

- *Developers:* Developers can access technical things like the capability to change some of the app settings through the Facebook API.

- *Testers:* Test users only have access to use the application when it is in Sandbox mode. They cannot alter or see any of the application settings.

- *Insights users:* Insights users only have access to the analytics and Insights settings for the app.

Web site

As I mention earlier, you can also integrate Facebook on your own Web site. Here is where you tell Facebook what Web site you will be integrating with. This also ensures that no other Web site can access Facebook on your behalf. See Figure 3-2 for a glimpse at what this page looks like. The settings on this page are as follows:

- ✔ **Application ID:** This is the unique identifier for your application, and it will be needed if you access the Facebook API through the JavaScript SDK.

- ✔ **Application Secret:** This is the unique identifier that you need when your application needs to make calls on behalf of users when they are not necessarily logged in to your application. Batch (cron) jobs and server-side operations are often where you use this. Note that you also have to get offline access permissions from the users when you do this, and you also need to store their session key.

- ✔ **Site URL:** This is the main URL for your Web site. If my site is `Social Too.com` (which it is), this would be `http://socialtoo.com`.

- ✔ **Site Domain:** If you want to use subdomains all managed by the same application, enter the base domain here. So, if I want to allow `app1. socialtoo.com` along with `www.socialtoo.com`, I would enter **socialtoo.com** in this field.

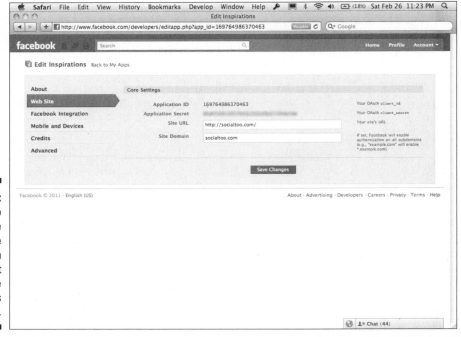

Figure 3-2: The Web site page in the application settings at the time of this writing.

Facebook Integration

If you're going to try the examples I've shown so far, this is the section that you need to fill out. In fact, if you filled out the minimum fields in Chapter 2, you're already somewhat familiar with this. Now I show you what the other fields mean. Figure 3-3 shows what this looks like.

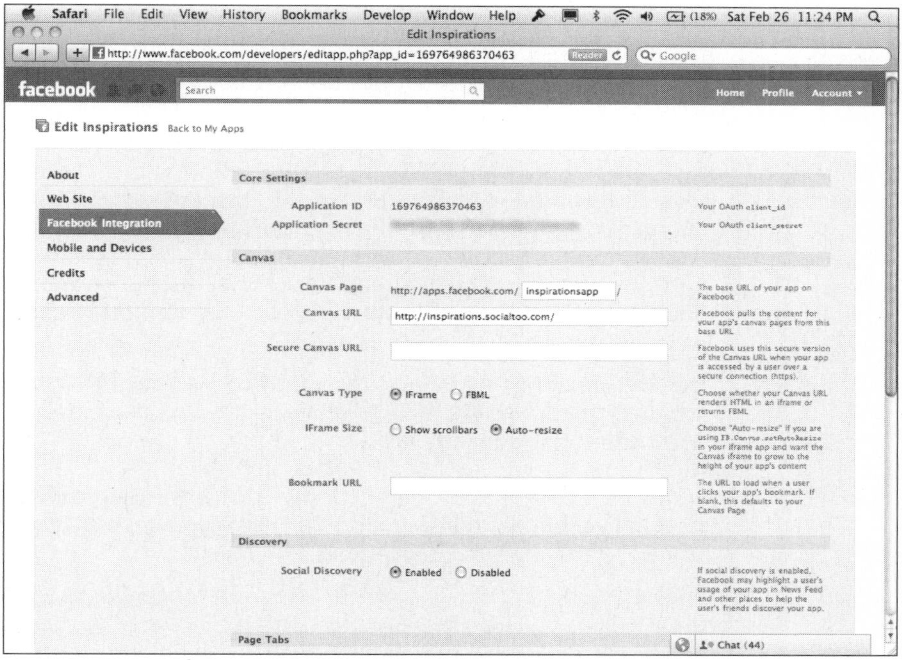

Figure 3-3:
Facebook
Integration
settings.

The settings on this page include the following:

- ✔ **Canvas URL:** You filled this out earlier. This is the unique identifier for your application. When users visit your application on `Facebook. com`, they go here. In my Inspirations application, I use the identifier `inspirationsapp`, and when users go to `http://apps.facebook. com/inspirationsapp`, they are taken to this application.

- ✔ **Canvas Callback URL:** This is the URL on your server that Facebook requests when users visit the Canvas Page URL. So, when users visit `http://apps.facebook.com/inspirationsapp`, Facebook calls your Canvas callback URL, which returns data that Facebook then formats and returns to the user with the Facebook header, footer, and sidebar ads that appear in all the applications.

✔ **Secure Canvas URL:** Users have the option to use Facebook entirely over a secure connection. By providing this, Facebook uses this URL when users use Facebook in that context. This way, they won't receive a warning stating that some of the elements on the page aren't secure.

✔ **Canvas Type:** You have the choice of FBML or iFrame here. Facebook is now pushing developers toward using the iFrame method if they can, and it will be deprecating the FBML type shortly. You might just be better off choosing an iFrame here, implementing a little JavaScript to be able to parse XFBML, and then going that route if you insist on having FBML in your application. Again, Facebook will be removing FBML in the future, so it's to your advantage to choose the iFrame option. I expect this field to go away because you won't have a choice in the future.

✔ **iFrame Size:** Here you have the option of Show Scrollbars or Auto-Resize. Use Show Scrollbars if you don't mind seeing scroll bars on the side of the iFrame and you don't want to worry about the height of the app as it changes throughout the user experience. If you choose Auto-Resize, you have a bit more responsibility to adapt the size of your app as it changes. You also won't see the scroll bars on the side of the iFrame. It will look more natural. If you can, I suggest going with the Auto-Resize option.

✔ **Bookmark URL:** This defaults to your Canvas Page URL (which you selected previously). Each application can allow users to bookmark the application. These bookmarks then appear in a prominent location in the left navigation pane of Facebook after users log in. This is a great way for you to get your application in an always-visible place for the user in Facebook. This specific URL is where Facebook takes users when they click your application's bookmark.

✔ **Social Discovery:** When enabled, as people authorize your application, their friends will also see that they authorized your application. For maximum visibility, I recommend that you enable this option.

✔ **Tab Name:** You can set up tabs (these are actually no longer tabs — they are now links on the left side of Pages) on Facebook Pages that pull in information that your application provides. This is the name of that tab (or link). You can have only one tab (or link) per application, but your application can actually spawn other applications (via the permissions API, currently part of the old REST APIs) that can technically each have its own tab (or link), all owned by the parent application. Find out more about this in Chapter 5.

✔ **Page Tab Type:** Just like the Canvas Type, this is going away soon, in favor of the iFrame type. I suggest that you choose iFrame. As I cover in Chapter 5, you can provide a custom link (formerly tabs) on the left side that reads your URL in an iFrame.

✔ **Tab URL:** This is the callback URL that gets called when the user opens the tab (or link) for your application on a Facebook Page. (See the example tab in Figure 3-4.) This is a path relative to your Canvas Page URL, so be sure that your Canvas Page URL either points to a directory or that your Web server controls the redirect based on the path if you use this.

✔ **Edit URL:** When you go into your Facebook Page settings, you can click an Edit link in the Applications section next to your application (assuming that your application has been installed on the Page). This URL is what that "edit" link points to. This can be a great place to provide configuration settings for your custom link/tab.

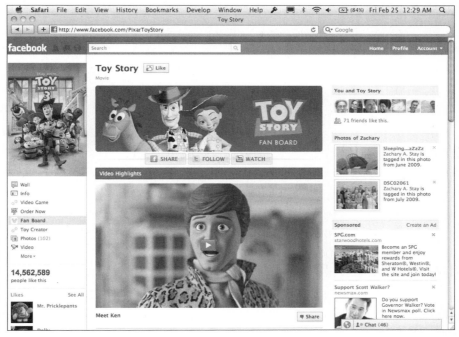

Figure 3-4:
A tab (also called a link) on a Facebook Page.

Mobile and Devices

If you're building a mobile app that integrates Facebook, configure this section for the optimal experience. Read Chapter 13 to find out more about this section and to see how you can build your own mobile app experience using Facebook. See Figure 3-5 for what this section looks like.

The settings on this page include the following:

✔ **Application Type:** You have the choice here of HTML5/Mobile Web or Native app. Choose the one that's applicable to you — Facebook uses this to identify what type of authentication experience to provide to the user.

✔ **iOS Bundle ID:** This is the value from your iOS app's `info.plist` file used for Facebook integration and for securing the login experience by Facebook in your iOS application. This should be in the format of, or similar to, `com.company_name.app_name`.

✔ **iTunes App Store ID:** This is the ID provided by Apple for your application in iTunes. Facebook uses this to provide a proper link to your app's iTunes Store entry. Unfortunately, at the time I write this, it's a bit unclear where this link can be found, but it might be wise to just fill this out anyway.

✔ **Key Hash:** I go over how to generate this in Chapter 13. This is the hash that you generate for your Android app if you're integrating with Android. It tells Android devices that have installed your app that it's okay to work with Facebook.

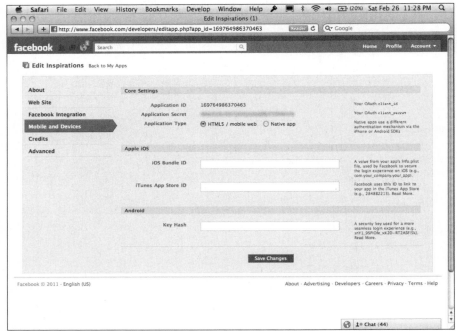

Figure 3-5:
The Mobile and Devices section in your app settings.

Credits

Credits are rather new at the time I write this. In fact, they were in beta just shortly before this book went to print. For that reason, I don't go far into detail on credits. However, if you're at all interested in social commerce, it will definitely be worth your while to find out what Credits can do for your application. Searching for the term *credits* on the Facebook Developer documentation provides you with information about things that you can do with Credits and how to use Graph API to access them. I strongly suggest that you check it out. See Figure 3-6 to understand the settings for credits that I'll cover here:

- **Company Name:** This is a drop-down list of companies that you have registered with Facebook for the Credits program. If you've never used Credits before, this drop-down will likely be blank. Click the Register link next to it to register your company and identify bank account information for funds collected from Facebook Credits. Then, make sure that this new company is selected.

- **Credits Callback URL:** When a new order using Facebook Credits is initiated, Facebook pings this URL to give you knowledge of the transaction. This is probably a URL that you'll want to use to track transactions, and maybe even give users access, knowing that they've now paid for what you're offering.

- **E-mail:** This is the e-mail address that Facebook uses when people have questions about payments.

- **Credits Test Users:** This is a comma-separated list of Facebook user IDs (the number only) that can use your application and make Facebook Credits transactions without ever being charged. This is a good way to be able to test your Credits integration and not get charged every time you test it.

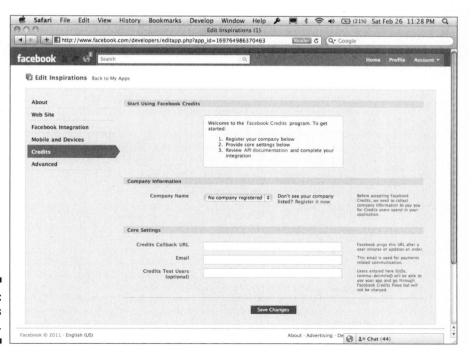

Figure 3-6: Credits settings.

Advanced

This section contains all sorts of advanced preferences that you can use to configure your application. In reality, this is just a miscellaneous section for anything that doesn't fit in the other sections. For many applications, you can ignore this section. As your application gets bigger, though, pay attention to this section to make sure that your app is fully optimized. See Figure 3-7 for an example of this section.

The settings here include the following:

- ✔ **Deauthorize Callback:** This is a URL that you can create to notify your application when the user removes the application. So, when a user removes the application from his or her profile (this can be done in the user's privacy settings), Facebook sends a request to this URL, and your application deletes the user record from the database, for instance. Or, perhaps it sets a flag saying that the user removed the application on Facebook so that you don't have to treat him or her as a Facebook user anymore.

- ✔ **Sandbox Mode:** You can choose Enable or Disable here. Usually when you first start building your application — at least if you want to keep it secret — you choose Enable here. This ensures that only registered administrators/developers/test users of the application are able to use and interact with the application. Other users cannot use the application when this is enabled.

- ✔ **Server Whitelist:** If you want to beef up security in your application, this is a great place to ensure that only your servers are the ones accessing the Facebook API for users. Enter a comma-separated list of IP addresses for the servers hosting your content here. If anyone ever gets hold of your API key, his requests would then be denied because he would not be making API calls from the servers listed here. This field is optional, so if none of this makes sense, you can leave it blank.

- ✔ **Update Settings IP Whitelist:** Through the old REST APIs, you can allow Facebook to update your application settings through code. This field is a whitelist of IPs that are allowed to make these changes. So, if you want to just be sure that no one takes over your application, fill this out with the IP addresses of your servers.

- ✔ **Update Notification E-mail:** If you fill this out, anytime a change to your application settings is made, it sends a notification to this e-mail address.

- ✔ **Advertising Account:** If your application accesses the Facebook advertising APIs, this tells Facebook what advertising account to associate ads with that you create on Facebook.

✔ **Preload FQL:** This is a useful way to speed up your application with little effort. If you specify a JSON-encoded string here, when users visit a specific URL or URL pattern in your application, Facebook will return the results of a specific FQL query in your application's POST parameters. This saves you a call to Facebook, and it makes the data much easier to access. Read more about it in the Facebook Developer documentation at `http://developers.facebook.com/docs/guides/performance`. (You may need to search for "preload FQL" if that URL is no longer valid when you read this.)

✔ **Preload FQL Multiquery:** This is just like the preload FQL text, but you can specify multiple queries to call when specific URLs are visited within your application. The values are returned as POST parameters.

✔ **Early Flush:** Like Preload FQL, this is an advanced topic that allows you to prefetch resources such as CSS and JavaScript files in the `<head>` section of your HTML for Canvas Pages and tabs (links). It's a JSON-formatted structure that you can find out more about at `http://developers.facebook.com/docs/guides/performance`. You will likely not need to use this if you're just starting to do Facebook development, but at least you know it's there.

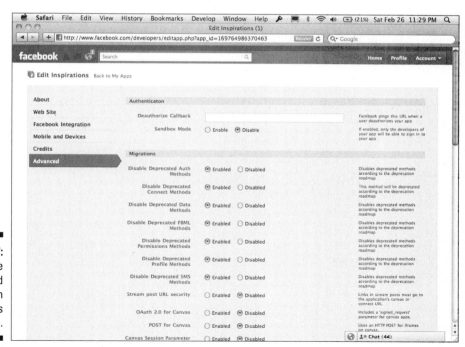

Figure 3-7:
The
Advanced
Application
Settings
page.

Migrations

This section will be different every time you visit. Facebook has made it convenient to allow users who want to add new features and settings to gradually incorporate those settings into their applications. In this section, Facebook lets you know new things that have changed in the Facebook API, and it allows you to enable those new features on your own schedule.

Follow the Facebook Developer blog for details on when these features will be automatically transitioned for you. Even though each feature starts out as Disabled (until you enable it), Facebook does eventually automatically enable all new features that it introduces into Facebook Platform. Facebook can't keep every feature around forever!

Part II

Integrating with the Facebook.com Environment

The 5th Wave   By Rich Tennant

"I know Facebook is great and you want to be a part of it. But you're my mom - you <u>can't</u> be my 'friend.'"

In this part . . .

If you're a marketer, you'll love this part. In Part II, I cover all the different places you can integrate an application. I show you how to build a business on Facebook and how to integrate Facebook into your own Web site. You find out all about Facebook Pages, and how you can customize your own with just a little knowledge of HTML.

The power of Facebook is in the capability to build technology that promotes itself and builds relationships. This Part shows you how to tap into that power, and will put you in the right mindset to build truly social experiences into your applications and Web sites.

Chapter 4

Targeting Integration Points

In This Chapter

▶ Working with integration points such as the Canvas Page, counters, and the News Feed

▶ Sharing with tabs or custom links

▶ Using the Add Bookmark button

▶ Keeping users updated

*I*n Chapter 1, I discuss the concept of "fishing where the fish are." The idea is that Facebook allows you, as a company or brand, to be where your customers are, enabling your most interested and loyal individuals to share and talk about your brand in their everyday conversations. The secret to successful development in the Facebook environment is to understand everything you can about the areas your application can interject on behalf of the user. Each of the areas that your application can participate in is called an *integration point*.

For instance, with some simple JavaScript, you can allow your application to share to a user's news feed. This would be an example of an integration point where your application can interject into the normal workflow of the user and his or her friends. Integration points are, quite simply, the touch points where your application can participate in the Facebook experience.

I'm going to take you through each of the possible integration points that your application can build upon, and I work with you to make your application even more useful by bringing it into as much of the Facebook experience as possible. The integration points that I cover in this chapter include the Canvas Page, Facebook tabs, bookmarks, counters, the News Feed, invitations, e-mail addresses, friend requests, and the Games and Applications dashboard.

Giving Your Application a Home on Facebook with the Canvas Page

I cover the Canvas Page in Chapter 2, the chapter in which you create your first application. Your Canvas Page is where you, as a software developer, get to paint your application in pretty much any way you choose, by providing a URL that renders a full page of what you want the user to see. The Canvas Page is essentially your application's Home — it's where you can make your application an extension of Facebook. It's a way to make other Facebook users feel your application or Web site is just another part of Facebook, keeping them from needing to leave the site.

Also, you can monetize this page as you like by putting ads by supported advertisers, selling products, and more. On the Canvas Page, you can do just about anything you choose, as long as it fits in the Facebook Developer Terms of Use.

Although you can monetize this page as you choose, Facebook does have specific guidelines surrounding advertising on this page. Make sure that you look up Facebook's advertising guidelines on the Policy page (www.facebook.com/ad_guidelines.php). In short, no deceptive advertising is allowed, and no incentives to click on advertising are allowed. You will probably be safe just making sure that there are no questions about what you can and cannot do on Facebook when using advertising on your Canvas Pages. In fact, Facebook just provided a list of accepted advertisers that you can advertise with. Using any other advertiser could get you banned. You can find out which advertisers are legit by going to http://developers.facebook.com/adproviders/ in the Facebook developer documentation.

Authorizing users to access more functionality

In Chapter 2, you created your Canvas Page, but admit it — it doesn't really do anything. All you did with it was display your name and profile picture, and these things are available to your application by default for all users, whether they have authorized your application or not.

Facebook has a small set of "publicly available information" that it makes available to the Web and to developers. This data does not require a user to authorize your application, and your application can access it any time. This data has changed only slightly in the past few years, but at the time of this writing, it includes the user's profile picture, name, Facebook ID, locale, gender, likes (interests), and list of friends and those friends' similar information. If you'd like to see what developers can see about you, log out of

Facebook and go to `http://graph.facebook.com/`*yourusername*. (Go ahead and try mine: `http://graph.facebook.com/jessestay`.) If users have enabled more data available via their privacy preferences, that data should appear as well.

So how do you access data beyond just the publicly available information? To do so, you have to authorize the user. You can do so with a protocol called OAuth, which I cover in Chapter 9. To put OAuth simply, you provide the user with a link, which takes that person through Facebook's login flow, and then returns the user back to your application.

Here is the code you need to add to the example you used in Chapter 2 to authorize a user with OAuth. When the user accesses your application with this code, he will be presented with a login link if he hasn't yet authorized the application. If he has, he'll see a logout link. After the user is authorized, you can start retrieving additional data about that person:

```html
<html>
<body>
<div id="fb-root"></div>
<script src="http://connect.facebook.net/en_US/all.js" charset="utf-8"></script>
<script>
    FB.init({appId: '169764986370463', status: true, cookie: true, xfbml:
        true});
</script>
<h1>Inspirations</h1>
<div id="quote">
            <div id="auth"></div>
            <span id="facebook_stuff">
            <div id="profile_pic"><fb:profile-pic uid="683545112"></
            fb:profile-pic></div>
            <div id="profile_name"><fb:name uid="683545112" useyou="false">
            </fb:name>
            </span>
            "When I examine myself and my methods of thought, I come to the
            conclusion that the gift of fantasy has meant more to me than any
            talent for abstract, positive thinking." -Albert Einstein
</div>
<script>
        FB.getLoginStatus(function(response) {
            if (!response.session) {
                    document.getElementById('auth').innerHTML = 'Click
            here to authorize and get a more personalized experience:
            <a href="http://www.facebook.com/dialog/oauth?client_
            id=169764986370463&redirect_uri=http://inspirations.socialtoo.com"
            target="_top">Authorize</a>';
             }
        });
</script>
</body>
</html>
```

In the above example, I add an additional blank <div> block where I can prompt the user to authorize the app if it isn't yet authorized. I then add some JavaScript to the end (just before the end </body> tag), using FB.getLoginStatus to detect if the current user is authorized yet. If the user isn't authorized, I add some HTML to the "auth" <div> block, prompting the user to authorize.

In the auth HTML is a simple link, the OAuth dialog link, which is in the format of:

```
http://www.facebook.com/dialog/oauth?client_id=APPLICATION_ID&redirect_
                uri=CANVAS_URL
```

When the user clicks on this, it takes him or her to an authorization dialog box, prompting the user to give permission for your app to access that person's information.

There's one caveat to this. In an iFrame app (on Canvas Pages and Tabs), Facebook requires your link to have target="_top" as I share in the example above. It's unclear if Facebook sees this as a bug or not, but if you don't do it, you'll get redirected to a page that just has the Facebook logo on it, and a link to Facebook.com.

In addition, notice that I set the redirect_uri, which is the place it sends users after they log in, to a URL directly on my own domain, inspirations. socialtoo.com, not apps.facebook.com/inspirationsapp. This is because you're in an iFrame, and the iFrame is already directly loading the HTML from your own domain. To use this, you also need to set your Site URL and Site Domain values under Web Site in your application settings — it should match this URL.

The login and logout links are a bit cumbersome, though. Maybe you just want to force the user to authorize so that you can get the data you need. Having a login button adds one unnecessary step. You can get around that by using a redirect to the login OAuth URL if the user has not yet been authorized. To do that, just replace the document.getElementById line in the example above with the following JavaScript:

```
top.location="http://www.facebook.com/dialog/oauth?client_
                id=169764986370463&redirect_uri=http://inspirations.socialtoo.com";
```

Note that again, instead of a location.href JavaScript call or similar redirect, I did top.location. This is equivalent to the target="top" attribute I include in the link before. See the tip above for why that's important.

So in the end, your full Inspirations application should automatically redirect the user to authorize the application if it has not yet been authorized. If the application has been authorized, it just stays there — your JavaScript does all the magic!

You might be wondering why not just use the JavaScript FB.login call to authorize the user? Facebook's JavaScript SDK does provide FB.login to do stuff like this, doesn't it? The truth is, this probably should work, but at the time of this writing it seems to have problems on Canvas Pages in iFrame environments. By the time you read this, you might be able to get this to work, but at the moment the OAuth method is the easiest and most fluid means to authorize a user. I suggest getting familiar with this method anyway, because in many ways, this way is much simpler than adding any sort of JavaScript into the flow to accomplish the same thing.

Another way of doing this is to use the `fb:login-button` XFBML tag. With this XFBML tag you can provide a JavaScript callback method that gets run when the user has logged in. This might be an easier way of doing it, but it does require the user to click the button, which may affect your user experience. Again, the OAuth technique is your friend! Get to know it.

Using a Canvas Page to promote a third-party Web site

One strategy I like to use when I integrate Facebook on a third-party Web site is to create a version of that Web site on Facebook, which allows users who discover your Web site through Facebook to avoid leaving Facebook to get your Web site's experience. In this case, your Canvas Page, in a way, becomes an advertisement for your Web site. Because you're "fishing where the fish are," you have the opportunity to re-create your Web site's experience right inside Facebook, and the user never has to leave Facebook to get to it.

Because you can monetize the Canvas Page however you like, this can actually be a great opportunity to build your brand right inside Facebook. Allow the user to get the experience that he or she would get on your Web site, right in the Facebook environment. Then you can sprinkle elements of your brand all throughout your Facebook application so that users will want to visit your Web site and start to interact there instead of just on Facebook.

I did this for my Web site, SocialToo.com. (See Figure 4-1.) On my Facebook application, I provided little features here and there to grasp the user's interest and allow him to find out about and use the application right inside Facebook. However, I still gave him opportunities to go back to the `SocialToo.com` Web site to upgrade his account, get more features (such as Twitter support), and get the full experience. The user never has to leave Facebook to use the Facebook features of SocialToo, though.

Because of this, SocialToo actually gets more traffic from Facebook than it does from Twitter in many instances, even though SocialToo has a strong Twitter focus. I talk more about that in the Part of Tens at the end of the book. The Canvas Page can be a powerful tool to seamlessly integrate the Facebook experience into your application, and your application into the Facebook experience itself.

The Canvas Page is only what your users see when they use the application. However, you can use many other places throughout Facebook to inject your application into the user experience for each user. If you have a loyal fan base, you should take advantage of the next few sections.

Figure 4-1:
Using the
Canvas
Page to
promote
features on
SocialToo.
com.

Sharing with New Visitors Via Tabs (or Custom Links)

A *tab* is just a custom link that your application can create that can be added to any Facebook Page. I cover more about creating a tab for a Facebook Page in Chapter 4, but it's sufficient here to say that this can be done, and it's an emerging market, with entire stores such as AppBistro looking to index these pages for page administrators wanting to find ways to customize their pages. You can see LiveScribe's custom tab in Figure 4-2. In this example, they actually set their custom tab as the page that appears by default as users visit the page. I show you how to do this in Chapter 5.

You may be wondering why they're called "tabs" when they're just links on the left-hand side of a Facebook Page. The truth is they actually used to be tabs. They existed at the top of Facebook Pages as little tabs you could click on. Just recently, Facebook redesigned its Facebook Pages so that all the tabs resided on the left-hand side as links. It's unclear at this time what those will end up being called in the future, but for now, everyone knows them as "tabs." For that reason, I call them tabs throughout the book.

Custom tabs can be a great way to bring a custom experience to a Facebook Page.

Figure 4-2:
The
LiveScribe
Facebook
Page
Welcome
tab.

Creating your first tab

What I'm about to show you next can automatically increase your value as a Facebook developer (or social strategist/marketer, if you would prefer not to "develop"). Entire businesses have surfaced around building custom tabs for Facebook Pages and user profiles for companies needing a little spice added to their Facebook strategy. It's actually quite simple to do — I'm going to take you through expanding your Inspirations application to include a list of a user's favorite quotes (or inspirations) on a tab on a Facebook Page that user owns. These could be pulled from a database, but for my purposes, you're going to just hardcode some quotes in place:

1. **Go to your application settings.**

   Go to these settings (go to the Developer application and click More next to the name of your application).

2. **Give your tab a name.**

   To tell Facebook where to look, go to the Facebook Integration link on the left in your application settings, as shown in Figure 4-3. The first thing you need to do is set the name of the tab. This can be up to 11 characters. I'm going to call mine Inspirations. You can do the same if you like.

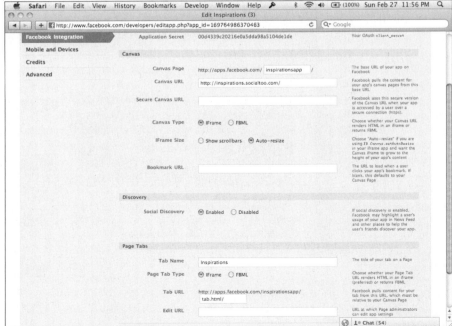

Figure 4-3: The Facebook Integration link is where you tell Facebook where to point your tab.

3. **Tell Facebook at what URL the content of your tab can be found.**

   Now you just need to give Facebook a URL to read what you want to display on the user's tab. This should be relative to your Canvas URL that you set in Chapter 2, so make sure that your directory structure is set up in a way that when you call `http://apps.facebook.com/inspirations/tab.html` (or the Canvas Page URL for your application), it calls `http://inspirations.socialtoo.com/ tab.html` (or the path to the Canvas URL plus the `/tab.html` path that tells your server to return the `tab.html` file). If you can't tell, I'm going to enter **tab.html** in the Tab URL field. You can choose what you like, but it might be good to follow along. At this point, your profile settings page should look like what is shown in Figure 4-3. Click the Save Changes button at the bottom to save your changes, and now you're ready to write some HTML!

4. **Write some HTML (or code).**

   If you keep it simple, this is the easy part! At a minimum, you need to know a little basic HTML. Understanding XFBML (which I mention in Chapter 3) is a bonus, and knowing how to integrate just a little bit of JavaScript may even give you more advantages. Or, if you're a coder, you can hack away, pull from a database, integrate some complex Ajax or PHP code, and have a fully integrated experience. It's all up to your expertise as to how your tab looks in the end.

   Face it — this is a *For Dummies* book, so I'm going to keep it simple. I'm just going to stick to simple HTML, and if you want to take it further, you can be creative. Share what you came up with on this book's Facebook Page, or in the Group!

   Creating your tab is simple. Consider that `http://inspirations. socialtoo.com /tab.html` points to a file called `tab.html` on your server. In that file, copy the HTML code below to your `tab.html` file. This is an adaptation of the same code I describe in Chapter 2 — this time it will appear on a Facebook Page tab, though:

```
<html>
<body>
<h1>My Favorite Quotes</h1>
<div id="quote">
        "When I examine myself and my methods of thought, I come to the
        conclusion that the gift of fantasy has meant more to me than
        any talent for abstract, positive thinking." -Albert Einstein
</div>
</body>
</html>
```

   Note that you can also add all the Facebook stuff you added in the other examples. This supports JavaScript, just like iFrames. To find out more about what you can do in a tab, refer to Chapter 8.

5. **Install the tab.**

   After you create your tab, users must add it to their Facebook Page for it to be usable. There are two ways users can do this:

   - **Click "Add to My Page":** If you go to the application profile page for your application (you can either click the Application Profile Page link on your app's settings page or go to the bottom of one of your app's Canvas Pages and click the name of your app in the lower-left footer of the page), on the left-hand side there is an Add to My Page link. If your users click that, they'll have the option to choose from the Facebook Pages they administer. When they select a Facebook Page, your app will be added as a new tab (or link) on the left side of their Facebook Page. This is the easiest way.

   - **Use the `add.php` dialog box:** Another undocumented way of adding your app to a user's Facebook Page is to provide a link to add the Page. Just create a link somewhere on the Page in the format of `http://www.facebook.com/add.php?api_key=API_KEY&pages=1&page=FACEBOOK_PAGE_ID`. Then set `target="_top"` in your `<a>` tags (don't worry about why right now — just know this will make it work).

   When you replace `API_KEY` with your app's API key and `FACEBOOK_PAGE_ID` with the page to add it to, it will prompt you to add it to the user's page. When you specify `FACEBOOK_PAGE_ID`, the prompt will default to the Page you specified. If you don't specify the `&page=FACEBOOK_PAGE_ID` part, it will give the user the option to choose. When that person chooses, it will automatically add the app to his Page and her fans can start using it! The page to select her Facebook Page looks like the one in Figure 4-4.

   It might be smart to add the above link to your Canvas Page somewhere. This way when people click the link to go to your app from your app's Application Profile page, users can add it from within your application itself.

Understanding the limitations of tabs

Tabs do have some limitations. A tab cannot include any advertising to third-party Web sites or any other Facebook application, and tabs cannot be monetized in any way (like, adding advertising or selling things). That said, some people do get away with monetizing tabs, so your mileage may vary — just be forewarned that this is the risk you take! You should consult the Facebook Developer Policy if you have any questions about what you can or can't do on tabs for Pages.

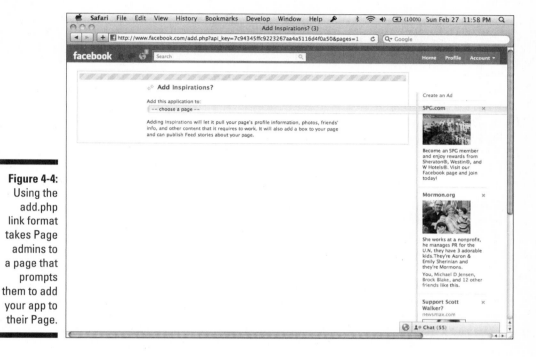

Figure 4-4:
Using the
add.php
link format
takes Page
admins to
a page that
prompts
them to add
your app to
their Page.

Giving Your Application Prominence through the Add Bookmark Button

One of the simplest things you can do to give your application more visibility is to add a Bookmark button at a visible location on your Canvas Page or Web site. Doing so is simple: To add one to the top of your Inspirations application, just add the `<fb:bookmark/>` XFBML tag, shown in the code below, to the top of your `index.html` file. The resulting app will look like the one shown in Figure 4-5. Now when users click the Add Bookmark button, your application will appear prominently on the left side next to their applications. Here is the XFBML code you need to add:

```
<fb:bookmark></fb:bookmark>
```

After users bookmark your application, you can notify them of new updates via counter notifications.

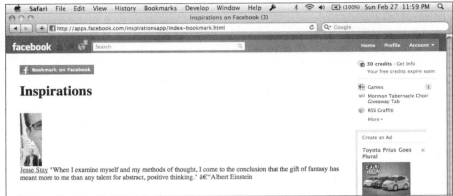

Figure 4-5:
What your
Inspirations
application
looks like
with the
bookmark in
place.

Keeping Your Users Updated through Counter Notifications

As you build your application, you need a way to notify users when they have new data. For instance, consider that a user's friend adds a quote to your application and you need to let the user know that he or she has new quotes to look at. How does that user know to go look? How do you notify the user?

Facebook has provided a way to increment a counter for your application that resides in the sidebar of Facebook for that user.

Remember the Add Bookmark button that I mention earlier in the chapter? Assuming that your user has bookmarked the application, your application should appear prominently in the left sidebar (under Applications) of Facebook for the user, where you can send these updates.

So how does the increment counter work? Here's how:

1. Your user's friend submits a new quote to the Inspirations application.

   I'll let you write the code for this. Basically, in your preferred language, you need to write code that takes the quote and submits it to the database and marks which user submitted that quote.

2. Your application notices this and sends an API call to Facebook, notifying it to increment your counter.

   You do this through the `dashboard.incrementCount` method (part of Facebook's old REST APIs, something which may be replaced by a Graph API method in the future, so be sure to check the Facebook Developer documentation!).

Assuming that your application is in PHP, your code will look something like this:

```
<html>
<body>
<?php
require 'facebook.php';

// replace "SECRET_KEY_GOES_HERE" with appropriate values
$facebook = new Facebook(array(
 'appId' => '169764986370463',
 'secret' => "SECRET_KEY_GOES_HERE",
 'cookie' => true,
));

if (!$_GET['uid']) {
        echo 'Failure! You need to pass a uid (with a username or user id)
            to increment the counter for the Inspirations app.';
        exit;
}

$admintoken = '8665218278|63qRuQs2GceTWSzTjA3bid4mOZk.';
$facebook->api(array(
'method' => 'dashboard.incrementCount',
'uid' => $_GET['uid'],
'access_token' => $admintoken
));
?>
Success!
</body>
</html>
```

You can test this by going to `http://inspirations.socialtoo.com/increment-counter.php` and passing in a `uid=USERNAME_OR_ID`. Be sure to go to `http://apps.facebook.com/inspirations-app/index-bookmark.html` and add the application via the Add Bookmark button at the top before you run it, though.

3. In a similar manner, say the user now goes and visits her application. She has now seen all her latest news items. To decrement the counter (and remove the notification), use the `dashboard.decrementCount` method in the old REST API. You can do this, similar to what I did above, with this code:

```
<html>
<body>
<?php
require 'facebook.php';

// replace "SECRET_KEY_GOES_HERE" with appropriate values
$facebook = new Facebook(array(
```

```
 'appId' => '169764986370463',
 'secret' => "SECRET_KEY_GOES_HERE",
 'cookie' => true,
));

if (!$_GET['uid']) {
        echo 'Failure! You need to pass a uid (with a username or user id)
           to increment the counter for the Inspirations app.';
        exit;
}

$admintoken = '8665218278|63qRuQs2GceTWSzTjA3bid4mOZk.';
$facebook->api(array(
'method' => 'dashboard.decrementCount',
'uid' => $_GET['uid'],
'access_token' => $admintoken
));
?>
Success!
</body>
</html>
```

You can test this out on your own with the code at `http://
inspirations.socialtoo.com/decrement-counter.php`, passing
in a uid just as you did in the increment counter example above.

You're done! With just a few server-side API calls, you can notify your users
of any new change that they need to know about within your application.
This is a valuable tool for bringing more attention to your application!

Sharing Your Application through the News Feed

One of the easiest and best ways to get attention to your application or Web
site is by sending updates to the Facebook news feeds of your users' friends
(via your users' walls). The news feed is one of the most frequented parts of
Facebook, and it's what all users see the minute they log in to Facebook. This
is where users go to find out what their friends are doing.

The news feed is the list of stuff that your friends are doing; you see it after
you log in to Facebook. That isn't to be confused with the wall, which is what
your friends see when they visit your profile. As you do stuff in applications
on Facebook, that stuff gets posted to your wall and then appears in your
friends' news feeds. The wall and the news feed are tightly interconnected.
You can view your wall at any time by clicking your name in the upper-left
corner of Facebook or by clicking the Profile link (usually in the upper-
right corner).

Posting to your users' news feeds is simple. In fact, it can be as simple as copying and pasting a simple social plugin (which I cover in Chapter 6) that automatically shares to their profiles. It can be some simple JavaScript that you install on your application or Web site, or it can be code that runs on your server and sends the update on behalf of your users.

For simplicity, I'm going to show you how to post to your users' news feeds using the Facebook JavaScript SDK, allowing your users to share their quotes on Facebook. Here's what you need to do:

1. **Create a simple JavaScript init statement.**

   For any JavaScript SDK calls to Facebook, you need to provide a simple init block, similar to the one you create in Chapter 2 that tells Facebook who your app is and authorizes your app to make calls to Facebook. Just use the same one for this:

   ```
   <html>
   <body>
   <div id="fb-root"></div>
   <script src="http://connect.facebook.net/en_US/all.js" charset="utf-8">
            </script>
   <script>
       FB.init({appId: '169764986370463', status: true, cookie: true, xfbml:
            true});
   </script>
   </body>
   </html>
   ```

   To get access to any information beyond the publicly available information (PAI) that I discuss earlier, you must always request permission from the user. You can view a list of all available permissions you can request from a user at http://developers.facebook.com/docs/authentication/permissions. For the FB.ui and feed dialog boxes you use below, you don't need any additional permissions, however, because Facebook handles all this for you.

2. **Use FB.ui to prompt the user to share his or her quote.**

   Now you just need to make an API call using the JavaScript SDK that prompts the user. Facebook makes this quite easy by doing all the heavy lifting for you. You just have to tell Facebook the text and images that you want to appear in the user's stream, and Facebook does the rest.

   So to start, you need to add a simple share link on your application's Canvas Page. Then, create an onclick that triggers a method that launches the share prompt. The HTML for that should look something like this, and just adds to the init block you created above:

```
<html>
<body>
<div id="fb-root"></div>
<script src="http://connect.facebook.net/en_US/all.js" charset="utf-8">
        </script>
<script>
    FB.init({appId: '169764986370463', status: true, cookie: true, xfbml:
        true});
</script>
<h1>Inspirations</h1>
<div id="quote">
        <span id="facebook_stuff">
        <div id="profile_pic"><fb:profile-pic uid="683545112">
</fb:profile-pic></div>
        <div id="profile_name"><fb:name uid="683545112"
useyou="false"></fb:name>
        </span>
        "When I examine myself and my methods of thought, I come
        to the conclusion that the gift of fantasy has meant more to
        me than any talent for abstract, positive thinking." -Albert
        Einstein
            <a href="#" onclick="FB.ui({method: 'feed',name: 'I\'m
        getting inspired!', link: 'http://stay.am/dummiesbook',
        picture: 'http://staynalive.com/dummiesbook.jpg', caption:
        'Inspirations', description: 'I\'m getting inspired through the
        Inspirations app in the book, Facebook Application Development
        For Dummies. Order your copy now!', message: 'Getting inspired
        through Facebook Application Development For Dummies!' });
        return false;"> Share this Quote</a>
</div>
</body>
</html>
```

In the example above, after you have a link to click, you just have to add the Facebook JavaScript call. Facebook provides a skeleton architecture for simple UI prompts like the feed dialog. This is the FB.ui method I used above within the onclick event. The FB.ui method calls the feed dialog method, which prompts users to share the quote to their Facebook News Feed.

You can try this out on the book's Inspirations app at http://apps.facebook.com/inspirationsapp/share.html. View the source of the frame to see what I did! If any of this sounds too complicated, try this — just copy my code above and insert your own text, adding your own application ID in place of mine. With this, you can really share anything you like on Facebook from your own Web site, app, or custom tab.

To find out more about dialog boxes and what is available to your FB.ui call, refer to Chapter 10. In fact, you don't even need JavaScript to call these dialog boxes. You could, technically, link to another page that takes the user through the sharing process. I share all the details on how to use that there.

Here are some explanations of each component of your feed dialog `FB.ui` call:

- ✔ **message:** The main message of the post shared on the user's wall. (See Figure 4-6 for what that looks like.)

- ✔ **attachment:** Attachments are JSON-formatted structures that let you attach rich data to the objects that users share on their walls. This can enable your application to insert a Flash file, for instance, or identify an MP3 file that the user's friends can play right in their news stream. This is where all the metadata, along with the main object of the item the user is sharing, should go, assuming that it's not just a text message. Be sure to read all the documentation on the Facebook developers site to find out everything you can do with this. (This is currently located at `http://developers.facebook.com/docs/guides/attachments`.)

- ✔ **action_links:** You usually see a Like and a Share link next to items on your news feed. If you are creating the item to be shared, you can add additional links next to the default links that Facebook provides. This is where you add those. You just need to provide a JSON array of text and links that get called when the user clicks that text.

- ✔ **user_message_prompt:** This is the text that the user sees when he is prompted to share the item on his wall.

    Your final code will produce a prompt that looks like what is shown in Figure 4-6.

Figure 4-6:
The prompt that the user sees when he or she clicks the link.

Inviting Your Users' Friends through Requests

Another way to get the attention of your users' friends is by sending those friends requests. Think of this as a way to allow your app's users to invite other of their friends to use your application in a personal, private manner. This is a method that you'll want to test, because it gives better results for some than others, and over time, this area has not been quite as used as others. Still, it is an additional way to get your users' attention, and you should take advantage of it.

Sending a request is mostly just a matter of sending a simple JavaScript `FB.ui` call as I describe in the sharing example above, or redirecting to the appropriate dialog box URL. Here's what your JavaScript for such a request would look like, using the Inspirations example:

```html
<html>
<body>
<div id="fb-root"></div>
<script src="http://connect.facebook.net/en_US/all.js" charset="utf-8"></script>
<script>
    FB.init({appId: '169764986370463', status: true, cookie: true, xfbml: true});

</script>
<h1>Inspirations</h1>
<div id="quote">
            <span id="facebook_stuff">
            <div id="profile_pic"><fb:profile-pic uid="683545112">
            </fb:profile-pic></div>
            <div id="profile_name"><fb:name uid="683545112" useyou="false">
            </fb:name>
            </span>
            "When I examine myself and my methods of thought, I come to the
            conclusion that the gift of fantasy has meant more to me than any
            talent for abstract, positive thinking." -Albert Einstein
              <div><a href="#" onclick="FB.ui({method: 'apprequests',message:
            'I just got inspired. Will you get inspired through Facebook
            Application Development For Dummies?'}); return false;">Invite
            your friends to use Inspirations</a></div>
</div>
</body>
</html>
```

Just as you did with the feed dialog box request above, request dialog boxes just take simple information to dictate what the `FB.ui` dialog box looks like, and sends to the user. The basic parameters you need to pass to this are:

- **message:** At a limit of 255 characters, this is the message that the receiving user will see in the request that user gets from the inviting user. The request will look like the one in Figure 4-7.

- **to:** This optional field, when specified, allows you to automatically select a single user by user ID or username. When this is not specified, a list of users the inviting user can select is presented, which looks like Figure 4-8. The user can then select up to 50 friends from this list.

- **filters:** This allows you to customize the list of friends presented if the "to" field is not specified. You have the choice between `all`, `app_users`, and `app_non_users` in this field. In addition, you can create your own lists by specifying a name and list of user IDs to include in that list. This can be useful when you have your own lists within your app that you want to include for the user to be able to invite from. This structure looks like this (as taken from Facebook's Developer documentation):

```
[{name: 'Neighbors', user_ids: [1, 2, 3]}, {name: 'Other Set', user_ids:
     [4,5,6]}]
```

  By default, with no filter selected, this will show all the user's friends.

- **data:** If you need to store additional JSON objects that can be retrieved with the request object ((I show you how to retrieve the request object later in this chapter)), you can store them in this field. This is great for tracking when you need to track where invites are coming from, and who invited whom.

- **title:** You can create a title for the friend selector dialog box (in Figure 4-8). This field is optional.

Figure 4-7:
The application request the receiving user gets when the sending user clicks "Send Requests."

In my `FB.ui` example earlier in this chapter, I just use the `message` and `method` parameters.

If you turn this into just a link, it would look like this (copy this into your browser and see):

```
http://www.facebook.com/dialog/apprequests?app_id=169764986370463&message=I%20
        just%20got%20inspired.%20Will%20you%20get%20inspired%20through%20
        Facebook%20Application%20Development%20for%20Dummies&redirect_
        uri=http://inspirations.socialtoo.com
```

When you initiate this dialog box, the user is prompted with an opportunity to choose from a list of friends to invite to use your application. The user will be able to select a number of friends, and all of those friends will get a request, which you defined, in their Games and Applications dashboards (see Figure 4-9). Sometimes this appears as a notification in the top navigation bar of Facebook.

The user is given the option to accept or decline the request. If she accepts it, she is sent to your application's Canvas Page, with the additional parameter, `request_ids`, added to the URL. This parameter contains a comma-delimited list of request IDs that the user attempted to act upon.

App Requests

Figure 4-9:
When the receiving user gets a new request, it appears as a new number in the user's Games and Applications Dashboard.

You can then make Graph API requests to identify the IDs and determine who referred the user. You can either do a generic GET request (either in your code, or using a tool like Curl) to get all the requests sent to the user, like this:

```
curl "https://graph.facebook.com/jessestay/apprequests?oauth_token=APP_TOKEN_
          GOES_HERE"
```

Or you can perform a GET on a specific request ID, like this:

```
curl "https://graph.facebook.com/10150404159370403?oauth_token=APP_TOKEN_GOES_
          HERE"
```

If all goes well, Facebook returns a JSON structure that looks like this:

```
{"id":"10150404159370403",
"application":{"name":"Inspirations",
"id":"169764986370463"},
"to":{"name":"Rebecca Day Stay",
"id":"895960402"},
"from":{"name":"Jesse Stay","id":"683545112"},
"message":"I just got inspired. Will you get inspired through Facebook
          Application Development For Dummies?","created_time":
"2011-02-28T06:12:27+0000"}
```

So from this structure you can easily tell who sent the request, to whom it was sent, and track referrals and any other data you passed into the request.

Lastly, you can perform a DELETE on specific request IDs to clear out your app's queue:

```
curl -X DELETE "https://graph.facebook.com/10150404159370403?oauth_token=APP_
          TOKEN_GOES_HERE"
```

Facebook suggests that it's best practice to delete requests that the user has already accepted or ignored. Facebook is unclear why it recommends this, but my guess is that it is to keep Facebook's own database clean and easier to manage. Facebook is also hinting that this interface may change slightly in the future, so the recommendation may have something to do with where Facebook is going with this.

Obtaining Your Users' E-Mail Addresses

Another way that you can notify your users, send them invitations, and so on is to just send them an e-mail. For each user in your application who gives you permission, you can obtain his or her e-mail address. You'll want to store this in a database somewhere when you get it, and as long as you regularly check that permission (or use real-time notifications to notify you when it changes — I cover this in Chapter 11), you can then use the e-mail address to send the user e-mail updates.

This method is only available to users of your own application. Because your users' friends may not have given your application permission to access their e-mail addresses, your application cannot send e-mail messages or invites to the users' friends. Use the request architecture I mention previously to do that.

To obtain the e-mail addresses of your users, you just need to do a few things — note that this may be a little advanced for some readers. You may want to point your developers to this section if you still need this functionality and it doesn't make sense to you. Here are the steps:

1. **Add the "e-mail" data permission to your list of permissions.**

   Your login link from the authorization example above in your Inspirations application should now look like what is shown below. Basically, I just added a scope parameter to the URL, and added "email" to the comma-delimited list of permissions that I want to prompt for:

```
<a href="http://www.facebook.com/dialog/oauth?client_
        id=169764986370463&redirect_uri=http://inspirations.socialtoo.
        com&scope=read_stream,email" target="_top">Authorize</a>
```

2. On your server, obtain the user's e-mail address.

To do this, in your preferred language, specify the path to the user's Graph API object (for `jessestay`, the path would be `/jessestay`), and in the returned results should be the e-mail address that the user has now given permission for you to see. You should make this call on your server, although you can certainly do it in JavaScript with a little Ajax.

3. Store the e-mail address in your database.

4. Send the e-mail!

Each programming language has its own way of sending e-mail. Consult the documentation for the server-side programming language of your choice to do this. This is something you will have to do on your server using a language such as PHP, Perl, or Python.

Making Friends Out of Your Users with the Friend's Dialog Box

One of my favorite calls is one that you can use with the `FB.ui` JavaScript method to send requests for friendship from user to user. The call is as simple as calling the friend's dialog box and passing it the ID of the user you want your user to be friends with. So, for instance, if you want to provide a list of other Inspirations users who aren't friends of your user, you could give your user the option to friend each of them, meeting new users of your application in the process. The code to do this is shown below. You can run this on your own site (`http://developers.facebook.com/tools/console/`) and see what it does, or see it in action at `http://apps.facebook.com/inspirationsapp/friending.html`:

```
<html>
<body>
<div id="fb-root"></div>
<script src="http://connect.facebook.net/en_US/all.js" charset="utf-8"></script>
<script>
    FB.init({appId: '169764986370463', status: true, cookie: true, xfbml:
          true});
</script>
<h1>Inspirations</h1>
<div id="quote">
          <span id="facebook_stuff">
          <div id="profile_pic"><fb:profile-pic uid="683545112">
           </fb:profile-pic></div>
          <div id="profile_name"><fb:name uid="683545112" useyou="false">
           </fb:name>
          </span>
```

```
              "When I examine myself and my methods of thought, I come to the
              conclusion that the gift of fantasy has meant more to me than any
              talent for abstract, positive thinking." -Albert Einstein
                <div><a href="#" onclick="FB.ui({method: 'friends',id:
              '773469922'}); return false;"> Now send a friend request to Eric
              Schmidt</a></div>
    </div>
    </body>
    </html>
```

Notice that all I need to do is pass it to Eric Schmidt's Facebook ID and it enables a simple friend request dialog box to appear. After your code runs, a pop-up appears that looks like what is shown in Figure 4-10. When the user sends the request and his friend accepts it, your users will now be friends.

Figure 4-10:
The pop-up that appears when your code runs.

In addition, you can just direct the user to the dialog box link for adding friends, which would look like this:

```
http://www.facebook.com/dialog/friends?app_id=169764986370463&id=773469922&redir
              ect_uri=http://inspirations.socialtoo.com
```

Sending More Updates through the Applications and Games Dashboard

The Applications and Games Dashboard is where you can go to get updates on all the applications and games that you and your friends are using. This is the place that you, as a developer or application owner, can update your users with new news about your application. You can use a series of APIs. Below, I show the code you could use (in PHP) to add news to your application on the Dashboard (taken from http://developers.facebook.com/docs/guides/canvas/#dashboards):

```
$news = array(array('message' => 'Come back and see our new quotes'));
$result = json_decode(file_get_contents(
    'https://api.facebook.com/method/dashboard.addNews?' .
    'news=' . urlencode(json_encode($news)) .
    '&format=json&access_token=' .
    $cookie['oauth_access_token'])); // this cookie is assuming you got their
                    access token elsewhere and have stored it for future access
```

The result looks like Figure 4-11 in your Applications and Games Dashboard.

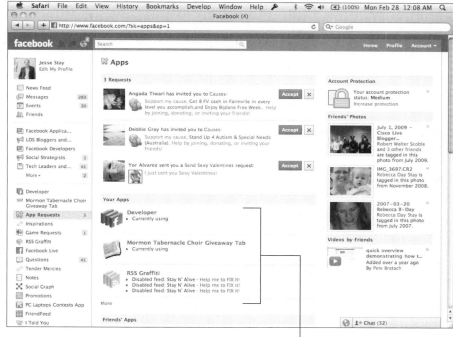

Figure 4-11: Updates to your Applications and Games Dashboard look similar to this.

Your Apps

Knowing Your Audience

One of the biggest advantages to social media is the capability to know who a user is through her profile and her friends. With Facebook, this is a huge advantage, because you can adapt the experience completely based on who is visiting your application.

At a very basic level, you can detect whether the person visiting the application has even installed the application before, and provide different content to the nonapp users that perhaps can target those users to authorize the application and start using it.

Knowing who your audience is can be key to a successful application. Knowing who each visitor of your application is and adapting the experience can increase his or her time spent and bring more users into your application.

Use the API to find out about each visitor. Track the usage of each user so that you can track the success of changes you put in place. All this can be beneficial to you, the application developer, in making a successful application.

Integrating as tightly into Facebook as possible is only the start of a successful Facebook application. After you do so, you should adapt the experience and make it unique to each user who visits your application.

Chapter 5

Targeting Brands through Facebook Pages

*B*y now, you may be thinking you are a whiz at Facebook development. Maybe you've never written a line of code in your life, and now you feel like you're actually creating cool, productive things with code. That feeling is the beginning of a pleasant journey that puts you in control of what you can do as a marketer, entrepreneur, or developer.

Or maybe you're still not very comfortable — all this is a little scary to you. That's okay too — you can still do many things, so don't give up! You are at the beginning of using powerful technology that shares itself, promotes itself, and builds your brand on its own, with little effort on your part.

Now it's time to apply these skills! One of the first things you should do is create a Facebook Page for you or your brand.

Facebook Pages are one of the strongest tools you can use to promote and share information about your company or brand. With a simple "like," enthusiasts of your brand can quickly, and virally, share with their friends their interest in your company. If you do not yet have a Facebook Page, this chapter is for you.

Just as powerful is the capability to interject your application into any brand's presence. Through custom tabs and links, and Graph API access to any Facebook Page, you can customize the user's experience on any brand's Facebook presence. I also show you how to do this in this chapter.

Discovering What Facebook Pages Can Do for You

What's a Facebook Page? It's a presence for any brand, like a Web site, within Facebook itself. Through Facebook Pages, people interested in your brand can like and show interest in you or your products and easily share that with their friends. A Facebook Page is the profile of your brand on Facebook.

That isn't to be confused with a Facebook profile. The Facebook profile is what you see when you log in to Facebook. You can see my Facebook profile at `http://facebook.com/jessestay` (friend me!). The profile is about the real you, a human being, and it can friend and follow people. A Facebook Page is different — it is built for brands and more anonymous perceptions of things and people. A Facebook Page can't friend anyone, but others can follow ("like") it. The page is public — search engines can see it. It's very simple for anyone to follow what is posted on a page (just by "liking" it). You can see the Facebook Page for this book at `http://facebook.com/fbdummies` ("like" it to get future updates!).

A Facebook Page can be your most powerful tool in your arsenal to engage, build community, and send a message to your customers that they can then pass on to their friends. Here are some advantages of using Facebook Pages:

- **Facebook pages are like giving a man a fish.** The old saying goes, "Give a man a fish, feed him for a day. Teach a man to fish, feed him for a lifetime." In social media, this is so true! With as simple a thing as a Facebook Page, you can post a message, and that message will be put in the hands of your customers to then share with their friends, and their friends, and their friends. In essence, you are teaching your customers to fish by giving them a message that they can then give to their friends, and that message will be passed from person to person, spreading your message in ways you never imagined! The tool itself is the teacher, enabling your message to be passed on for a lifetime!

- **People are the new search engine optimization (SEO).** More and more, it is becoming so important for you to permeate your brand on social networks like Facebook. Gone are the days that you can rely solely on link-building strategy. Now it is becoming increasingly more important for you to put your message in the hands of people, rather than just Web sites, so that they can then spread your message and your links throughout the Web. Just shortly before I wrote this, Bing partnered with Facebook to show search results based on the things your friends on Facebook like and search for. Google is rumored to be doing something similar.

Already, Facebook ranks its own search results by the things your friends have liked and shown interest in (go ahead — search for "Dummies" in Facebook and see what gets returned!). Your brand and your message will be in many more places than ever if you can have your customers spreading links for you, rather than building those links yourself. People, not links, are the new SEO. Pages should be your first way of putting those links in the hands of your customers or users.

✔ **Facebook Pages are easy to advertise.** Facebook advertising is something I cover in much more detail in Chapter 15. However, it's important to know that Facebook ads can be one of the most important reasons to build a Facebook Page. Facebook users, in general, do not like to leave Facebook. Advertising a Facebook Page can be a great way to promote your brand, build a distribution channel for potential customers, and keep them on Facebook at the same time.

With Facebook advertising, you can finely target who sees the ad, and with one click and never leaving their news stream, they can easily "like" your Facebook Page, right from the ad! With the right ad campaign, you can see great results, perhaps even better than traditional search engine or display advertising, with much better long-term results.

Customizing Your Facebook Page

Now that you understand the benefits of Facebook Pages, it's time to build and customize your Facebook Page in a manner that gets results. To build your first Page, follow these steps:

1. **Go to** `http://facebook.com/pages`.

2. **Click the Create Page button in the upper-right corner. (See Figure 5-1.)**

   Facebook is a constantly changing environment. This button could very likely look different by the time you read this book. Be sure to ask on `stay.am/dummiesgroup` if you need help finding it.

3. **On the resulting screen, choose the type of page you want to create. Then choose a category for that type. (See Figure 5-2.)**

   You have numerous choices here — choose the one that is closest to what your brand does. Don't worry if it isn't exactly the same — as long as you have fewer than 100 friends you can change it later if you like.

   Keep in mind that even if you create a community page, you must still respect certain trademark concerns. For instance, if Facebook gets a request from lawyers representing the brand whose page you created, your page will likely be removed. Always respect copyright and trademark laws when creating your page! You can find out more about Facebook's Page policies at `http://www.facebook.com/terms_pages.php`.

The Create Page button

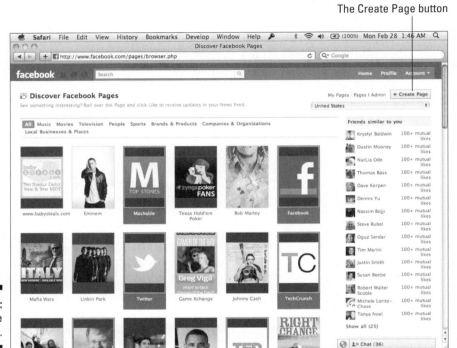

Figure 5-1:
The Create
Page button.

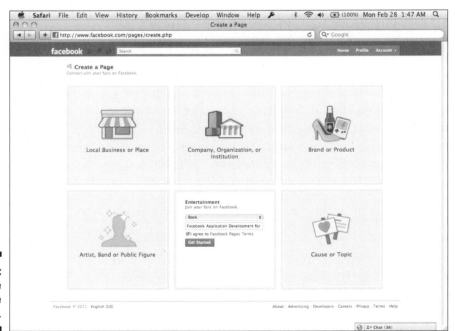

Figure 5-2:
The Create
a Page
screen.

4. **Select a page name (I used** `Facebook Application Development For Dummies`**), and denote that you agree to the terms.**

Select the best page name you can. After you select a name, you can change it, so long as you have fewer than 100 fans. After 100 fans, you can't change it again. If you do not select a username, your page name also appears in your page's URL, which makes it one of the first things search engines see when they index your page. Remember that pages are public and visible to search engines, so every little thing counts. The page name should be one of the first things that you think about when targeting your page to index well in search engines.

Choosing the correct category for your page is very important so that the proper fields are available for you to describe what you are trying to represent. For instance, if you select `Government Official`, the wording of the fields that describe the official will appear targeted to someone who is in a government office. Selecting `Local Business` can present specific fields such as operating hours, menu items, and so on. When you have 100 fans, you are also unable to change the category name, so choose carefully!

See `http://stay.am/fbcategories` for a great overview of what fields you get for which categories.

5. **Click the Get Started button.**

That's it! You're now taken to the screen in which you can start customizing your Facebook Page. (See Figure 5-3.)

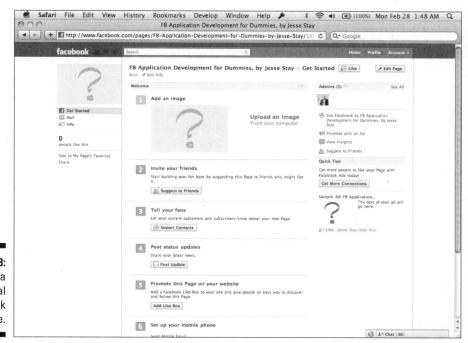

Figure 5-3:
Creating a new official Facebook Page.

Selecting the main image

After your page is set up, the first thing you should do is choose a main image. To add an image, just mouse over the main image in the upper-left corner and select Change Picture. A drop-down menu appears, allowing you to upload a picture, take a picture using your Web cam, choose a picture from an existing Facebook album, edit the thumbnail for an already uploaded image, or remove an already uploaded image.

Whichever method you choose, crop your image to your preference. I like to maximize the size of my image so I get maximum screen real estate, making my page look even more customized toward my brand's look and feel. Facebook allows main images up to 200 pixels wide by 600 pixels high, so take advantage of that real estate if you can! (See Figure 5-4.)

Entering other miscellaneous information

Your page is a great way to build SEO for your brand. Be sure to maximize everything you can to appear high in search engines as a result of your Facebook Page. Here are some things you should enter next:

- **Fill in the Info tab.** The category you select determines what fields appear here. Fill these in as much as you can; these fields contribute to the index inside Facebook's own search engine. In addition, they are a great way to give visitors more information about you or your brand.

- **Post a status update.** This is also important, and you should do this frequently. Posting links here can also give high ranking value to those things you are linking to, because they appear high on the page.

- **Add some masthead graphics.** There are five spots for featured masthead graphics at the top of your page. This is a great location for you to further customize your look and feel. Add graphics that are natural and complement the main profile image.

See `http://stay.am/fboptimize` for a great overview on what you can do to improve SEO for your Facebook Page.

Figure 5-4:
Facebook allows images up to 200 x 600 pixels. Here is what my Facebook Page looks like.

Creating a username for your page

After you create your page and start pointing people to it, you should set up a unique username for your page. This can both improve your SEO and give people an easy way to remember where your Facebook Page is. Later in this chapter, I show you some other cool things that you can do with the username and text messaging (SMS) as well.

To create a username, follow these steps:

1. **Build at least 25 "likes."**

   For some unknown reason — some say it's to prevent spam — Facebook requires Facebook Pages to have at least 25 likes before any page can create a unique username. If you don't have 25 friends who can like a page so that you can get the username you want, go to this book's Facebook Page at Facebook.com/dummiesbook and ask for some help!

2. **Go to** http://facebook.com/username. **(See Figure 5-5.)**

   This is the URL where you can set up your custom username. After you have 25 likes, you can choose a username for your page.

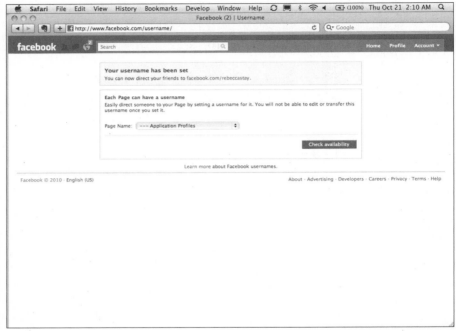

Figure 5-5:
The
username
selection
page.

3. Select your page, and select a username.

Facebook lets you know whether your username has already been taken. Unless you pay a lot of money for advertising to Facebook, you will be limited to using no less than five characters for your username. It will be difficult to come up with such a short username that hasn't already been taken, so try to think of short names that aren't too short but are easy to remember.

If your trademark is being used as a username, you can probably secure the username of your choice under your current trademark by filling out the trademark infringement form at `http://www.facebook.com/help/ contact.php?show_form=username_infringement`.

Integrating Your Own Application into a Facebook Page through Tabs

Tabs, which are now links on the left side of a Facebook Page, are a way you can integrate your application into a brand's presence on Facebook. I show you how to build a simple custom tab in Chapter 4. Setting up an application into a Facebook tab is as simple as creating that first application (refer to Chapter 2).

For consistency's sake, I call the little links on the left of your Facebook Page "tabs." This is because as I started this book, those links actually were tabs, spanning across the top of each Facebook Page. However, they're now just links on the left side of the page. Facebook hasn't called these links anything else at the moment, so I'll just keep calling them tabs.

Setting up your custom tab

Just as with your first application, you need to set up where Facebook points to for your custom tab. The Custom Tab application works just the same — the user opens the tab and Facebook calls your server to get the code to display for the user (through an iFrame).

To set up your custom tab, follow these steps — these may be a bit of a repeat of Chapter 4 if you went through tab creation there:

1. **Go to** `Facebook.com/developers`, **and go to your application's settings.**

   If you haven't yet created an application, go back to Chapter 2 and create an application. (In this case, you really don't have to write any code for your Canvas Page — you just have to pretend it's there and set a location so that Facebook knows where to find your tab.)

2. **Go to the Facebook Integration section and set the tab name and tab URL.**

   Be sure that you have set your Canvas URL first, which is the base to which your tab points. Then, select the name of your tab (I call mine `We <3 Dummies!`), followed by the name of the file or path that includes your tab code. I like to put mine in `tab.html` or `tab.php`. (See Figure 5-6.)

   Adding a URL in the Edit URL field supplies a URL to another Canvas Page that appears when the page admins click the Edit link next to your app in their page administration interface. This can be a great place to add administrative functions for the setup of your tab. For instance, on a promotions app created for SocialToo, page admins can go into their Page settings and configure their promotion, who won, and so on, all from the page itself. I'm not going to go into much further detail on how to do this, however. The Edit URL is just another Canvas Page and works exactly like any other Canvas Page in your application.

Figure 5-6:
The contents of my We <3 Dummies! Facebook Integration page after filling in the tab information.

Building on the server

Next you must edit your code, just like you did with the app you created in Chapter 2. In this case, you can provide a simple welcome message, or you can get down and dirty and use the Facebook API with a language like PHP to determine whether the user has liked the page, figure out who his or her friends are, and display information accordingly. Because I haven't covered the details on the Facebook API yet, just know that you can do all that stuff here; I cover all that in detail starting in Chapter 7. This code is now hosted on your own server, and you can dynamically render whatever content you want now! The following code renders a simple welcome message, hosted on your own servers in `tab.html`. Just enter this into a file named `tab.html` on your own server (the location you pointed to in your Application settings above):

```
<html>
<body>
<div style="text-align:center">
<h1 style="margin: 20px">CLICK "LIKE" ABOVE FOR PROMOTIONS AND MORE INFORMATION
                ON WHEN THE BOOK GOES TO PRINT!</h1>
```

```
<div style="margin: 20px"><img src="http://staynalive.com/dummiesbook.jpg"
         border="0" width="300" height="300" alt="Facebook Application
         Development For Dummies" /></div>

<h2 style="margin: 20px">Facebook Application Development For Dummies, by Jesse
         Stay</h2>

<p style="text-align:center;margin: 20px">Buy it in Stores or on Amazon late
         2011!</p>
</div>
</body>
</html>
```

You can have only one tab per application! If you want to have multiple tabs, you need to create multiple applications. With some advanced skills, an application API is available (at the time of this writing) that may allow you to dynamically create these applications and tabs, but that is beyond the scope of this book.

Creating a Welcome tab

Did you know that you could make a custom HTML page show up whenever a new visitor visits your Facebook Page? This only works for people who have not yet liked your Facebook Page, so it's a great way to welcome new visitors to your page and encourage them to like it. To set this up, follow these steps:

1. **Click the Edit Page link in the upper-right of the page.**

2. **Click Manage Permissions.**

   After you do this, click the Default Landing Tab drop-down menu and select the tab you just created.

3. **Test!**

   Remember, you aren't going to see your Welcome tab appear by default because you're the administrator of the page. Create a developer account, or just create a test account of some sort and visit the page without liking it. Now your custom tab appears by default!

After you create your custom tab and set it as the default, you now have a great tool in your SEO arsenal. Be sure that you create content for this page that search engines can index well for the search terms that you want to rank under. Just as new visitors can see this page, so can search engines, which also have not "liked" the page.

Picking a third-party application

Now that you've created a custom tab, what do you put on it? Sure, if you're a 1337 h4x0r (that's code for *hard-core coder*), you may be able to sit down and code a really cool app (which I cover next), but it might be faster just to use someone else's code.

You can use a couple of resources to find cool apps for your page — here are some of my favorites:

- **AppBistro:** This is by far the most thorough listing of applications for Facebook Pages. Built by former Facebook employee Ryan Merket, it is a full index and marketplace of third-party applications for Facebook Pages. With AppBistro, you can find just about anything you need for your Facebook Page — some are free, some at a cost. This should be your first stop for finding custom applications for your Facebook Page.

- **Involver:** Involver builds a few of its own custom Facebook applications for pages. It has a cool Twitter stream app and RSS app for importing content. Involver also provides analytics around those applications. Be sure to check out the custom apps that it has built — some are at a cost, some are free.

- **SocialToo:** This is pure shameless self-promotion, but I have to share. By the time you read this, `SocialToo.com`, my own site, should have several applications available to you. SocialToo currently has a great contest application that allows you to target and incentivize people to become fans of your page, providing unique ways to target your customer base and build likes, places check-ins, and sales. Stay tuned to SocialToo for more applications and tools in the near future. SocialToo can also build custom applications for you based on your needs. If this isn't available by the time you read this book, contact me and maybe I can build something custom just for your needs.

Basic Tips Every Page Owner Should Know

A chapter on Facebook Page customization wouldn't be complete without a few tips on how to make your page successful after you create it. Here are a few of my favorite tips and techniques:

- **Post regularly!** This is one of the most beneficial and easy techniques that you can use to keep fans engaged and interested in your page. Keep in mind that posts that have more likes and more comments are the ones that are more likely to appear in your fans' news streams, so you want to give them lots of content to catch their attention.

There is no magic number for this. Be sure to use Facebook Insights to determine at what point people stop interacting or liking your page if you end up posting too much or too little.

✔ **Use SMS to your advantage.** This is one of Facebook's best-kept secrets. Right now on any page or user profile, you can click a Subscribe via SMS link. What Facebook doesn't tell you is that you don't even have to visit `Facebook.com` to like a page. You can actually like a page through simple SMS or text messaging.

To like a page via text message, just have your customers send `like` *username* (so, `like stay` if it were my personal Facebook Page) to 32665 (which is FBOOK on a cell phone). After they do, they will automatically be subscribed to your page's updates, and updates will go straight to their cell phones after that!

This can be incredibly useful if you have a physical location such as a store. Be sure that you have a signup saying where your Facebook Page is and encouraging customers to like it on their cell phones. Not everyone has a Web browser on his or her cell phone, but you can pretty much bet that users have text messaging!

✔ **Provide incentives for your visitors to become fans.** One of the greatest techniques that you can use to build your page is to come up with unique ways of encouraging your visitors to become fans. Be careful — this is a sensitive issue. Review the rules carefully at `http://www.facebook.com/promotions_guidelines.php` to be sure that you are keeping in line with Facebook's rules surrounding promotions.

Here are some basic guidelines:

- *Get a Facebook account representative.* This can be one of the greatest tools in your arsenal, because when you have one, you can get around issues such as trademark infringement and other problems much faster. It usually involves paying Facebook ad money, though. You can apply to get an account representative at `http://www.facebook.com/business/contact.php`.

- *Make it clear that you're not Facebook.* Facebook asks that each promotion includes the following text: "This promotion is in no way sponsored, endorsed or administered by, or associated with, Facebook. You understand that you are providing your information to [recipient(s) of information] and not to Facebook. The information you provide will only be used for [disclose any way that you plan to use the user's information]." You also find other guidelines listed in the previous URL.

- *Don't automatically pick winners based on them just liking your page.* I personally think it's okay to have a separate tab where the contest only appears if they've liked the page, but do not just randomly pick your winners from the fans of the page. Make them enter the contest first, and then you can choose from those entrants.

- *Be careful how you notify users.* Facebook says that you can't notify users that they have won through Facebook messaging such as their Facebook inbox, their wall, or chat. You should instead get their e-mail addresses (you can use the API and permissions to get that automatically) and send them an external e-mail to notify them.

Although some of the terms are unclear, use your best judgment as you build your contest or promotion. One thing a lot of page owners really like to do is have a tab with a promotion that users can enter, but that promotion appears only if they are fans of the page. It's unclear whether this is legal per Facebook's terms, so ask your account representative whether this is okay (or just take the risk knowing that your page could be taken down). If you need an application that helps with this, my own site, SocialToo.com, offers a contest application that you can install and customize to provide promotions to your fan base.

✔ **Provide incentives to encourage your visitors to check in.** As always, remember the preceding promotion guidelines. However, another technique that is rather new at the time of this writing is to require fans to check in to a specific location to get a special deal on your Facebook Page.

Facebook's API supports reading the Facebook check-ins of a specific place or location. So, technically, you can write an application that reads these check-ins, matches them to the Facebook ID of the current visitor, and renders different content if they've previously checked in to that specific place. I think that huge possibilities exist for this strategy that have yet to be tapped.

✔ **Write with a call to action.** I've seen huge results from this. Make sure that your posts on your page's wall always end with a call to action. I like questions — "What do you think?" "How does this make you feel?" "Tell us your story." All of these encourage the users to comment and like the post. As they comment, their friends also feel motivated to comment, and those posts will naturally get more comments and likes.

This is important because the more comments or likes your posts have, the more likely they are to appear in your fans' news streams. Facebook has an algorithm that determines this, and that algorithm weighs heavily on how many comments and likes each post has.

✔ **Post updates.** This is infrequently used, and maybe rightly so. Under the Edit Page Administration section for your page, you can see a Send an Update link on the right. If you click that, you can choose a specific audience for your update to go to.

What this does is send a message to each of targeted fan base member's Facebook inbox. Those who have Facebook set to send inbox notifications to their e-mail will also get an e-mail about it. This is a great way to ensure that your fan base sees the message you have to share.

Note one caveat to posting updates — be careful not to spam! Keep in mind that anything that goes to the users' e-mail inboxes has the potential to annoy them. Therefore, any update you send also has the potential to encourage them to dislike your page, reducing the overall effectiveness. Try this out, but weigh it with the response that you get from your fan base after you do.

✔ **Target your audience.** Pages have a powerful tool that few people use. With each post you make on Facebook, you have the capability to finely target the country and language you want that post to appear to.

So, perhaps you have a large Spanish-speaking audience. With a single update, you can click the Lock button, select Customize, and choose Spanish as the language, and now only those who view Facebook in Spanish will see that update. (See Figure 5-7.) The English-speakers will never see it. That's powerful, because it builds community in not just English, but in any language and for any country. Not enough people take advantage of internationalization, and that has the potential to be a powerful tool in your arsenal.

Figure 5-7:
Click the Lock button to target your updates by language or country.

Part III

From Fishers to Farmers — Building Facebook on Your Own Site

The 5th Wave   By Rich Tennant

J. MONK OPTOMETRIST

"Games are an important part of my Web site. They cause eye strain."

In this part . . .

In Part I, I talk about the concept of "fishing where the fish are," meaning providing a means for your message to spread to people on the social networks they're on (like Facebook). After you master this concept, you'll want to try what I call "farming."

Facebook has provided many ways that you can put the message or product you want to share in the hands of your customers, right on your own Web site (your turf). Through a few simple techniques, you can integrate Facebook into your own Web site, and your users and customers will never have to leave your site to participate with, share, and expand your message to their friends on Facebook.

Chapter 6

Turning Your Web Site into a Facebook Page with Open Graph Protocol and Social Plugins

In This Chapter

▶ Introducing social plugins

▶ Working with OGP

▶ Linking Facebook users as admins

*I*n 2010, Facebook launched new, simpler methods to allow anyone, regardless of where he or she is on the Web, to seamlessly integrate a social, Facebook-integrated experience into a Web site, mobile app, or desktop product. Facebook introduced *social plugins,* enabling Webmasters to easily enter parameters into a few simple forms, and immediately get simple HTML code to just copy and paste into their Web site. Facebook also released Open Graph Protocol (OGP) to make indexing of Web sites easy, putting the content that you want into Facebook's search and interests fields, not just the content the Web site provides.

All of a sudden, Facebook is becoming a new form of search. Just as it has become an index of people around the Web, Facebook is now actually indexing the Web itself but allowing the people on its network to index the Web for them. Through this, Facebook is quickly becoming its own search engine for the Web. With Facebook, people are the new SEO, as they are the ones that through their likes and shares will actually be indexing and adding your Web sites to the new search engine that is Facebook.

SEO, or search engine optimization, is a technique used to get your Web site to the top of search engine results when people search for specific keywords that you want to rank high under.

Going the Easy Way with Social Plugins

Social plugins are a nice, easy way to build a Facebook-integrated Web site on the fly with little effort by anyone who can do a simple copy and paste. In the past, Facebook provided Facebook Markup Language (FBML), a tag language giving shortcuts to things like comment boxes and simple nav bar structures and other shortcuts in your code. Social plugins are Facebook's next evolution in this, moving from FBML to simple HTML iFrames; you can copy and paste these little pieces of Facebook into any HTML document on or off `Facebook.com`.

Understanding social plugins

Before you start working with social plugins, go to `http://developers.facebook.com/plugins` and look at the various plugins that Facebook has available.(See Figure 6-1.) By the time you read this, you will probably find many more than those I mention here.

The best way to convince you that social plugins are valuable is by working with them directly, right on Facebook itself. If you do anything in this chapter, I want you to try this exercise, and I promise that you'll see the benefit of integrating Facebook on your site almost immediately!

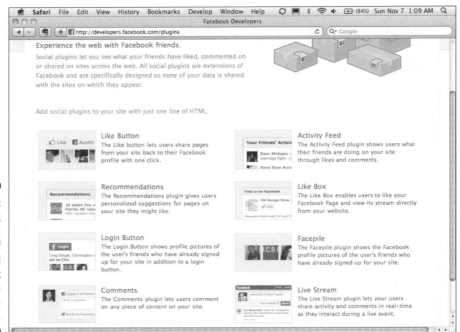

Figure 6-1: Facebook offers a range of social plugins that you can choose from.

To see the full potential of social plugins, follow these steps:

1. **Go to** `http://developers.facebook.com/plugins.`

2. **Click the Activity Feed plugin.**

   On the following page, you'll see a form with all kinds of options that you can configure.

3. **Start by changing the height to 700, and then click another field so that it saves.**

   I chose 700 for the height only because I want to show you a long list of people's activities. You see why in a second.

4. **In the Domain field, enter the name of your Web site. I'm going to enter** SocialToo.com.

   Look on the right — see anything interesting? Now you're presented with an activity stream of all your friends who have shared or liked your Web site on Facebook. See how long the list is?

   If you need any excuse — this is it. People are sharing your content on Facebook, whether you know it or not. You may as well embrace this and make it even easier for them to share and like using social plugins!

5. **Click the Get Code button.**

   You're presented with some HTML code that you can use to create the Recent Activity plugin that you see on the right. Copy it, paste it into your Web site, and you're done! (See Figure 6-2.)

As you can see, it's extremely simple to set up and install new social experiences that interact with Facebook right on your Web site. You just fill out a form, click a button, copy, and paste — and you're done!

Although you can perform most customizations just by filling out the Web form on each plugin page, with a little URL hacking, you can also customize the plugins even further by editing their parameters in the URL fields of the HTML iFrame tags that you copy and paste into your Web site. Occasionally you will see parameters here that do not exist on the Web form.

In addition, you can always update the Cascading Style Sheets (CSS) for your Web site and edit the look and feel of your social plugins that way. To figure out what the IDs and class attributes are for your plugin, use a tool like Firebug for Firefox or the Console tool for Chrome to inspect the HTML and find what you need to alter. This is for serious HTML hackers only!

Figure 6-2:
The Activity plugin shows visitors all their friends' activity on your site.

Choosing a social plugin

Now that you've implemented a simple social plugin, it's time to find out what other plugins are available. In the following sections, I discuss the plugins that were available at the time of this writing, but don't rely on me — check them out for yourself! If my calculations are correct, you will find many more of these in the future, and you'll have many more options to choose from. You can also refer to `facebook.com/dummiesbook` for more ideas (seriously — just ask us a question!).

The Like button

The Like button gives your users the capability to "like" basically anything on your Web site. Essentially, anything with a unique URL can have a Like button. This is valuable for several reasons:

✓ **More visibility for your Web site:** Every time someone clicks a Like button on your Web site, it appears in his or her news feed as "So and so likes such and such on *yoursite.com*." Note that "such and such" is the title of the page or thing that person is liking (which can be configured using Open Graph Protocol), and it links right back to your Web site, *not* `Facebook.com`. Therefore, every time someone clicks Like, his or her friends see your Web site, and they also have the opportunity to click Like and share with their friends as well. Like buttons also allow people to add their own comments, and those comments appear in the stream, just like in a normal share (see Figure 6-3).

✔ **Links:** Every Like button produces a link on `Facebook.com` back to your Web site (when people click it). Facebook, at the time I wrote this, had a page rank on Google of 10/10. That basically means that for any public profile that clicks the Like button, you get a very strong link back to your site. Get lots of those, and you have continually relevant content and links back to your site, hopefully improving your own site's rank in search engines. The Like button is a great SEO technique.

✔ **Interests:** For each item people like on your Web site, that item gets added to the user's Interests section on the Info tab in his or her profile. Although this doesn't necessarily appear by default to search engines (depending on their privacy preferences), it does provide additional visibility for the items on your Web site that people are liking. This means more likes, and even more visibility. Again, you can use Open Graph Protocol, which I talk about later in the chapter, to configure the categorization of where each item to be liked will be placed.

✔ **Search:** With Facebook, people are the new SEO. This is why: For every Like button clicked on your site, that item appears in the search drop-down box when users are searching for things similar to the item they liked. (See Figure 6-4.) Their friends can also see this as a search suggestion as they are typing things into search, especially if a lot of people have liked it.

At some point, thanks to this method, all you will have to do is search in Facebook to find the sites you are looking for. The best thing about it is that you will now start seeing search results, not on what Facebook is guessing you might like, but ordered instead by the things that your friends have liked and shown interest in. The Facebook Like button is a powerful concept, and if you have to choose only one plugin, this is the one to implement on your Web site.

Figure 6-3:
When a user comments on the Like button, objects on your Web site get more visibility.

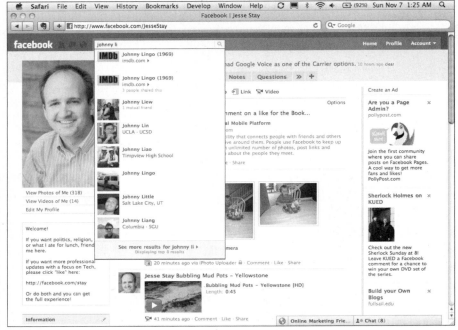

Figure 6-4:
The Like
button helps
prioritize
objects
on your
Web site in
Facebook
Search.

You can also link your Like buttons to a specific Facebook Page instead of an actual URL on your Web site. To do so, just enter the Facebook Page URL into the URL field of the form on the Plugin Configuration page (`developers.` `facebook.com/docs/reference/plugins/like`). Now when users click the Like button, it will be liking the actual Facebook Page instead of the URL they are currently on.

Case Study: IMDb, a popular site dedicated to indexing movie titles and actors, integrated Like buttons throughout its site for actors, movies, and other types of objects. Since integrating Like buttons, IMDb's referral traffic from Facebook doubled! (See Figure 6-5 and Figure 6-6.)

The Like box

Like boxes are plugins that you can place on your Web site that allow users to "like" a specific Facebook Page (not a URL, like a Like button). In addition, Like boxes can display the names of the user's friends who have also "liked" that Facebook Page, along with an optional news feed of the latest posts by admins on the page.

Like boxes can be a great way to introduce your Facebook Page to users visiting your Web site. You may have visitors, for instance, who are not familiar with the fact that you have a Facebook Page. This introduces your page to them, and it keeps them from having to leave your Web site to "like" the Facebook Page.

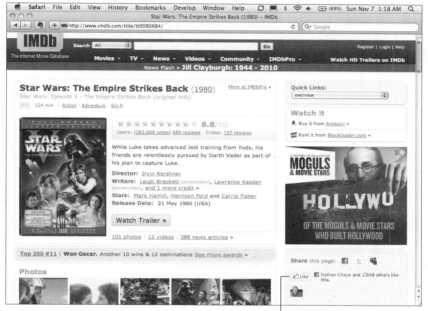

Figure 6-5:
This is what the Like button looks like on IMDb.com.

The Like button

Pressing the IMDb Like button adds this line to my news feed.

Figure 6-6:
This is what that like looks like in my news feed when I click the button.

What is the difference between a Like box and a Like button?

The answer is, "not much." The main difference is that a Like box focuses solely on Facebook Pages. Although you can certainly configure a Like button to link to a Facebook Page, the Like box was built with the sole purpose of promoting Facebook Pages. This is in contrast to the Like button, which was built with the sole purpose of promoting actual Web site content that has a unique URL. If you're going to promote your Facebook Page from your Web site, or if you need to display a news stream along with the Like button and list of friends who have liked the page, consider using a Facebook Like box first.

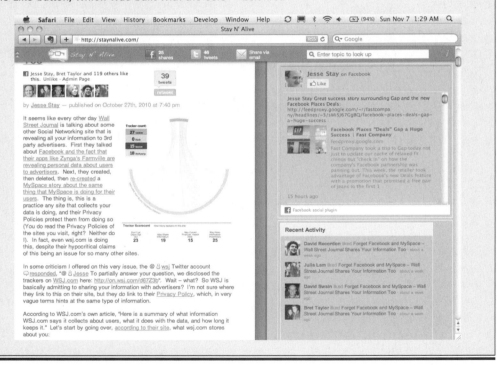

Recommendations

Recommendations can be a great and simple way to suggest content to your visitors based on what their friends are liking and sharing. For instance, if you visit StayNAlive.com, my blog, you see a very large version of the Recommendations plugin on the main page, suggesting articles that you should read based on what your friends are reading, liking, or sharing. Or, perhaps you want to share the top items that your users' friends are purchasing, liking, and sharing. This can be a great way to provide relevant items that your users can purchase, bringing more purchases, more page views, and greater engagement to your Web site. See Figure 6-7 for a great example of this.

The Login button

The Login button (see Figure 6-8) is most useful to you if you're using Graph API to access data about logged-in users, which I cover later. If you know a little about the Facebook JavaScript SDK, you can make calls on behalf of the user after the user has logged in with simple JavaScript. This means, as a user, you get a more relevant experience. After the user is authenticated, you can customize the experience to that user's interests, and likes, and friends.

You can read more about the Facebook JavaScript SDK by searching for *JavaScript* in the Developer documentation or by going to `developers. facebook.com/docs/reference/javascript`.

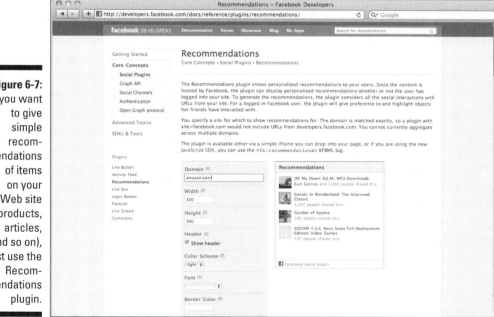

Figure 6-7:
If you want to give simple recom-mendations of items on your Web site (products, articles, and so on), just use the Recom-mendations plugin.

Comments

The Comments social plugin is great to use when you need to add a simple Comments section to any part of your Web site. (See Figure 6-9.) Users can also choose to publish their comments to Facebook when they're done commenting, giving more attention and page views back to your Web site. You can choose whether you want users to be logged into Facebook before they can comment, giving you a lot of flexibility over how you want your comments to work using this plugin. Comments can be a great way to increase engagement and keep users on your Web site longer.

The activity feed

This is a simple activity feed (which you set up earlier in the chapter) that shows all of a user's friends who are "liking" or sharing a particular URL. This can be a great way to keep a sense of community on your Web site, keeping your users talking with their friends about your brand.

Facepile

This is just what it sounds like: a "pile" (or at least a row) of faces. (See Figure 6-10.) The feature displays the profile pictures of friends of the user who have previously logged in to the site. If you don't need a Login button, this feature can be used creatively to keep users coming back to your site because they know their friends are using it.

The Login button

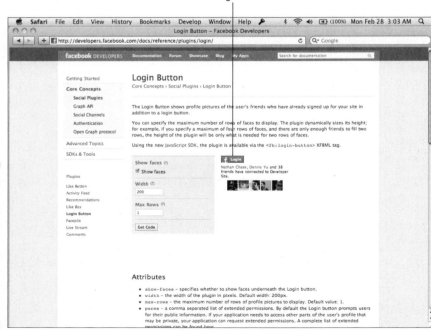

Figure 6-8:
To authenticate users of your Web site and access the Graph API, integrate a Login button like this.

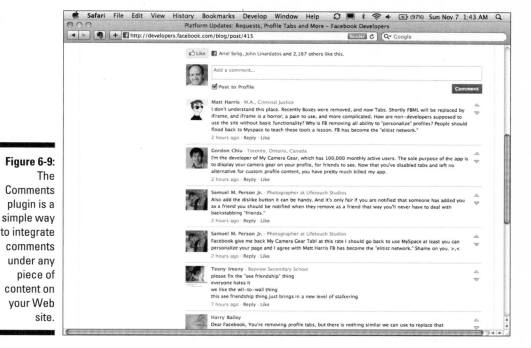

Figure 6-9:
The Comments plugin is a simple way to integrate comments under any piece of content on your Web site.

Figure 6-10:
Facepile is just a compilation of profile photos of all your users' friends who have logged in to your Web site.

Live Stream

The Live Stream plugin is great for events, and it provides a live stream of user updates for people viewing the page they are currently on. (See Figure 6-11.) Facebook uses this for its own Facebook Live channel, where it often broadcasts live events and training from Facebook headquarters. Users watching the event live on video can comment as they are watching the event, see what others are posting in real time, and even choose to post their comments back to their Facebook profile, bringing more attention back to the event. This works best for live events and current videos.

Figure 6-11:
Facebook
uses the
Live Stream
plugin on its
Facebook
Live video
streams.

The New SEO: Introducing OGP

In 2010, Facebook introduced a new way for Web sites to integrate seman-
tic metadata into its HTML that can declare the identity or function of the
site and can specify the way the site owner would like the site indexed
by Facebook. This metadata is known as Open Graph Protocol, or OGP.
Overnight, as Web sites began to integrate OGP and social plugins into their
own HTML for Facebook to discover, Facebook turned from a social network
focusing on just friends and family connections on Facebook.com to a global
network of hundreds of thousands of Web sites, all being indexed by people
rather than bots. With this move, Facebook moved from a walled garden to
a global, distributed Web platform that anyone could integrate and add to
Facebook's index. Open Graph Protocol is the organizer of this index of Web
metadata for Facebook.

Open Graph Protocol is certainly not necessary to be able to use social graph
plugins. The plugins will still work, and Facebook will guess the data that it
needs to populate in user news feeds and likes and Interests fields. However,
if you want to be even more specific on how your articles and products
appear in a user's news feed, help Facebook to index this data by specifying
some simple Open Graph Protocol tags in your HTML.

Using OGP meta tags can help your Web site appear better in news feeds, likes, and Interests fields, as well as search results as users are searching throughout Facebook for relevant terms related to your Web site. It would be wise to index your data as much as possible so that Facebook doesn't have to do as much work in indexing your Web site in the future.

Open Graph Protocol is just a series of meta tags that identify what a specific Web site or URL is about. It is a standard created by Facebook based on the RDF (a protocol you probably don't need to worry about). As you set up your Facebook Page in Chapter 5, you selected a category and page type under which to classify your page. You also selected a page name, and maybe even added some additional information such as a phone number and e-mail address. Open Graph Protocol allows you to do this very same thing with a Web site, effectively turning your Web site into a Facebook Page, now part of Facebook's network but part of the open Web and fully under your control.

Here are a few OGP tags you should be aware of — you may want to add these to each page on your Web site. You can do so by just adding them to your site's meta tags, in the format of `<meta property="og:title" content="Title goes here">`:

- `og:title` — The title you want to show up in the user's stream when he or she clicks the Like button for your page. If this isn't specified, it defaults to the `<title>` tags of your Web site.

- `og:type` — For the item being liked, this is where it will be placed in a user's Likes and Interests section on the user's Info tab for his or her profile. This can be anything from the list specified at `developers.facebook.com/docs/opengraph#types`.

- `og:image` — When the user likes the page and comments on the like, this is the image that appears for that specific item being liked in his or her news feed. Choose something that stands out here, so it attracts more likes from the user's friends! Facebook automatically chooses one of the first images on the page if none are specified.

- `og:url` — This defaults to the URL of the current page, but if you want a user's like or interest to link back to a different URL, specify that here.

- `og:site_name` — This defaults to the title of the Web site, but you can set it to something different if you like.

- `og:description` — When the user likes the page and comments on the like, this is the description that appears in his or her news feed with the image and comment. You want this field to be dynamic for each page that is liked — the more specific and descriptive, the better!

- `fb:admins` — I talk more about this later in the chapter, but this is a comma-separated list of Facebook IDs of people whom you want to be able to administer the current Web site (which is also a page, remember!) on Facebook.

In addition, consider these OpenGraph types (again, as meta tags in your HTML) to further describe each page on your site (which I think describe themselves):

- og:phone_number
- og:email
- og:latitude
- og:longitude
- og:street-address
- og:locality
- og:region
- og:postal-code
- og:country-name

I've integrated these on my own blog, StayNAlive.com, and you can view them today by just viewing the source of the page and looking between the <head> tags at the top. Here is what StayNAlive.com's OGP implementation looks like:

```
<meta property="fb:page_id" content="12327140265" />
<meta property="fb:app_id" content="293151070252" />
<meta property="og:title" content="Stay N&#039; Alive" />
<meta property="og:type" content="website" />
<meta property="og:url" content="http://staynalive.com" />
<meta property="og:phone_number" content="801-853-8339" />
<meta property="fb:admins" content="683545112" />
<meta property="og:description" content="Converging the World of Marketing and
          Technology" />
<meta property="og:email" content="jesse@staynalive.com" />
<meta property="og:site_name" content="Stay N&#039; Alive" />
<meta property="og:image" content="http://staynalive.com/wp-content/themes/
          staynalive/images/Logo-20080519-113612" />
```

Notice the tags are just simple <meta> tags, with the name of the ogp tag as the property value and the value of the tag as the content value.

Linking Facebook Users as Admins on Your Web Site

As I mention in the list of OGP tags, one tag you can add to your list of meta tags is the fb:admins tag. This is an underused but powerful tag that you can use to now publish updates to any and all users who have "liked" a specific page on your Web site. It also specifies who can view analytics (Facebook Insights) for Facebook users who visit that specific page.

Consider an example from my blog. If you go to `staynalive.com/articles/strategy-build-relationships` and view the source, you can see that I've added the `fb:admins` meta tag at the top. My Facebook ID is one of those admins in the content portion of the tag:

```
<meta property="fb:admins" content="683545112" />
```

Now, whenever I visit that page on `StayNAlive.com` when I'm logged in to Facebook, I see a small Admin Page link below the Like button.(See Figure 6-12.) If I click that link, I'm taken to a page on `Facebook.com` that looks a lot like a Facebook Page. I'm the only person who can see this page (and any other admin I specify in the `fb:admins` tag).

Figure 6-12: If I'm the admin and I visit an article with the fb:admins tag in the source, I see an Admin Page link like this.

On this page on `Facebook.com` (see Figure 6-13), I can post updates, view Insights, and see a few other things. This is where it gets fun. Now, just like on any other Facebook Page, I can post updates to all the people who clicked the Like button on my article, "How do I get people to interact and build lasting relationships?"

Specifying an `fb:admins` OGP tag enables you to now be able to post very targeted updates to people who have just liked a specific page on your Web site, not even the entire Web site itself! Basically, this makes every single object on your Web site its own Facebook Page, with its own audience and its own community, and it gives you full power to post updates, track gender, see demographics, and view other information for anyone who clicks Like on the page. Your Web site now has all the same functionality as a traditional Facebook Page hosted on `Facebook.com`.

You have now felt the full effect of building your own farm and managing Facebook on your own turf, rather than on `Facebook.com` itself!

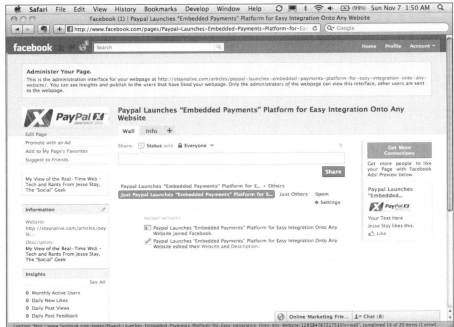

Figure 6-13:
When I click
Admin Page,
I'm taken to
a page on
Facebook.
com that
looks like
this, where
I can post
updates that
appear in
the news
feeds of
people who
liked the
article.

Instant Personalization

You should be aware of one more element of social plugins. Some of this probably fits well in some of the Graph API chapters of this book, but because it's so similar from site to site, I include it here. I'm referring to the product that Facebook provides called Instant Personalization.

Instant Personalization is a feature that Facebook provides only to selected partners, but it enables those partners to instantly be able to personalize the experience of any visitor to their Web sites without that user ever having to physically log in to Facebook. As long as that user is logged in to Facebook elsewhere, he or she should instantly see what his or her friends like on the site and what those friends are participating in.

One example of this is `RottenTomatoes.com`. (See Figure 6-14.) When you visit `RottenTomatoes.com`, you are instantly greeted with a list of movies that your friends on Facebook like, your friend activity, and even movies that RottenTomatoes recommends to you based on your Facebook friends' activity.

Instant Personalization sites all must have an opt-out message prominently displayed on the site, and users can also turn it off in their Facebook privacy settings. However, if you have some money and a great idea, you can quite possibly convince Facebook to include you in its list of select partners for this program.

To sign up for Instant Personalization, you need to get an account rep. This usually means that you will need to spend a lot of money on advertising and have a pretty good relationship with Facebook. You can request an account rep by filling out the form at www.facebook.com/business/contact.php.

Figure 6-14:
Rotten Tomatoes.com instantly customizes the experience for any Facebook user who visits its Web site.

Chapter 7

Integrating Facebook on Your Web Site through Graph API

My book shows you some simple ways to make your Web site a part of the already powerful Facebook network. Adding Facebook to your Web site can be a terrific way to build relationships among your users, while allowing them to still participate in the environments they frequent daily, all in a comfortable environment. Integrating your site with Facebook allows you to "think socially," bringing your users' close friends and family and relationships right into your own environment. When they are all of the sudden experiencing your site alongside their friends, it becomes a much more intimate environment for them. They want to stay longer. They want to interact longer. They are influenced to buy your product as a result.

Now it's time to get your hands a little dirtier by integrating simple code like JavaScript or PHP to make your Web site a little more social. I start with some basic tips as you design your Facebook integration.

Understanding the Fundamentals of Graph API

Facebook Graph API was announced at Facebook's F8 Conference in the spring of 2010 as an easier, simpler way to access anything on Facebook. At its simplest form, Facebook Graph API allows anyone to access data about any object on Facebook in an organized form through his or her Web browser. Data is requested by typing **https://graph.facebook.com/** into the browser, followed by the name or ID of any object, followed by anything you want to retrieve about that object.

So, to retrieve my own information, I type **https://graph.facebook.com/ JesseStay** into my Web browser, and immediately I get results similar to those shown in the following code (notice that I can also type **https://graph. facebook.com/683545112** — 683545112 is my Facebook ID — and it returns the same data). To access my friends, I just need to pass `https://graph. facebook.com/JesseStay/friends` and I'm given a JSON-formatted list of my friends (per Facebook privacy limits, which I discuss in a bit).

You may be asking yourself, "What is JSON?" JSON stands for JavaScript Object Notation. If you're a Perl programmer or JavaScript coder, JSON is a format that you might be familiar with — curly brackets encapsulate key-value pairs containing information (or "objects" in JavaScript). Square brackets encapsulate lists of data — these can be lists of strings, lists of objects (the curly brackets), or lists of numbers. If you open any of the links shown in the next section, you can see a great example of JSON in action. The goal of JSON is to provide a minimal way of presenting data that a program can parse very easily.

```
{
    "id": "683545112",
    "name": "Jesse Stay",
    "first_name": "Jesse",
    "last_name": "Stay",
    "link": "http://www.facebook.com/JesseStay",
    "gender": "male",
    "locale": "en_US"
}
```

By following this format, the API is mostly self-explanatory. To retrieve data about an object, a Facebook library for any language (Facebook's own JavaScript SDK included) needs to provide only an interface to the paths associated with what the developer wants to retrieve and that developer will know how to access the API. Accessing a Graph API object in Facebook's Javascript API is as simple as accessing the `FB.api` method and passing the path to the object data being requested. The following example would return an alert box that says, "Jesse Stay."

```
FB.api('/JesseStay', function(response) {
    alert(response.name);
});
```

To access a Facebook Page, just send the username or Facebook ID of the Facebook Page, just like you do in the preceding example. For this book's Facebook Page, you send `https://graph.facebook.com/dummiesbook`. To get an event, pass the ID of the event. To get a video, pass the ID of the video — seeing a trend here? To get my profile picture (this is useful in `<img>` tags, for instance), pass `http://graph.facebook.com/JesseStay/ picture`. (See Figure 7-1.)

Figure 7-1:
Sending
a simple
`<img>`
tag returns
my profile
picture —
try it with
your own
profile ID!

Getting data from just a Web browser

Graph API was designed so that, with a simple GET request — or in simpler terms, by typing the URL into your browser — you can get all the data you need about an object. Here are some fun queries — be sure to replace my username for yours where applicable:

- ✔ `https://graph.facebook.com/me`: Gets the basic information about the currently logged-in user

- ✔ `https://graph.facebook.com/JesseStay/friends`: Gets a list of my friends, with their Facebook IDs and profile URLs (assuming my friends list is public). Programming languages like PHP and JavaScript can easily parse this data:

```
{
   "data": [
      {
         "name": "Jared Morgenstern",
         "id": "…"
      },
      {
         "name": "Randi Zuckerberg",
         "id": "…"
      },
      {
         "name": "Sasha Rush",
         "id": "…"
      },
      {
         "name": "Francisco Ramos",
         "id": "…"
      },
      {
         "name": "Dan Rose",
         "id": "…"
      },
      {
         "name": "Tamar Weinberg",
         "id": "…"
      },
      {
         "name": "Justin Smith",
         "id": "…"
      },
      …
```

✔ `https://graph.facebook.com/dummiesbook`: Gets the basic information about this book's Facebook Page

✔ `https://graph.facebook.com/472512064641`: A note on my profile (and all commenters, assuming this Note is public)

✔ `https://graph.facebook.com/23667699117`: A photo on my other book's Facebook Page

✔ `https://graph.facebook.com/dummiesbook/feed`: The feed for this book's Facebook Page

All data returned by Facebook gets returned in a nice JSON structure, which, if you're using JavaScript, should parse almost automatically. If you're using something like PHP or Perl, some simple serialization routines can turn the data into a structure that you can easily read.

```
{
    "data": [
        {
            "id": "120809261289270_185523121484550",
            "from": {
                "name": "Facebook Application Development For Dummies",
                "category": "Product/service",
                "id": "120809261289270"
            },
            "message": "Yes, there are many undocumented tricks in Facebook
                Application Development For Dummies. This book will take you
                places the Facebook Developer documentation doesn't!",
            "type": "status",
            "created_time": "2011-02-27T20:36:27+0000",
            "updated_time": "2011-02-27T20:36:27+0000",
            "likes": {
                "data": [
                    {
                        "name": "Sait Mara\u015fl\u0131o\u011flu",
                        "id": "756753195"
                    },
                    {
                        "name": "Mike Grainger",
                        "id": "754115069"
                    },
                    {
                        "name": "Ren R. Shore",
                        "id": "818427795"
                    },
                    {
                        "name": "Rob Mazur",
                        "id": "662251027"
                    }
                ],
                "count": 7
            }
        },
        {
            "id": "120809261289270_184959428207586",
            "from": {
                "name": "Facebook Application Development For Dummies",
                "category": "Product/service",
                "id": "120809261289270"
            },
...
```

CRUD! GET'ing versus POST'ing versus DELETE'ing

Thus far, I show you various ways that you can "get" data about users, photos, events, and other objects on Facebook in format you can easily be parsed. Entering this data into a Web browser is essentially a GET request in HTTP (Hyper Text Transfer Protocol, the protocol that drives requests between your browser and your server) terms.

There are numerous types of HTTP requests: GET, POST, and DELETE are commonly used in this book. There is also PUT. Each of these types of requests tells your server to treat the data slightly different. For instance, a POST request typically expects form variables from an HTML form, or similar as part of the request. A GET request takes those variables and parses them straight from the URL. All of this is somewhat more advanced stuff, but you should probably spend some time getting acquainted with it if you really want to understand the Web.

For now, just know that these are all different types of requests, and you should probably understand how your Facebook library of choice and the language of your choice can send requests using these methods. I show you how you can do this with a tool called Curl later in the chapter. I also show you how to do it in PHP and JavaScript. You probably want to learn how to do this in your own language as well.

In the HTTP protocol, you have various other ways of sending requests to Facebook. A GET tells Facebook that you want to "get" data — simple enough. However, Facebook also supports the POST request format, which tells Facebook that you want to "post," or send, data to Facebook. This is something that you have to do in your language of choice, because it involves altering the HTTP request sent by your application to POST data instead of GET it (although some browser plugins can enable even this through the browser if you know what you're doing). After all, I'm trying to create an application, not surf Facebook.

Technically, you find more than just GET and POST in the HTTP protocol. In typical REST ("Representational State Transfer"; this is a protocol Facebook uses that employs CRUD to send and receive requests from developers in a standardized way), DELETE tells the server that you want to delete a record. PUT tells the server that you want to update a record. In REST, this is called CRUD, or Create, Read, Update, Delete. To be fully REST compliant, a site should technically support all four. Facebook doesn't support all four yet, but it is pretty darn close! In fact, most sites aren't fully REST compliant, but we usually say they are if they are implementing some part of the CRUD architecture.

POST'ing requests

You already know that a GET request gets the data you're sending to Facebook. You can also tell Facebook to create information as well. You do this through an HTTP POST request. Consider that I want to post a message to my wall (feed). Assuming that I've already authorized the user, I would send a POST request to the following (sending the variables as POST variables, not necessarily in the URI, Uniform Resource Indicator):

```
https://graph.facebook.com/JesseStay/feed?message=Here's my
          message!&picture=http://graph.facebook.com/JesseStay/
          picture&link=http://staynalive.com&name=Message goes
          here&caption=This is the caption&description=a nice
          description&source=Dummies Book
```

Sending this request creates a simple status message ("Here's my message!"), a picture with my profile picture, a link back to my blog, and a simple title, caption, and description to go along with it. All that from a simple URL! The following code shows how this would look in JavaScript (assuming that you're loading the JQuery scripting libraries):

```
$.ajax({
    type: 'POST',
    url: 'https://graph.facebook.com/JesseStay/feed',
    data: {
      'message': 'Here\'s my message!',
      'picture': 'http://graph.facebook.com/JesseStay/picture',
      'link': 'http://staynalive.com',
      'name': 'Message goes here',
      'caption': 'This is the caption',
      'description': 'a nice description',
      'source': 'Dummies Book'
    },
    success: function() {
      alert('Success!');
    },
    error: function(event, xhr, settings) {
            alert("error: "+xhr.content);
        }
});
```

With the POST, you can do all sorts of stuff. Think to yourself, "With this GET request, what would happen if I could update the content I was retrieving?" and you probably have a good idea what the POST does. For example:

- ✔ `https://graph.facebook.com/post_id/likes` with a POST likes the post that you're specifying.

- ✔ `https://graph.facebook.com/profile_id/checkins` with a POST checks in the user to a specified location on Facebook.

As always, check `developers.facebook.com` for many more details on this topic. There you can find what variables you need to pass along with a POST, what objects are available to you, and what has updated since I wrote this. This particular documentation in the Facebook Developer documentation is one of the most interesting parts on the site — get to know it well.

DELETE'ing requests with Graph API

In addition to POST and GET, Facebook also supports DELETE for specific types of objects. For instance, to unlike, or "delete," a like, you can send a DELETE to `https://graph.facebook.com/`*post_id*`/likes` (where *post_id* is the ID of the post that has the like that you want to unlike).

Note that some clients don't support the DELETE HTTP method. In these cases, just pass a POST HTTP request with the variable (and value), `method=delete`, and it will accomplish the same purpose.

In the ensuing chapters, I cover many other ways that you can use Graph API, such as searching for things and getting updates for things you're searching for in real time, among many other things that you can accomplish.

Objects, fields, and introspection

You see how objects work in Graph API. Facebook also provides ways that you can specify fields you want to have returned. This is useful in cases where bandwidth is critical and expensive, and you need faster results that can often be bogged down by large data sets. To specify what fields you want to have returned, just pass the `fields` parameter in your URL, like this:

```
http://graph.facebook.com/JesseStay?fields=name,picture
```

Load that in your browser, and it only returns the name and picture of the individual (`JesseStay`, in this case) you just requested. Try that with any field or set of fields — you can get very specific!

Getting Multiple Objects

Perhaps you don't want `JesseStay`'s profile data. Maybe you also want `LouisGray`'s data, and maybe `Scobleizer`'s data; I also throw in the Facebook Page, `dummiesbook`. You can specify select lists of objects just by passing the `ids` parameter to the URL:

```
https://graph.facebook.com?ids=JesseStay,LouisGray,Scobleizer,dummiesbook
```

The resulting data looks something like what is shown below — a JSON object keyed by the IDs of each object requested. This can resolve the problem of sending multiple requests to Facebook just to get the same data — now you can do it in one request!

```
{
   "Scobleizer": {
      "id": "14090190332",
      "name": "Scobleizer",
      "picture": "http://profile.ak.fbcdn.net/hprofile-ak-snc4/188038_1409019033
            2_6863516_s.jpg",
      "link": "http://www.facebook.com/scobleizer",
      "category": "Journalist",
      "website": "http://scobleizer.com",
      "username": "scobleizer",
      "location": {
         "street": "Pinehurst Lane",
         "city": "Half Moon Bay",
         "state": "CA",
         "country": "United States",
         "zip": "94019"
      },
      "phone": "+1-425-205-1921",
      "bio": "Tech enthusiast, video blogger, media innovator, fanatical about
            startups. Searching the world for world-changing technologies at
            Rackspace, home of fanatical support and Web hosting for Internet
            entrepreneurs. ",
      "affiliation": "Rackspace Hosting",
      "birthday": "01/18/1965",
      "personal_info": "My community-edited bio is at: http://en.wikipedia.org/
            wiki/Robert_Scoble and all my various sites, video feeds, and
            other things are at: http://www.google.com/profiles/scobleizer",
      "personal_interests": "technology, gadgets, photography, my kids, silicon
            valley, innovation, business, geeks, rackspace, web, mobile,
            hosting, tech, entrepreneurs, startups, Internet, net, social
            media, journalism, iphone, xbox, google, microsoft, facebook,
            apple, consumer",
      "likes": 12995
   },
   "dummiesbook": {
      "id": "120809261289270",
      "name": "Facebook Application Development For Dummies",
      "picture": "http://profile.ak.fbcdn.net/hprofile-ak-snc4/27524_12080926128
            9270_4376_s.jpg",
      "link": "http://www.facebook.com/dummiesbook",
      "category": "Product/service",
      "website": "http://amzn.to/dummiesbook",
      "username": "dummiesbook",
      "company_overview": "Like this Page for important updates and information
            on the upcoming book, Facebook Application Development For
            Dummies!",
      "products": "Facebook Application Development For Dummies, by Jesse Stay",
      "likes": 423
   },
   "JesseStay": {
```

```
        "id": "683545112",
        "name": "Jesse Stay",
        "first_name": "Jesse",
        "last_name": "Stay",
        "link": "http://www.facebook.com/JesseStay",
        "gender": "male",
        "locale": "en_US"
    },
    "LouisGray": {
        "id": "589638695",
        "name": "Louis Gray",
        "first_name": "Louis",
        "last_name": "Gray",
        "link": "http://www.facebook.com/louisgray",
        "gender": "male",
        "locale": "en_US"
    }
}
```

Identifying the Logged-in User

You can identify the current logged-in user just by using the me object in your requests. So, assuming that I'm the one logged in to the browser when my application makes the request, if I make a GET request to https://graph. facebook.com/me, it is the same as making a GET request to https// graph.facebook.com/JesseStay. Both provide a JSON-serialized object with data about me. This can be useful if you don't particularly know the person who is logged in, and you don't want to go through the trouble of parsing his or her Facebook ID from a signed request, for instance (I cover signed requests later).

There will be many times you come across the need to use /me – if /me returns nothing or an error, the user isn't logged in. This can be an easy way, in a Canvas app or tab, to tell that the user is currently logged in, without needing to parse the signed request.

Knowing associated connections through Introspection

Introspection is a way of knowing what things are associated with a known object without knowing what an object's type is. As I mention earlier, the object you pass as the first part of a Graph API call is a Globally Unique ID (GUID). This means across all of Facebook, there will never be a repeated instance of that ID. That's no matter whether the object is a user, a Facebook Page, an event, a group, a note, or just a post or comment. There's no way to tell by the ID alone what that ID actually represents. For this reason, you may not know what the Graph API methods (or connections) are that are available to that object.

For instance, if I'm using an object ID that is a user type, but I don't know that object is a user (I only have the ID, after all), I may not know that I can call the `friends` connection to that user (like `http://graph.facebook.com/JesseStay/friends`). As far as I know, that object ID could be an event type, or a group type, or a request type object. I don't need to know that though, to find out what API calls are available to me to get more information about that object. To find out what connections are available for a given object, pass `metadata=1` to the given URI.

So, sending `https://graph.facebook.com/dummiesbook?metadata=1` returns an additional object of connections that can now tell me what additional information I can pull about `dummiesbook`. I don't even have to know what the object is to know what types of data I can find out about it. The following code gives a great example of what this additional data looks like:

```
"connections": {
    "feed": "http://graph.facebook.com/dummiesbook/feed",
    "posts": "http://graph.facebook.com/dummiesbook/posts",
    "tagged": "http://graph.facebook.com/dummiesbook/tagged",
    "statuses": "http://graph.facebook.com/dummiesbook/statuses",
    "links": "http://graph.facebook.com/dummiesbook/links",
    "notes": "http://graph.facebook.com/dummiesbook/notes",
    "photos": "http://graph.facebook.com/dummiesbook/photos",
    "albums": "http://graph.facebook.com/dummiesbook/albums",
    "events": "http://graph.facebook.com/dummiesbook/events",
    "videos": "http://graph.facebook.com/dummiesbook/videos"
}
```

Now I know every possible piece of related information that I can pull about an object. Add in an `oauth_token` parameter (I cover this slightly in the next section, "Privacy," and in more detail in Chapter 9), and you get even more information. That's where privacy comes in.

Privacy

Graph API is respectful of users' privacy. By default, only data allowed as public (Everyone) in the user's privacy settings is permitted for access by Graph API. Facebook makes it clear that privacy is a top priority.

So how do you access private information? The answer is simple — the user has to give you permission. With a user's explicit permission, your application can access all the data (with a few exceptions) about any user on Facebook. You do this through OAuth, which I explain later in the chapter and in thorough detail in Chapter 9.

Basically speaking, though, you need an OAuth token, and after you have it, you pass the `oauth_token` parameter to your GET, POST, and DELETE requests.

Although a user must grant permission before you can access his private data, there are times that Facebook just wants to know what your application is before you can access the data. Sometimes Facebook doesn't need the users to authorize your permission (often because they already have in their privacy settings), but because the information is more sensitive, Facebook just wants to be able to control which applications do and don't have access to this data. Because of this, you need a special token called an "Application Access Token" to make these types of requests. To get your application's OAuth token, go to any UNIX shell prompt (or download and install Curl for Windows) and type the following:

```
curl -F grant_type=client_credentials \
     -F client_id=your_app_id \
     -F client_secret=your_app_secret \
     https://graph.facebook.com/oauth/access_token
```

Replace *your_app_id* with the application ID for your Web site's application (which I set up next), and add the secret key from the same location to replace *your_app_secret*. This call returns an OAuth token that you can now use in your calls to Graph API.

Now when I make a call to `https://graph.facebook.com/JesseStay?oauth_token=INSERT_OAUTH_TOKEN_HERE` (notice the `oauth_token` attribute — be sure to replace its value with your own that you got above), a few extra fields appear. That's because I've authorized this OAuth token earlier to provide a little more information, even if I'm not logged in. Notice in the following response from Facebook that for my user object (`/JesseStay`), the additional fields for e-mail and Web site are included. This is because I, the user, authorized Facebook in my privacy settings to reveal that information to the public (yes, I openly share my e-mail address — this won't be normal for most users unless they explicitly grant your application permissions), and you identified your application to be able to make the calls and access that additional data:

```
{
    "id": "683545112",
    "name": "Jesse Stay",
    "first_name": "Jesse",
    "last_name": "Stay",
    "link": "http://www.facebook.com/JesseStay",
    "location": {
        "id": "109377132415537",
        "name": "Taylorsville, Utah"
    },
    "gender": "male",
    "email": "apps+8665218278.683545112.9b7f749430bc561961e1102e0aabcc44@
               proxymail.facebook.com",
    "website": "http://staynalive.com\r\nhttp://socialtoo.com\r\nhttp://facebook.
               com/stay",
    "locale": "en_US"
}
```

How do you deauthorize an application to which you have previously allowed access to your data? You have to go into your privacy settings (click on "Account" in the upper-right, then "Privacy Settings"), and under "Edit Settings" under Applications and Websites (toward the bottom), you can individually remove applications that you have previously authorized. On this page, locate the offending application, and click the "X" button (or equivalent "remove" or "deauthorize" function). Keep in mind that if you authorize them again, you have to repeat this process!

Setting Up Your Web Site to Use Graph API

Now that you have a sense of the basics about how Graph API works, it's time to set up your Web site to start making calls to Graph API.

First, just like I do with the application setup in Chapter 2, you need to set up your Web site so that Facebook knows who you are, and it can authorize your requests. Web sites get set up just like applications, and in fact, sites can be a great extension to an existing application, as you soon see. Facebook needs you to register, though, to keep out fraudulent use of its API.

Setting up your Web site on Facebook

To set up your Web site, go to your Inspirations application that you set up in Chapter 2. Here are the additional steps you need to take to get your Web site up and running:

1. **Go to** `facebook.com/developers`.

   Next to your Inspirations application, click the More link and select Edit Settings from the drop-down box that appears. (See Figure 7-2.)

2. **Click the Web Site tab from the choices on the left.**

   You're taken to a page that looks like the one shown in Figure 7-3. Here you can enter information pertaining to your Web site, which gives requests from your Web site's URL permission to access the Facebook API.

3. **Enter your site's URL.**

   In the Site URL field, enter the main URL for your site (prefixed by `http://`). This will be used to point users back to your site on various parts of Facebook.

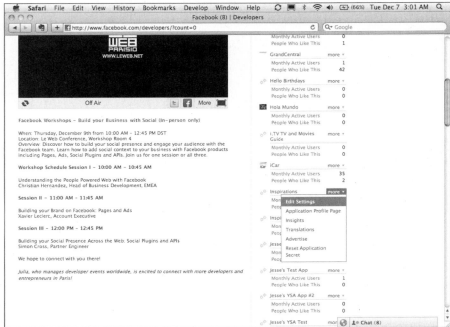

Figure 7-2:
Click Edit Settings under the More link next to your application.

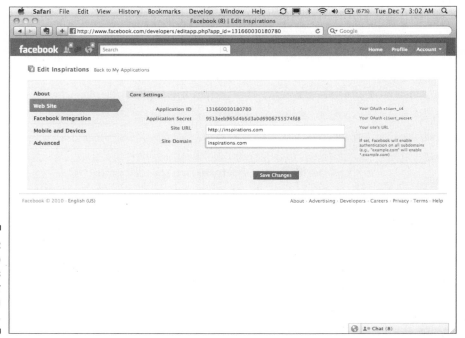

Figure 7-3:
The Web Site settings page in your application setup.

4. Enter your site's domain.

This is the base domain for your site. All subdomains for this domain will be approved for access to Facebook (meaning that `dummiesbook. com` will allow `this.dummiesbook.com` and `that.dummiesbook.com` to access Facebook).

5. Click the Advanced tab (see Figure 7-4), and make sure that all appropriate options are checked.

At the time of this writing, Facebook was in the process of transitioning its API from an older, REST API to the new Graph API. Therefore, it gradually allowed developers to turn on the features of Graph API as they needed them.

At the time of this writing, I enabled OAuth 2.0 for Canvas. You need to understand what each option is and whether you need to enable any of them. When in doubt, leave them all disabled, try the examples here, and if something doesn't work, try enabling various options to get the example to work.

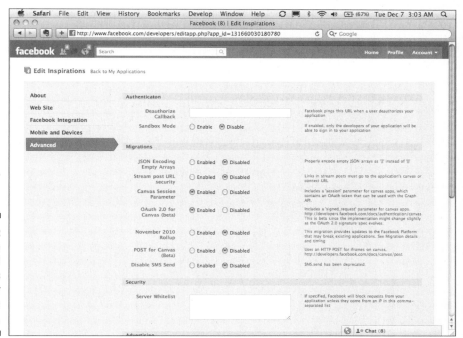

Figure 7-4:
The Advanced settings page in your application setup.

Now that you've set up your Web site on Facebook, you need to add some simple things to your site to get it going. You can do this either in JavaScript or in your language of choice on the server. For the server-side examples, I use PHP in my examples in this book, because of the ease of understanding the language and the global use across the Web.

You really don't need any additional code if you only want to add Facebook social plugins. Review Chapter 6 if you don't want to get your hands any dirtier than you need to. The next section is for people who want to go a little further with what they can do with Facebook development.

Preparing your Web site to use JavaScript

Before you can do anything on your Web site with Facebook, after you set up your Web site in your application settings as described in the preceding section, you need to add some simple `init` calls that tell Facebook who you are, and associate your Web site with the application that you just set up. Here's what you need to do:

1. **On the page where you want to work, open that page's file in your favorite editor.**

   The code I include in Step 2 can be added to every single file (like an `index.html` file), or you can use your language of choice and create a header that gets imported automatically at the top of each page. The latter will be much less effort for you if you already know or feel like learning a little Web scripting to automate this.

2. **Right below the `<body>` tag, add the following code.**

   ```
   <div id="fb-root"></div>
   <script src="http://connect.facebook.net/en_US/all.js"></script>
   <script>
           FB.init({appId: 'yourappidgoeshere', status: true, cookie: true,
               xfbml: true});
   </script>
   ```

   This is all you need to get going! This code identifies your application and initializes the Facebook object in JavaScript so that you can make more calls to Facebook on the page. (Be sure to replace *yourappid-goeshere* with the application ID you took from your application setup in the preceding section!)

In this code, I call a simple `FB.init` method and pass to it a JavaScript object with the `appId`, `status`, `cookie`, and `xfbml` parameters embedded. `appId` is the application ID that you can get by going to the application settings you set previously. `status` just forces it to get a fresh status from Facebook, telling your client whether the user has logged in or not every time you load the page. `cookie` sets a special cookie that contains the user's

Facebook ID when that user is logged in. `xfbml` enables you to use Facebook's special markup language called XFBML right on your own Web site.

When you set `cookie` to true, a cookie gets set, entitled `fbs_app_key` (`app_key` is the application ID number from your application settings). When you read this, it should return information about the logged-in user, including his or her Facebook ID if the user has authenticated with Facebook.

Preparing your server to access Facebook using PHP

Because Graph API works the same regardless of which language you use, you'll find that PHP's setup looks similar to JavaScript's. If you prefer to use PHP over JavaScript, you can download the PHP SDK at `https://github.com/facebook/php-sdk`. Then open up a new php file in the Web directory of your server. You can call the file `index.php`, or whatever you like. Then add your `init` block, similar to the JavaScript example I share earlier. Your `init` block for PHP is shown in the following code:

```php
<?php

require './facebook.php';

$facebook = new Facebook(array(
  'appId'  => 'YOUR APP ID',
  'secret' => 'YOUR API SECRET',
  'cookie' => true, // enable optional cookie support
));
```

After you include this code in your PHP, you can start making API calls with the `$facebook` object returned in your PHP code.

Identifying Your Users

In the olden days (just five years ago in Web terms), Web sites often had a registration form that each user had to fill out before she could get started on that Web site. That user would have to reenter her name, address, and other types of profile information for each Web site visited. This was a painful process, so much that many of the browsers began to store some of this information and autopopulate forms for the user as he or she surfed the Web.

As the Web evolved, sites like Facebook began to provide application programming interfaces (APIs) and other means to allow Web sites to access this data on behalf of the user. Protocols such as OpenID and OAuth came about, and very quickly it became much less necessary for Web sites to require users to reenter their information on every Web site they visited.

OpenID is a way for developers and Web sites to identify their users, without users ever having to store their information on the Web site that they're logging in to. At a raw level, users can enter a Web site, such as `Gmail.com`, and they'll automatically be redirected to Google to authenticate with their Google username and password. Google then redirects them to your site with some basic information about the users.

Although OpenID is about *authenticating* users, *OAuth* is about *authorizing* users. Many sites have moved from a model of just authenticating the user to instead getting permission to access additional information about the user. OAuth makes it possible to retrieve additional information about a user by providing a series of letters and numbers, called an *access token,* that your Web site or application passes back to the site (such as Facebook) to identify and retrieve more information about that user. I cover the latest version of OAuth, OAuth 2.0, in Chapter 9.

At the time of this writing, a new version of OpenID, called OpenID Connect, is being specified, which places OAuth on top of OpenID, providing a federated way of authentication (meaning that it doesn't matter where your data is stored) while providing access data through an access token that gets attached to the response. Facebook is currently in the process of migrating to this model. The new model encrypts the data, providing a secure way to access data about a user, no matter where his or her data is stored.

Identifying users the more modern way

You may be saying to yourself, "But I still have a Web form to register my users!" That's okay, and in fact, you're probably still in the majority of Web sites today. A better way exists to create your Web site registration, though, and that's through a one-click, single sign-on that pulls information about the user from the sites that he or she is most familiar with.

CinchCast.com

Cinch, a former client of mine, did just that. If you go to `CinchCast.com`, you see two buttons: a Facebook Login button and a Twitter Login button. (See Figure 7-5.) To register with Cinch, all you have to do is click one of those buttons, provide your Twitter or Facebook credentials, and, you're in! Cinch is able to obtain your name and all the information it needs to set up an account in its system. In fact, Cinch doesn't even need a separate login because after you authenticate through Facebook, Cinch now knows who you are, so you don't need to provide a separate username or password.

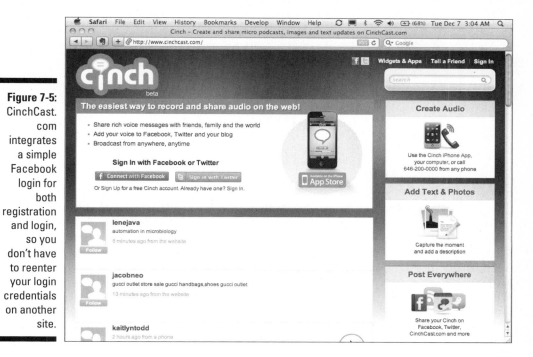

Figure 7-5:
CinchCast.
com
integrates
a simple
Facebook
login for
both
registration
and login,
so you
don't have
to reenter
your login
credentials
on another
site.

Of course, Cinch also provides a means of access for users without Facebook or Twitter accounts, but that is the fallback. In addition, Cinch also integrates with BlogTalkRadio's powerful VoIP system, enabling you to also sign up by just calling a number. The registration form is practically no longer needed — keep your registration as simple as possible, and your users will thank you!

SocialToo.com

SocialToo is my business. I build tools to help you manage the social networks that you or your brand is on. SocialToo's tools currently focus only on Facebook, Twitter, and Myspace. (See Figure 7-6.) Because I know that every one of my users is either a Facebook, Twitter, or Myspace user, I don't need a traditional registration or login form.

Right now when you visit SocialToo.com, you are greeted with three Login buttons. No registration is necessary. Just log in through your favorite network, I supply the tools you can use with that network (and logins to add more tools for additional networks), and you're done! It will be the fastest registration process you've ever participated in. As you can see, registration by using Facebook's authentication is much simpler than doing it "the old way."

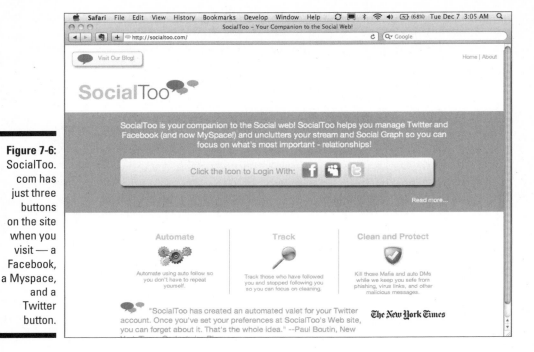

Figure 7-6: SocialToo. com has just three buttons on the site when you visit — a Facebook, a Myspace, and a Twitter button.

Integrating a Facebook Login button on your site

Here are the basics of what you need to integrate a Facebook Login button on your Web site. Facebook makes this really easy. Follow these steps to set up a basic Login button:

1. **Set up a new application through the Developer app.**

   For any new Facebook integration you do, you need to set up a new application. I show you the fields you need to fill in earlier in this chapter.

2. **Identify your application or Web site.**

   This is what you did with the `init` block in the PHP and JavaScript examples earlier in this chapter. You can do this with some simple JavaScript on the page or by sending the user to a separate page (or pop-up window) where you send your application's application ID in the URL parameters of the request. Going the JavaScript route takes care of everything for you. Doing the redirect involves a little more effort, but it will return an access token that you can use to both identify your application and access information on behalf of the user in the future.

3. **Place the Login button on your Web site.**

This can either be a social plugin, the code for which you can copy and paste from `developers.facebook.com/plugins`, or you can use your own image and either do an on-click event handler to have JavaScript do the login process or link to an authentication page for that user. Again, I show you how to do this at the end of the chapter, and I go into even further detail in Chapter 9, where I discuss the intricacies of OAuth.

4. **Identify the user and adapt the page to his or her new, logged-in status.**

After users have authenticated, they'll either be redirected to a page that you identify or a JavaScript callback on your page will be notified, and you can do things in JavaScript to change the content of the page and/or redirect the user to a state that you've set for users who are logged in to your Web site. From here, you can access information about the user and customize the entire experience for him or her!

Now you'll write some code. Here's what you need to add to the page that you set up in JavaScript earlier in the chapter (in the section "Preparing your Web site to use JavaScript") with the `init` block. Make sure that the `init` block code from the JavaScript section is in place somewhere at the beginning of the page, and then follow these steps:

1. **Add the following code anywhere on the page.**

```
<fb:login-button></fb:login-button>
```

This needs to go anywhere on the page where you want to add a Facebook Login button:

Want your Facebook button to automatically change to a Logout button after the user has logged in? You can use the `autologoutlink` attribute (set to `true`) to dynamically change the Facebook Login button. You can also always provide your own custom button to do the login/ logout process.

2. **Add the code in Step 1 to establish a callback that gets run after the user logs in or logs out.**

Now you need to do something when the user logs in. The code in this block runs when the user logs in or logs out. This can be a place to refresh the page so that server-side code can detect the user and present a logged-in view, or you can use it to just dynamically welcome the new user:

```
FB.Event.subscribe('auth.sessionChange', function(response) {
    if (response.session) {
        // A user has logged in, and a new cookie has been saved
    } else {
        // The user has logged out, and the cookie has been cleared
    }
});
```

At this point, you can now start building social experiences for your users. I talk about that next.

Turning Your Web Site into a Social Experience

You've identified your user, but that's just one piece of the puzzle. After all, how can a social network be "social" if it's all about just the individual? You can't be social unless you bring a person's friends into the picture, and the Facebook API makes that really easy.

With Facebook API, you not only can bring your user's information to your Web site, but you can also bring all that user's friends and those friends' information as well. This enables you, with just one click, to automatically have a social experience right out of the box on your own Web site.

Here's a sample "social experience," assuming that you have a blog, and how it could work on your Web site:

1. The user logs in to your blog (if the user is already logged in, it moves to Step 2).

2. Now, whenever the user visits your blog, rather than seeing a chronological view, immediately the user sees what her friends are reading, and it gets sorted by the most-read and -shared articles on the site, providing a much more interesting experience for the user. HuffingtonPost.com, for example, creates a social experience for users on social networks by presenting all their articles in a view sorted by what their readers' friends are reading. (See Figure 7-7.)

3. For each article that the user reads, he or she can see similar articles that his or her friends have read.

4. Users can share each article to Facebook with their friends. Friends can comment on the article on Facebook or on the article itself, building a two-way dialogue among users on the blog.

Figure 7-7:
Huffington
Post.com
creates
a social
experience
for its users.

Now that you understand the concept, hopefully you've done some planning around how your Web site might work within a social experience. Graph API has a few basic calls that you can make to retrieve a user's friends and match them with content on your own Web site. I use JavaScript in this case to show you how, but always know that you can do this in your server-side language of choice (like PHP). Follow these steps to identify the user and organize your content based on the interests of their friends:

1. **Detect the user's login status.**

   You can initiate this through the callback that you set up earlier, but what if that user is already logged in (meaning that the *action* of logging in hasn't been initiated)? You need to look for that cookie I talk about earlier and render content accordingly. Add the following code to detect the user's login status:

   ```
   FB.getLoginStatus(function(response) {
       if (response.session) {
           alert("user is logged in!");
       } else {
           alert("user is not logged in!");
       }
   });
   ```

If you decide to do this in PHP rather than JavaScript, on the server side, detecting the login status is almost as easy, if not simpler, than in JavaScript. To detect the status of a user in PHP, call something similar to the following code:

```
if ($facebook->getSession()) {
  echo '<a href="' . $facebook->getLogoutUrl() . '">Logout</a>';
} else {
  echo '<a href="' . $facebook->getLoginUrl() . '">Login</a>';
}
```

This code looks for that cookie that Facebook sets, and if the cookie is detected, it automatically returns true. If not, the user is not logged in, so it returns false.

2. **Get the user's list of friends from Facebook.**

To get the list of a user's friends, make a simple Graph API call. The path to get a user's list of friends is /*objectname*/friends, where *object name* is the username or ID of the user. In JavaScript, this is made using the FB.api() method call somewhere below your init block. The following code shows what this would look like:

```
FB.api('/JesseStay/friends', function(response) {
  console.debug(response);
});
```

console.debug is a method that outputs the full object of the response to your browser's error log. You can use the developer mode in Chrome or Safari, or an extension like Firebug in Firefox to access this value.

The following code shows how it is done in PHP — just dump $friends to see the contents and know how to parse the data:

```
try {
  $friends = $facebook->api('/JesseStay/friends');
} catch (FacebookApiException $e) {
  error_log($e);
}
```

3. **Organize your content by what the user's friends have done with that content.**

Now that you know who the user's friends are, you can do cool things with that information and the data you host on your Web site. For instance, perhaps you sell CDs and you want to show all the CDs that the visiting user's friends have shared. In JavaScript, you can make a series of JavaScript Ajax calls, or on the server side, you can access the data directly. To get and organize your data "socially," follow these steps:

   a. *Make a query to your content.* This could be either a JavaScript Ajax call or a simple query to your database.

b. *Determine what other things friends of the user have done with that content.* Hopefully in your database you are tracking when users share things to Facebook, like things, or interact with your content. When they do, store that in the database. Now, take that list of friends and match it to each piece of the content that you just retrieved to sort it by how many friends have interacted with that piece of content the most.

c. *Present that content to the user in a social way.* Now that you've sorted the content socially, you can present the content back to the user, sorted by the most interactions with his friends. You could also list thumbnails of those friends who are interacting with the content so that they see the pictures of the friends and that their friends are interacting with your Web site.

If you don't have time to track interactions that your users are having with your content, you have another excellent way to retrieve content that your users are interacting with. Instead of querying your database, you can make a query to Facebook using its Facebook Query Language (FQL). (See the next sidebar, "What is FQL?"). The following code shows how you could retrieve the items that your users are sharing within a list of friends of a particular user. Also, note that certain social plugins can provide this data as well.

```
var query = FB.Data.query('SELECT post_id FROM stream WHERE app_id = {0} AND
          actor_id IN  (SELECT uid2 FROM friend WHERE uid1 = {1}'), app_id,
          user_id);
query.wait(function(posts) {
  console.debug(posts);
});
```

In the example, insert your application ID from your app settings, and the user ID of the user you're trying to access data about.

What is FQL?

FQL stands for Facebook Query Language, which is a simple, standardized way for developers to access data from Facebook's API that may not always be available via simple Graph API methods. It uses simple SQL-like syntax to access various "tables" that Facebook makes available for you to get the data you need. Get really familiar with this, see what tables are available, and see what data is available within those tables — you might find some secrets that give you that added edge your competitors haven't figured out yet by embracing FQL! I cover FQL in thorough detail in Chapter 10. In the meantime, look over the documentation at `http://developers.facebook.com/docs/reference/fql` to start getting familiar with this powerful way to access Facebook data.

To see how this all works in a real-life scenario, check out how `RottenTomatoes.com` does it.

`RottenTomatoes.com`, a Web site devoted to news and reviews about film, gives each user a social experience right out of the box. (See Figure 7-8.) RottenTomatoes uses a feature Facebook provides to select partners called Instant Personalization, but you can still assume that the same experience would occur if the user had to log in through Facebook.

Instant Personalization is a way for sites to automatically provide a social experience without forcing the user to first log in. It is something select partners can get for their sites if they have an ad account. Basically, if you spend enough in advertising dollars and if your concept is something that users won't be offended by for automatically having a social experience built in (without needing to log in), your site might be eligible for Instant Personalization. If you meet these criteria (most sites don't), consider Instant Personalization for your site.

Here's how `RottenTomatoes.com` works:

- ✔ Users can see the top-ranked movies that their friends on Facebook rated.
- ✔ Users can see the top movies that their friends liked on Facebook.
- ✔ RottenTomatoes provides a list of movie suggestions based on movies the user liked on `Facebook.com`.
- ✔ The site welcomes and greets the user by name as he or she visits.
- ✔ Like buttons proliferate the site and allow users to Like movies right on `RottenTomatoes.com`.

Immediately users are greeted with a very social experience, sorted by a list of their friends, rather than a traditional, chronological, or categorized view of topics that is much less personal. (See Figure 7-8.) With Graph API and Facebook, you can provide an interesting, relevant, exciting experience for your users that actually involves their real-life friends, rather than trying to guess like the Web has had to do for more than a decade now.

Automating the friendship process with Graph API

With Graph API, you no longer need to re-create a "friends list" and identify who a user's friends are. In fact, the whole concept of a social network is almost ubiquitous with Graph API, because you can now just import users' friends from the social networks like Facebook.

The list goes on and on with ways that you can build a two-way relationship between your content and your users and their friends. Just like the registration and login, you no longer have to re-create the friend-building experience for your users either.

Automating the friendship process is quite simple. It works like this:

1. A user identifies himself on your network and associates a Facebook profile with that identity. This can occur through the Facebook login I mention earlier. After the user does this, you now know his friends.

2. You do a search for other users in that user's friend list that are in your system. This is actually a very simple FQL query (which I discuss later in this chapter) that keeps you from having to do anything in your own database.

3. You present the list of the user's friends who are in your system to your user, asking if he or she would like to friend those individuals on your own system. This list you provide will probably look very familiar to the individual, who will very likely want to add many if not all of them.

4. You prompt the user, asking if he wants you to automatically add future users in his friend list as they log in to your site. This piece is powerful. Now you have an ongoing contract with that user, where, as he gains more friends on Facebook, those friends also get added to your Web site as friends of that user. Or, maybe some of the user's friends are not friends on your Web site. As soon as those friends log in to your Web site, they will automatically be added as friends to that user on your own Web site. Now they can worry about adding friends on Facebook, while your Web site can focus on providing the unique value to your brand. Every Web site can become its own social network this way.

   Keep in mind, to do this, you need to create some automated scripts that run regularly on your servers, checking for new friends of that user who may have recently logged in to your Web site for the first time. Thanks to Graph API, this is not a difficult task, though, and if you have just a little scripting knowledge, you'll have a script written in no time! In fact, in Chapter 11, you find out how to get the user's new friends in real time, simplifying the need for any automated scripts even further.

5. You invite the user to invite his friends on Facebook who are not on your Web site. Because you know which of his friends on Facebook are not yet members of your site, this is a great opportunity to encourage him to invite those friends to log in through Facebook. You can easily do this with a simple request form that allows him to invite those friends.

Now that you've automated the friending process for your users, you can sit back and watch interactions happen automatically. As your users gain new friends on your site from the friends they build on Facebook, be sure to notify them when that happens. They'll see that lots of their friends are also using your site, and they'll be encouraged to keep coming back and using your site as well.

To perform friendship automation on your own, you first need to understand two things. The first is how to get the list of your user's friends on Facebook who are members of your site. The second is how to present a form of the user's friends who are not members to the user so that he can invite them to your site and become friends there as well.

Getting a list of a user's friends who are already members of your site

You can do this through a simple FQL query. In this query, you make a call to the user and friend tables, looking for the field in the user table called `is_app_user`. The resulting call and query (in JavaScript) look something like this:

```
var query = FB.Data.query('SELECT uid FROM user WHERE uid IN  (SELECT uid2 FROM
          friend WHERE uid1 = {0}) AND is_app_user = 1', user_id);
query.wait(function(friends) {
  console.debug(friends);
});
```

This code performs a search for all the friends of the current user (that you'll need to pass to the `user_id` variable) and returns the `uid` of those friends who have `is_app_user` set to 1 for your app. The resulting data set is a list of all friends of the given user who are already users of your app!

Keep in mind that you can also do this by making a `/me/friends` call in Graph API and then searching through your database to find out who is already in there. Some developers have found the latter method to be faster, but I leave that for you to discover. At least you know two simple methods for accessing a user's friends who are already in your system!

Creating a form that the user can use to invite his or her nonmember friends to become members

After you know who in a list of the user's friends are members of your site, take the remaining friends and encourage that user to invite them. Facebook provides simple controls for you to do that.

To create this form, you need to take that list you made and put it in the `exclude_ids` parameter of the XFBML `fb:multi-friend-selector` tag. Now, just create the form as shown in the following code, stick it somewhere on your Web site, and you're done!

```
<fb:request-form
   action="<? // url to redirect the user after submitting form ?>"
   method="post"
   type="<? // name of your app - appears as "so and so sent you a 'type'
           request" ?>"
   content="<? // content of the request to be sent - 'so and so is using z.com
           and would like you to try it!' ?>">

   <fb:multi-friend-selector
           actiontext="Here are your friends who haven't joined z.com yet.
           Invite them now so you can interact with them!"
   exclude_ids="<? echo $friends; ?>" ></fb:multi-friend-selector>
</fb:request-form>
```

Keep in mind that the above XFBML will go away soon in favor of the request dialog API I share in Chapter 4. Refer to that chapter for even better ways to do this.

Digg.com, a social news Web site, is a great example of friendship automation using Facebook. The site allows users to log in through a simple Facebook dialog box, and immediately does a search on that user's friends to determine which ones are using Digg. After it determines this, Digg suggests that the user's friends become friends on Digg.com as well. (See Figure 7-9.)

After becoming friends on Digg.com, Digg also allows Facebook users to automatically add other Facebook friends as friends on Digg as they too log in to Digg.com through the Facebook login. (See Figure 7-10.) Digg then sends e-mail notifications to users as their friends on Facebook join the site. As a user, this feels like lots of my friends are constantly joining the site, and I feel like Digg.com is a site that I should pay attention to and use alongside my Facebook friends.

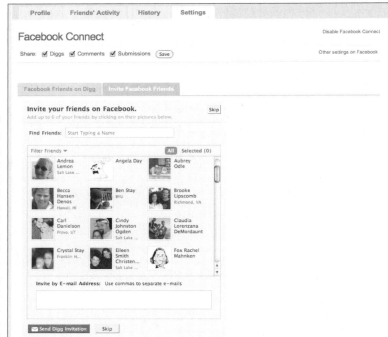

Figure 7-9:
Digg automates the friending experience by presenting a list of friends to invite after you log in through Facebook for the first time.

Figure 7-10:
Figure 7-10:
As users'
friends join
the site in
the future,
Digg allows
you to auto-
matically
add them
as friends
on Digg
as well,
continually
increasing
your social
graph in
Digg.com as
your friends
join.

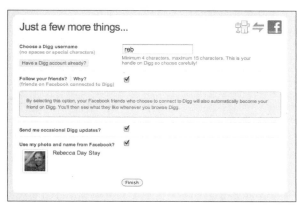

Tips for building social experiences with Facebook

There are some basic guidelines that you should consider when building social experiences for your Web site using Facebook. Keep these in mind as you plan your Web site's Facebook integration:

✔ **Don't reinvent the registration process.** Use a Facebook Login button and Graph API to determine a user's information rather than making users reenter it into a registration form.

✔ **Don't reinvent the login process.** Use Facebook to identify whether a user is real, and then match that Facebook ID with an ID in your system and create the session for the user. If the user is already a Facebook user, there is no reason to make him or her enter a username and password that are specific to your site.

✔ **Don't reinvent the friending process.** After being authenticated, you can get a user's list of friends from Facebook and create friends out of that from the existing users on your Web site who are in that user's list of friends.

✔ **Think in social experiences with your content.** Rather than organize your content in a hierarchal, categorized, or chronological structure, search for the content on your system that each user's friends are doing things with. Then present it sorted by the content that a user's friends are interacting with most. A user should see his or her friends in a much more prominent position than your content!

✔ **Use every opportunity to invite new friends of your users to your Web site.** You know which of a user's friends on Facebook are not using your Web site. Now invite them every chance you get! The more you can get a user's friends using your Web site, the longer that user will stay on your Web site and the more he or she will come back.

✔ **Use social plugins to simplify the process.** You can already use many social plugins to create social experiences on your Web site. Find one or two that suit your experience and use those where applicable. Then, where you need a more customized experience, write your own code to customize it further for the user. You can also hire a third-party programmer to step in where things get too difficult.

Putting It All Together — Integrating Facebook into Your Web Site in Five Minutes

Now it's time to put everything I discuss into action. Pretend that you have a Web site that is a CD store and you want to give your customers an easy way to find the CDs their friends are liking and sharing on Facebook. I add a simple Recommended CDs section to the bottom of that page. Here's the minute-by-minute account of what you need to do to set that up.

Minute 1: Create the login and registration

I start by adding the `init` script and Login button that you created earlier. Start by creating an application for your Web site, or adding your Web site URL and domain to an existing application. Then follow these steps:

1. **Add the `init` script somewhere right below the opening `<body>` script.**

```
<div id="fb-root"></div>
<script>
  window.fbAsyncInit = function() {
    FB.init({
      appId  : 'YOUR APP ID',
      status : true, // check login status
      cookie : true, // enable cookies to allow the server to access the
            session
      xfbml  : true  // parse XFBML
    });
  };

  (function() {
    var e = document.createElement('script');
    e.src = document.location.protocol + '//connect.facebook.net/en_US/all.
        js';
    e.async = true;
    document.getElementById('fb-root').appendChild(e);
  }());
</script>
```

2. **Add your Login button anywhere on the page.**

```
<fb:login-button autologoutlink="true"></fb:login-button>
```

3. **Establish a callback that runs when the user has logged in.**

```
FB.Event.subscribe('auth.sessionChange', function(response) {
    if (response.session) {
      // A user has logged in, and a new cookie has been saved
    } else {
      // The user has logged out, and the cookie has been cleared
    }
  });
```

Minutes 2 and 3: Detect the user's friends on Facebook and add them as friends on your site

Now that you can tell when a user is logged in, it's time to get that user's friends. I get the list (remember — you just want the friends who are already members of your site), submit the list to an internal friends table in your database, and then add the friends to a simple box on the site with their profile pictures. Follow these steps:

1. **Get the list of the user's friends who are members of your site.**

   You did this earlier, so I just plug that code into the callback:

   ```
   FB.Event.subscribe('auth.sessionChange', function(response) {
       if (response.session) {
       var query = FB.Data.query('SELECT uid FROM user WHERE  uid IN (SELECT
           uid2 FROM friend WHERE uid1 = {0}) AND is_app_user = 1', user_
           id);
       query.wait(function(friends) {
        console.debug(friends);
       });
       } else {
          // The user has logged out, and the cookie has been cleared
       }
   });
   ```

2. **Submit that user's friends to your database as friends there, and create a box with the friends' profile pictures in the HTML of your site.**

   Put this in place of the `console.debug` line in Step 1:

   ```
   for (i=0; i++; i<friends.length) {
       // add the friend to your database as a friend
       // (assumes we can get the user id of current user through the session)
       $.post('/add_friend',{'id': friends[i].uid});
       $("#friends").append("<img src='http://graph.facebook.com/"+friends[i].
           uid+"/picture' width='50' height='50' />");
   }
   ```

   `/add_friend` is a script that you would have written on your server somewhere, which creates the friendship on your Web site. I leave it up to you to create this piece of code — I share it to show you how it can be done.

   Then, in your HTML, include a piece of code like this, which provides a `<div>` block that you can use to dynamically insert the friends' profile images with the code (via the line that starts with `$("#friends")`):

   ```
   <div id="friends"></div>
   ```

Minutes 4 and 5: Sort the list of CDs by what the user's friend is sharing and liking on Facebook

Now it's time to build a social experience around all the data you've collected so far. Assume that you have a `cds` div, and then add each recommended CD with it's own `cd` class assigned to it. I now replace those instead with a list of CDs that their friends have recently purchased.

I'll start with a simple JavaScript Ajax call to your server. I assume that you
have a script on the server somewhere that performs the query and returns
the CD records for CDs purchased by individuals in the list you provide it.
The query is done on the server by Facebook IDs of each user in your system.
The following code shows how that might look:

```
$.post(
   '/get_cds',
   {
     'facebook_ids': friends
   },
   function(cds) {
     for (i=0; i++; i<cds.length) {
       $("#cds").append("<div class='cd'>"+cds[i].name+"</div>");
     }
   }
);
```

The HTML for this example looks like this:

```
CDs your friends also like: <div id="cds"></div>
```

Putting It All Together

If I take all the examples that I wrote previously and put them in one `index.
html` file, it looks this:

```
<html>
<head>
 <script src="/js/jquery-1.3.2.min.js" type="text/javascript"></script>
</head>
<body>
  <div id="fb-root"></div>
  <script>
  window.fbAsyncInit = function() {
    FB.init({
      appId  : 'YOUR APP ID',
      status : true, // check login status
      cookie : true, // enable cookies to allow the server to access the session
      xfbml  : true  // parse XFBML
    });
  };

  (function() {
    var e = document.createElement('script');
    e.src = document.location.protocol + '//connect.facebook.net/en_US/all.js';
    e.async = true;
    document.getElementById('fb-root').appendChild(e);
```

```
}());

FB.Event.subscribe('auth.sessionChange', function(response) {
  if (response.session) {
      var query = FB.Data.query('SELECT uid FROM user WHERE    uid IN
          (SELECT uid2 FROM friend WHERE uid1 = {0}) AND is_app_user = 1',
          user_id);
  query.wait(function(friends) {
  for (i=0; i++; i<friends.length) {
    // add the friend to your database as a friend
    // (assumes we can get the user id of current user through the session)
    $.post('/add_friend',{'id': friends[i].uid});
    $("#friends").append("<img src='http://graph.facebook.com/"+friends[i].
          uid+"/picture' width='50' height='50' />");
  }

    $.post(
      '/get_cds',
      {
        'facebook_ids': friends
      },
      function(cds) {
        for (i=0; i++; i<cds.length) {
          $("#cds").append("<div class='cd'>"+cds[i].name+"</div>");
        }
      }
            );
  });
  } else {
    // The user has logged out, and the cookie has been cleared
  }
});
</script>
<fb:login-button autologoutlink="true"></fb:login-button>
<div id="friends"></div>
CDs your friends also like: <div id="cds"></div>
</body>
</html>
```

That's it! You should now be hacking Graph API like the pros!

Chapter 8

Knowing What Information You Have Access To

*W*ith an accessible API and such a broad set of information you can get about each user, it's good to know exactly what information that you, as a developer, have access to. This is a source of frustration for many; notice that many of the calls to Graph API that you make in Chapter 7 give some sort of message about an "access token." Although Facebook makes this information available to developers, ultimately users decide what elements of information they allow developers access to. Facebook is strict on ensuring its users' privacy, and this bleeds from every piece of the UI on Facebook.com all the way into the applications and Web sites to which users access and provide information through Facebook.

In this chapter, I show you how to prompt the user to get the information you need as a developer. I discuss what you have access to without any permissions (other than an authenticated user), and how to get access to more detailed information when the user gives you the permission you need. In addition, I show you a few ways you can know what users are visiting your site (hint: without authorization this isn't always possible).

Getting the Defaults with Publicly Accessible Information

Every Web site or application has access to a default set of information about every user. If you visit any profile on Facebook (see Figure 8-1), you'll notice that the information there is pretty much the same information that you can find in the user interface for Facebook as well. This information is what Facebook, regardless of the privacy preference, always reveals about each user.

The default pieces of public information about each user, according to Facebook, are called "Publicly Accessible Information" (PAI). This is the information that, as a developer, you see about each user.

Here is what everyone has access to by default:

- Name
- Profile picture URL
- Gender
- Any networks the user belongs to
- User ID
- Locale
- Friends, and the same information for your friends
- Any information that the user sets to "Everyone" access in his or her privacy settings

The best way to know what you have access to without any login by the user is to just make a query to `https://graph.facebook.com/`*username* (go to `https://graph.facebook.com/jessestay` for mine) with no `oauth_token` parameter added. Here is what Mark Zuckerberg's Graph API data looks like:

```
{
  "id": "4",
  "name": "Mark Zuckerberg",
  "first_name": "Mark",
  "last_name": "Zuckerberg",
  "link": "http://www.facebook.com/zuck",
  "gender": "male",
  "locale": "en_US"
}
```

Figure 8-1:
A default
profile as
visible to
other users
who haven't
logged in to
Facebook
and are not
friends with
the user.

Getting More Detailed with Permissions

Aside from Publicly Accessible Information, the Facebook users who visit your Web site have complete control over the information they give your Web site access to. To get a user's birthday or e-mail address, for example, you must explicitly prompt him for permission to access his birthday or e-mail address before you can access it.

You can prompt the user for this permission in several ways. Here's the simplest way to prompt the user for permission:

1. **Set up your** `init` **block.** If you've already added the `init` JavaScript (see Chapter 7), you're halfway there. If not, do it.

2. **Add the** `perms` **key/value pair as an object at the end of your** `FB.login` **call.** The `FB.login` call will both log in the user if she isn't already logged in and prompt her for the appropriate permissions if she is. To assign

what permissions to get, just add a {perms} block (like the following) to the end of the call:

```
FB.login(function(response) {
  if (response.session) {
    if (response.perms) {
      // user is logged in and granted some permissions.
      // perms is a comma separated list of granted permissions
    } else {
      // user is logged in, but did not grant any permissions
    }
  } else {
    // user is not logged in
  }
}, {perms:'email,user_birthday'});
```

Adding the {perms} block to the end prompts the user for access to his birthday and e-mail address. After you add this code, when the user logs in through Facebook on your site, he is prompted with a message that looks like the one shown in Figure 8-2.

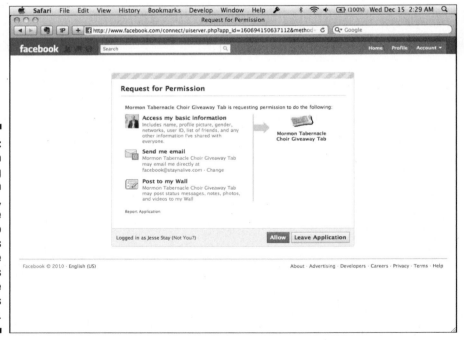

Figure 8-2: When users log in through your site, they'll be prompted to give access to these permissions to your site with this prompt.

Requesting access via OAuth

Authenticating the user in JavaScript is the simple way to authenticate. However, using OAuth to authenticate the user with Facebook is also not that difficult if you know what you're doing. To request extended permissions for a user in OAuth, just pass the scope parameter to your OAuth URL when you redirect the user and pass to it a comma-separated list of permissions that you would like to request. So the basic flow would happen like this:

1. Check to see whether the user is logged in and has the appropriate permissions (you have numerous ways to do this — see Chapter 7 f or a few examples).

2. If the user is not logged in, or does not have proper permissions, redirect him to the appropriate authorize URL, passing in the permissions that you would like to extend. The following code segment shows one example of the URL that you would redirect him to (also note that you could do this in a pop-up window as well). Notice the scope parameter and permissions passed to the end of the URL:

   ```
   https://graph.facebook.com/oauth/authorize?
       client_id=...&
       redirect_uri=http://socialtoo.com/login/callback&
       scope=email,user_birthday
   ```

3. When the user has logged in, he will be prompted to grant the permissions you requested. This will look just like the prompt shown in Figure 8-3.

4. Facebook then redirects to the redirect_uri that you specified in your authorize URL, and you can then do things with the newly granted permissions!

Knowing how to make requests in OAuth pretty much solves any problem that you run into. Even if the JavaScript doesn't work for you, you can always resort to the OAuth method and get what you need.

Facebook actually uses its own OAuth process on the back end for its JavaScript libraries. So know that OAuth is always the answer when you get into a bind.

I go into much more detail on OAuth in Chapter 9, so if you want to really know what OAuth is, feel free to skip ahead to that chapter.

Knowing what permissions you can request

What data can you request? Facebook provides a slew of data that you can get access to. This list will probably change by the time you read this book, so consult the Developer documentation (search for "permissions") to be sure. Here are the permissions, according to Facebook's own documentation, that were available at the time of this writing:

- **Publishing permissions:** Whether it's creating an event or posting a message to your friends through your news feed, these are all publishing events. In order to do these types of things on behalf of the user, you will need to get one or all of these permissions from the user:

  - **publish_stream:** Gives access to your application to publish status updates on behalf of the user. These can be links, videos, photos, plain status updates, and more. You don't need offline access to send these on a user's behalf when you have this permission, although Facebook does ask that you prompt the user before posting anything on his or her behalf.

  - **create_event:** Gives access to create events on behalf of the user.

  - **rsvp_event:** Gives access to RSVP to events on behalf of the user.

  - **offline_access:** Gives access to make calls when the user is not logged into your Web site or application. Normally, access tokens you get from Facebook have a very short time limit. This gives your access token a very long expiration time (Facebook does not say this is infinite, though).

  - **publish_checkins:** Your Web site can check in on behalf of the user with this permission.

- **Data permissions:** For almost all these permissions, you are required to request the same permission for the user's friends if you want to access the same data for that user's friends. There are some types of data that you simply cannot request about a user's friends — I specify where that is the case. I add in parentheses the connection or property that you use to access the information you are requesting permission for.

  - **user_about_me, friends_about_me (about):** Gives access to the user's or her friends' "About Me" section.

  - **user_activities, friends_activities (activities):** Gives access to the user's or her friends' activities section.

- **user_birthday, friends_birthday (birthday_date):** Gives access to the user's or her friends' birthday.

- **user_education_history, friends_education_history (education):** Gives access to the user's or her friends' education section on the profile.

- **user_events, friends_events (events):** Gives access to the user's or her friends' list of events that they are attending.

- **user_groups, friends_groups (groups):** Gives access to the list of a user's or her friends' groups that they are a part of.

- **user_hometown, friends_hometown (hometown):** Gives access to the list of a user's or her friends' hometown information.

- **user_interests, friends_interests (interests):** Gives access to the user's or her friends' list of interests.

- **user_likes, friends_likes (likes):** Gives access to the user's or her friends' list of Pages that they have liked.

- **user_location, friends_location (location):** Gives access to the user's or her friends' location information.

- **user_notes, friends_notes (notes):** Gives access to the user's or her friends' list of notes.

- **user_online_presence, friends_online_presence:** Gives access to the user's or her friends' online/offline status on Facebook (useful for chat).

- **user_photo_video_tags, friends_photo_video_tags:** Gives access to the user's or her friends' list of photos and videos they have been tagged in.

- **user_photos, friends_photos (photos):** Gives access to the user's or her friends' list of photos they have uploaded.

- **user_relationships, friends_relationships:** Gives access to the user's or her friends' list of family and personal relationships (lists), as well as their relationship status (married/single/it's complicated).

- **user_relationship_details, friends_relationship_details:** Gives access to the user's or her friends' relationship preferences (likes boys, likes girls, and so on).

- **user_religion_politics, friends_religion_politics:** Gives access to the user's or her friends' religion and political information.

- **user_status, friends_status:** Gives access to the user's or her friends' current status update.

- **user_videos, friends_videos:** Gives access to the user's or her friends' list of videos that they have uploaded.

- **user_Web site, friends_Web site:** Gives access to the user's or her friends' Web site URL.

- **user_work_history, friends_work_history (work):** Gives access to the user's or her friends' list of work history.

- **e-mail (e-mail):** Provides access to the user's (not her friends) e-mail address. Keep in mind even though you have this you are required to still abide by Facebook's rules on the matter, as well as the CAN-SPAM act.

- **read_friendlists, manage_friendlists:** Provides access to the user's or her friends' friend lists.

- **read_insights:** Provides access to the user's (only) insight analytical data about the domains and Pages that user owns. This is read-only.

- **read_mailbox:** Provides access to the user's (only) mailbox — this is read-only.

- **read_requests:** Provides access to the user's (only) list of friend requests. This is read-only — you can't accept friend requests via Graph API.

- **read_stream (feed):** Provides access to the user's (only) news feed. This is read-only — to publish to the stream, request publish_stream access.

- **xmpp_login:** Provides access to Facebook Chat and gives your application the capability to log in users to Facebook Chat.

- **ads_management:** Provides access to the Facebook Ads API on behalf of the user. See the Facebook Developer documentation for more information on this API.

- **user_check-ins, friends_check-ins:** Provides access to a user's or her friends' list of check-ins.

✔ **Page permissions:** If your users are admins of Facebook Pages, and your app requires that you access those Pages (edit the Page, post to the Page, and so forth), you need to get these types of permissions from the user:

- **manage_pages (accounts):** Gives your application or Web site access to retrieve an access token specifically for Pages the user administrates. This allows you to perform specific page administration tasks on behalf of the user.

It's important that you get to know the permissions that are available to your application. Knowing what data your Web site or application has access to can give you the added edge that's needed to automate some of the process, prompting your users to want to stay on your Web site longer.

Knowing Which Facebook Users Are on Your Web Site

You now know how to access data about your users and you know what data is available. Now how do you identify those users? You can't pull identifying information about a Facebook user without having him or her log in first. However, you do have a few ways to get the user to log in so that you can access his or her data. Here are a few ideas:

✔ **Include a Login button.** When the user clicks this button, you can call `FB.login` and get the proper permissions that you need to access data about that user.

✔ **Detect the user's status and automatically log him in if he's not logged in.** This can happen two ways:

- *On your Web site:* You can use `FB.getLoginStatus()` to determine whether the user is logged in and then prompt him if he is not, or if he doesn't have the appropriate permissions.

- *On a Canvas Page:* `FB.getLoginStatus()` should work on Canvas Pages as well, but I have some issues with it. Instead, I parse the signature for the user and look for a `user_id` parameter. If it exists, I know that the user is logged in (I also know his Facebook ID). If it doesn't exist, I need to redirect him through the OAuth process to log in.

Parsing the signature is something that most language libraries should do automatically for you. For instance, in PHP, `$facebook->getSession()` should automatically parse the signed request for you and determine whether the user is logged in. In Perl, I use the `Facebook::Graph` libraries and call `$fb->parse_signed_request`, and then I look for the `user_id` parameter in the resulting `hashref`. Because of this, I don't go into a lot of detail on how to parse a Facebook signed request here. Refer to the Facebook Developer documentation to discover the nitty-gritty details on how signed requests can be parsed and used.

Instant Personalization

I mention earlier in this chapter that you can't pull identifying information about a Facebook user without having him or her log in first. I actually lied — you have one way to automatically detect a Facebook user on your site. You can request Instant Personalization from Facebook, and if it deems your site worthy (very few sites are), it can approve you for Instant Personalization.

Instant Personalization is the access that Facebook gives some applications and Web sites, allowing them to access data about Facebook users who are visiting their sites. It is an opt-out feature, which is why Facebook doesn't allow just any Web site to join. Web sites that enable Instant Personalization must prompt the user to opt out if she doesn't want to be identified when she visits. `RottenTomatoes.com` is one example of a site like this — see Figure 8-3 for an example of how this works on RottenTomatoes.

Figure 8-3: Rotten **Tomatoes. com** uses Instant Personalization to identify movie tastes of users and their friends.

Logging users

Facebook provides a certain level of analytics for each application that you can access in your application settings. They provide such data as monthly active users and other information about how many people are using your Web site or application who are users of Facebook.

However, although Facebook provides an overview of how many people are using your site, it's impossible to find out through Facebook exactly who has visited your site, possibly because Facebook wants users to give permission before they identify themselves to your application.

For this reason, I strongly suggest that you prompt your users to log in and give the permissions you need (in a Canvas app, this is just approving permissions — they don't need to log in because they are already logged in), and then as they approve your Web site or application, you store their Facebook ID in your database. When you store their Facebook ID in your database, you have a listing of exactly who is using your application or Web site from Facebook, and you can do neat stuff with that data. I share some ideas for that next.

Creating Scripts to Access Offline Data

After you have permissions to access user data, you get to do cool things with that data. One of the most powerful permissions that you can get from a user is the `offline_access` permission. This permission allows your application almost indefinite access to that user's data, even when he or she is not logged in to Facebook. The only way for the user to turn off your access is to go into his privacy settings and revoke access to your application.

Making offline calls is just like making calls when you're interacting with the user online. You just pass in the `oauth_token` parameter to Graph API, and Facebook gives you the data you need.

Here are some useful things you can do with `offline_access`:

✔ **Find out information about your users:** Some Web sites like to process stats about demographics, age, gender, interests, and more about their users. If you have a database full of Facebook IDs and access tokens, you can run a script on a regular basis that makes Graph API calls to get information about each of those users. You can then report that in useful ways.

✔ **Queue requests for later:** It doesn't always make sense to make a request to Facebook at the exact time that the user requests to do so. For example, perhaps the user wants to publish something to Facebook, but she's on a cell phone and doesn't have access at the time she wants to publish. You can queue up her request and use her permanent token to publish the request to her feed later.

As always, when in doubt, consult the Developer documentation on `developers.facebook.com`! Facebook data access constantly changes, and it's good to stay up on what's new.

Part IV
Delving into APIs

The 5th Wave   By Rich Tennant

"That's the problem-on Facebook, everyone knows you're a dog."

In this part . . .

In this part, I go a lot deeper into Graph API, what types of information you have access to, and how you can access that information. I cover how to identify users and describe the technology behind that. I cover real-time APIs and search APIs. I also show you how to "check in" someone. By the time you're done with this part, you'll be a seasoned professional!

If you're a marketer and have not done much if any programming before, have no fear — I keep this part nice and simple for you. You have a great opportunity to learn here, so don't give up yet!

Chapter 9

Understanding OAuth 2.0 — The Basics of Facebook Authentication

. . . .

In This Chapter

▶ Learning about standards

▶ Understanding OAuth

▶ Implementing and integrating OAuth into your own environment

. . . .

*T*o retrieve any information about a user, you have to identify the user. Facebook currently uses OAuth 2.0 (although it's currently contemplating another revision of OAuth, called OpenID Connect, which could be the next version of the authentication system) as the way that it wants developers to identify users and obtain permission to make calls on behalf of those users. OAuth 2.0, an open standard for authorization, is intended to make development easier for you, the developer.

Adopting Open Standards

You can identify users on various sites throughout the Web in many ways, and if you're going to embrace all of them, it can be a lot of work! Having to rewrite new code for each platform you write for can be a time-consuming process that is frustrating for the developer. After all, you're essentially authorizing users for each Web site you connect to — you just have to do it in a different way for each one!

In order to save effort, Facebook is trying to embrace open standards. A *Web standard, or open standard,* is an established practice of architecting your software so that whatever you implement on your site is done in the same way that other sites throughout the Web are doing it.

For example, sites like Facebook, Google, and Twitter are all embracing standards that interoperate so that you, the developer, don't have to reinvent the wheel designing new APIs for each one. Protocols like HTML or HTTP are standards that are understood by Web browsers and Web servers no matter what browser or Web server reads them. You, the developer, only have to write once (ideally), and it works on all of them.

The frustration of standards incompliance

You may have built a Web site before, and while it may work on Firefox, it doesn't work on Internet Explorer. Or, perhaps you have a camera that takes a normal SD Card, and you buy a Sony device that requires its proprietary storage. This lack of compliance to standard technologies causes frustration among both developers and users.

For this reason, sites like Facebook are starting to embrace standards and even work together with their competitors at times to make your life as a developer easier. There are many advantages to doing so.

The benefits of standards

Standards benefit both the end user and the developer for many reasons:

- **Standards reduce the amount of code you have to write.** Because multiple sites are supporting one protocol, you only have to write code once. Ideally it should work in the multiple places you're trying to integrate it with because they all understand that same protocol.

- **Standards reduce the number of tools and experiences the end user has to learn.** If the end users are going through the same path to give you, the developer, access to the sites they participate in, they don't have to figure out new ways of doing this for each site they belong to. A consistent path means money, especially if your site sells products, as it means fewer points of abandonment in the purchase process.

- **Standards end up being cheaper for those who are implementing them.** Because you're writing less software, you're spending less time implementing standards. In addition, you often don't need to buy expensive software packages or consulting services because you don't have the time to integrate with the services yourself. This ends up saving you money in the long run.

- **Standards can often evolve faster than their proprietary counterparts.** "The whole is greater than the sum of its parts." That holds true when everyone is working together to build the software, libraries, and processes needed to build a good standard. Usually the top minds in the industry are all working on solving the various problems occurring with the standard. Because of this, you often have some of the most secure software and some of the best software, all being developed at a much faster pace than you could afford to keep your own software going. Facebook is smart to be adopting these standards.

✔ **Standards allow you to reuse the code that others have already written.** If a standard exists, your language of choice probably has an SDK or library built for that standard. Because so many people are all working together for one cause, you can use and reuse code rather than having to rewrite it every time.

 Encourage the sites that you work with to adopt standards. If your service of choice isn't adopting standards, demand that it does! It is to your advantage as a developer that the services you integrate are making it as easy as possible for you to integrate with as many services, on behalf of your users, as possible.

Understanding OAuth

OAuth (Open Authorization) is an authorization standard used by Facebook to authorize applications to access its platform. OAuth works by sending users through a Facebook-hosted login process, in which they authorize your application to access specific bits of information about them. In return, Facebook returns a token back to your application for further requests on Facebook Platform.

OAuth is intended to be a much more secure way of accessing an API on behalf of a user. You don't have to store passwords in your database this way, mitigating any risk of attack from a hacker down the road.

Saving yourself from security woes

OAuth and open standards like it can save you from security breaches. Take Gawker, for example. In 2010, this Web media company, which owns such popular Web sites as `Gizmodo.com` and `Valleywag.com`, fell victim to a series of security crackers (people who break into computers maliciously) who cracked the passwords on their servers and exposed the usernames, e-mail, and passwords of all the commenters on their blogs. Tens of thousands of passwords were exposed, many that were also the same passwords used on other sites. Afterward, a worm spread on Twitter as a result of hackers taking these passwords and abusing them.

Gawker got caught by surprise (see Figure 9-1). The company was forcing its users to trust it, storing usernames and passwords in its own database, when it could have been relying on third-party services that use OAuth to access user credentials and identity information, without ever having to store any passwords in its database.

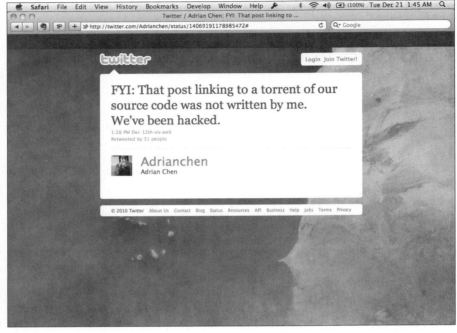

Seeing how an OAuth application works

Simply put, the entire goal of OAuth is to get an access token from the information provider (such as Facebook) that you are trying to access on behalf
of the user. Here's how the flow for a typical OAuth application works
(see Figure 9-2):

1. **Click a Login button.**

   Your application redirects the user to a page on the information provider's Web site to log in.

   In Facebook's case, you usually see a pop-up or pop-over unless you
   specify otherwise.

2. **Log in to the Web site.**

   After the user logs in, the Web site redirects to a callback URL on your
   site that you passed over to the Web site in the original redirect, and
   passes a token with it as a parameter to the URL if the user authorized
   the application.

   Your application then takes that access token and makes API calls to get
   information about the user according to the access that the user just
   gave your application.

In previous versions of OAuth (Twitter currently still uses OAuth 1.0, for example), you would also have to pass back "request tokens" to and from the information provider. However, in OAuth 2.0, which Facebook uses, you rely on Secure Socket Layer (SSL), so the browser handles all the token passing and ugly security stuff for you.

In all, it's a pretty simple process.

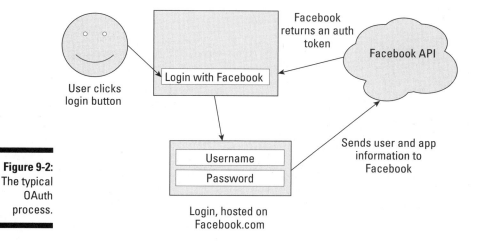

Figure 9-2:
The typical
OAuth
process.

Architecting OAuth 2.0

After you understand how OAuth 2.0 works, you can start building your own implementation. You need some basic pieces set up to manage a simple OAuth flow:

- ✔ **An initial redirect:** This code redirects the user to the identity provider's authentication flow. In Facebook, this is the login screen on `Facebook.com` that usually appears in a pop-up on Web sites you visit. Your code just needs to redirect (or initiate a pop-up for) the user to a given URL on the domain where you are trying to get permission. You also need to pass a callback URL with that to identify where the user will be sent after he logs in. Check your site of preference's Developer docs to know what this URL is.

- ✔ **The callback:** You pass this URL with the redirect so that the identity provider knows where to take the user after she logs in. After the user logs in to the authenticating site (such as `Facebook.com`), the user is taken back to this URL on your servers. You need to write code at this URL that receives the access token and either stores it somewhere or makes API calls with it when the user comes back to your site.

The above callback works simply with OAuth 2.0. In earlier versions of OAuth, it wasn't quite this simple. If you have done OAuth before, you might be familiar with "request tokens." These are tokens that you get on the back end (server side) to identify yourself with the identity provider. Those were features of OAuth 1.0 and are still in use at the time of this writing by sites like Twitter. Because the focus of this book is on Facebook, I stick with OAuth 2.0, which removes the need for request tokens and instead uses SSL, a secure encryption layer that accomplishes basically the same thing, using built-in browser technology so that you don't have to do it.

✔ **The storage:** In your callback, you are given the access token usually as a parameter in the URL, which you need to make calls on behalf of that user in the future (or present, depending on permissions). In the callback, take this access token and store it in the database somewhere with the user and his Facebook ID. You can then use this to make calls for that user. Note that you can also store this in a cookie or in a session, or just use it from the parameters you were sent if you don't need to use it for very long.

On Facebook, a code is returned from the server in your callback URL (as the `code` parameter). You then have to send this code to your token endpoint URL, provided by Facebook (I discuss this more fully in the next section), which returns your access token.

This process works on many implementations. However, on some other Web sites, just the OAuth token is returned in the URL. In such a case, your callback URL looks like this:

```
http://socialtoo.com?oauth_token=OAUTH_TOKEN_GOES_HERE
```

In Facebook's case, the callback URL looks like this:

```
http://socialtoo.com?code=CODE_FOR_TOKEN_ENDPOINT_HERE
```

✔ **The caller:** After you have the access token, you can make calls on behalf of that user using a specified API. With Facebook, this API is Graph API (see Chapters 7 and 10 for more on Graph API). This could also be standard APIs such as OpenSocial, which is used on sites like Myspace and Google. In addition to making your standard API call, you simply pass the access token with the call as defined in the API, and you will then be given the information about the user that you need.

Is the access token always necessary? It really depends on the API — some APIs require it for every call. Others, like Facebook, only require it if you want to get more than the default set of information about each user. In really good APIs, the default public information doesn't need an access token because that is data that could be indexed by a search engine anyway.

You also have other ways of implementing an OAuth workflow. The preceding process is the manual way to implement a workflow, but you can find a lot of libraries and SDKs for OAuth, in almost every language, which you can use to shortcut the process. Each of those uses the process I mention previously in the back end, but you don't have to worry about it because they take care of the heavy work for you. One example of this is Facebook's JavaScript SDK and `FB.login` process.

Implementing OAuth 2.0 in a Facebook Environment

Facebook makes implementing OAuth 2.0 easy (and easier with libraries and SDKs), so after you know the URLs to call, it's just a matter of writing the code on your server to handle the requests.

You can get all the URLs you need from the Developer documentation at `developers.facebook.com`.

Here's how a sample Facebook OAuth 2.0 flow works:

1. **Register your application.**

   Go through the application setup process (see Chapter 7). After that is done and you've set up your Web site URL and domain, you are given an application ID and secret. Note that information, because you need to copy and paste it later.

2. **Redirect the user to** `https://www.facebook.com/dialog/oauth`.

   Pass to it your application ID in a parameter called `client_id` and a callback URL that you want to process and get the access token when the user is done logging in. This URL should be passed to a `redirect_uri` parameter. So, your URL should look something like `https://graph.facebook.com/oauth/authorize?client_id=...&redirect_uri=...` (passing in the appropriate values as specified).

   Want to request permissions for additional data about the user? It's in this step that you can request permissions, by passing the `scope` parameter in addition to the preceding parameters in the `authorize` request. Simply attach a comma-separated list of the permissions you want to access (see Chapter 8), and when the user is done logging in, he is prompted to give access to those specific permissions.

You must use the `https` protocol when making your authentication requests! This takes the place of the request token passing done in OAuth 1.0. Put simply, it ensures that you are who you say you are, and that the data being passed back and forth can't be intercepted by an intermediary service. That way, no one but you can authenticate that user and get permission to access information about that user!

3. The user logs in.

The user enters his username/e-mail/phone number and password into the ensuing form, and then if you passed a `scope` parameter to the `authorize` request, the user is prompted to give permissions to your application. Note that the user may not have to log in or grant permissions here if he has already granted permissions and is logged in. Facebook handles all that automatically for you. Redirect the user here and let Facebook handle the rest.

4. The user gets redirected to your callback URL specified in the `redirect_uri` **parameter in Step 2.**

Here is where you do some magic to get the access token, so get ready to do some magic in your code to make a GET request on the back end to get the access token.

5. Get the access token.

You make the call on the back end. The URL that you need to call is `https://graph.facebook.com/oauth/access_token`. The parameters you need to pass to it are as follows:

- `client_id`: This is the application ID that you got in your application registration.

- `client_secret`: This is your application secret that you got in your application registration, something hopefully only you and Facebook know (never reveal this to anyone but Facebook!).

- `code`: This is the verification string. It came as a parameter in your callback URL that Facebook sent the user to after she logged in, so pull this from the URI parameters. You use this to exchange for the access token for the user.

- `redirect_uri`: This is the same URL that you specified for your callback. It must be the same and is used for verification purposes.

6. Make Graph API calls.

After you make your call, your access token will either be returned as a parameter in the URI if you did a redirect, or as the body of the content of the request if you made your call on the back end. At this time, store your access token with the Facebook ID of the user if you got offline access permission on behalf of the user and need to make calls later, or you can store it in a cookie or just make calls right now. Simply make your Graph API calls in the form of

```
https://graph.facebook.com/object/connection?access_token=...
```

Of course, replace *object* and *connection* with the appropriate API object (`jessestay`) and optional connection (`friends`), and insert your `access_token` in its appropriate place.

That's it! You just got all the permissions necessary to start making API calls for your users. It's really that simple, and it involves very minimal code on your part.

Guess what? You can make the preceding workflow even simpler. Facebook and others have put together libraries for some of your favorite programming languages that do all the stuff I list in the workflow for you. Ideally, with just a couple of function calls in your preferred language, you can authenticate and authorize your users like a pro!

Taking Shortcuts with OAuth Libraries

Facebook provides several libraries out of the box that you can use to make authorization of your users on Facebook Platform even easier. Some libraries Facebook provides for you include

- JavaScript
- PHP
- Python
- iOS Platform (Objective C)
- Android Platform

In addition, you can search and find libraries for just about any language out there. Perl, my personal favorite (I like my one-liners), has Facebook::Graph, which you can use to initiate authentication. You can also find libraries for Ruby, .Net, and many others. Check the Developer Forums at `forum.developers.facebook.com` for support for your language.

Authorizing on Your Web Site or in an iFrame Environment

In this section, I show you how to do a simple authentication, which uses OAuth 2.0 on the back end, in PHP. In Chapter 8, I also show you how to authenticate in JavaScript, so you have plenty of examples. Your language of preference probably operates similarly to the examples covered thus far and those I provide in this section.

Because your PHP library automatically handles things for you, you can authorize in both an iFrame `Facebook.com` environment and on your own Web site, all using the same code. Your PHP handles all the differences for you. (Hopefully by the time you read this, you will find no differences — currently Facebook is moving in this direction.)

Here's how you authorize in PHP:

1. **Initialize your application or Web site.**

    You can do so with the following code:

    ```php
    require 'facebook.php';

    // replace "…" with appropriate values
    $facebook = new Facebook(array(
     'appId' => '…',
     'secret' => '…',
     'cookie' => true,
    ));
    ```

2. **Determine whether a user is logged in.**

    You do so with the `getSession` method of your `$facebook` object. The following code shows how this works:

    ```php
    if ($facebook->getSession()) {
        // do stuff with the user - you've read their access token and the PHP
              libraries will automatically append it for you
    }
    else {
        // start the OAuth login process to authorize the user
    }
    ```

3. **If the user isn't logged in, give him the option to log in (or just redirect him).**

    In this example, I print a Login button in HTML, but you can also redirect the user to the URL you get here as well. The following code shows how to create your Login button with the right login URL:

    ```php
    if ($facebook->getSession()) {
        ?><a href="<?php echo $facebook->getLogoutUrl(); ?>">Logout</a><?php
    }
    else {
        ?><a href="<?php echo $facebook->getLoginUrl(); ?>">Login</a><?php
    }
    ```

4. **In your callback, get the access token.**

    You do this by calling the `getSession` method again. This time, it notices the `signed_request` parameter in the URL, and it automatically does some parsing to get out the access token from that signed request. You don't have to do any of the extra heavy lifting to make the GET requests or anything to get the access token with that. The following code shows how simple this piece is:

```
$session = $facebook->getSession();
if ($session) {
    $access_token = $session['access_token'];
}
```

Or, you can get even simpler by just calling `getAccessToken`, and it handles all the `getSession` stuff for you:

```
$access_token = $facebook->getAccessToken();
```

5. **Make API calls.**

   Now you just need to make the API calls necessary to get the information you need. Your PHP libraries handle all the appending of access tokens for you — in fact, you don't even have to make the preceding call to do what you want. Just make the API call after you know you have a session, and it all "just works"! Your API call in PHP looks like this:

   ```
   $user = $facebook->api('/me');
   ```

After you make all your calls in PHP, your final block of code should look like the code that follows. Notice how simple it is? This is why you want to always use libraries where possible — libraries take all the heavy work out of OAuth for you!

```
<?php
require 'facebook.php';

// replace "…" with appropriate values
$facebook = new Facebook(array(
  'appId'  => '…',
  'secret' => '…',
  'cookie' => true,
));
if ($facebook->getSession()) {
    ?><a href="<?php echo $facebook->getLogoutUrl(); ?>">Logout</a><?php
    $user = $facebook->api('/me');
}
else {
    ?><a href="<?php echo $facebook->getLoginUrl(); ?>">Login</a><?php
}
```

Knowing the Future of OAuth

OAuth is a moving target. In just the last year, three or four versions have been proposed and implemented by different organizations. Twitter uses OAuth 1.0 at the time of this writing. Facebook uses OAuth 2.0, and became one of the first implementations of the standard. Before OAuth 2.0, another site, `FriendFeed.com`, was the first to implement an OAuth 2.0 precursor called OAuth WRAP.

Here are a few of the alternative standards you should know about that are similar or parallel with OAuth. Familiarize yourself with these, because you may need to know them some time in the future, or for other Web sites you develop.

OpenID

Pre-OAuth, developers would, and still, use a protocol called OpenID to identify users. OpenID's intent was to give users a way to delegate to whom they want to handle the identification process for them. After the user was identified, the delegate would then return the identifying information for him. Using this method, a site like Facebook could authorize a site like Google to log the user in, and a basic set of information about the user would be returned from Google.

The problem with OpenID, however, is that its entire focus was on authentication and identifying the user. No privacy was attached to it. No level of permissions existed as to what and how much information a developer could retrieve about the user. It was all or nothing.

OpenID Connect

At the time of this writing, a new protocol is being formalized: the next revision of both OAuth and OpenID, called OpenID Connect. The protocol was originally suggested by Chris Messina (who, ironically, now works for Google) and then formalized by Facebook and discussed by many other parties, including Google, Microsoft, Yahoo!, and others.

The idea of OpenID Connect is to strap OAuth on top of OpenID, with the goal being to allow the user to specify a URL or e-mail address as her ID (or you, the developer, pass that along for her if you don't want to just give her an open form), and you, the developer, can then detect where to send that user to get identified. After she is identified at the location that she prefers, simple information about that user is returned, along with an access token that you can then use to access additional information about her.

OpenID Connect is intended to offer the best of both worlds when it comes to authentication (identification) and authorization (access and privacy) of users. It's intended to give users full control, while at the same time making your job as a developer easy if you ever want to implement your own API and access to that API.

Facebook appears to be on a path to be one of the first to adopt OpenID Connect. Because it is not yet fully formalized, no one is currently using it at the time of this writing. This is something that you should watch for, though, as you look toward what you need to adopt next.

As always, consult the Facebook Developer documentation to know how to fully embrace Facebook authentication and OAuth in the most modern way possible!

Chapter 10

Understanding the Essentials — Basic API Calls Every Developer Should Know

- -

In This Chapter

▶ Working with objects and accessing their data

▶ Publishing to Facebook and deleting objects with Facebook Graph API

▶ Understanding FQL to simplify API requests

- -

Facebook Platform is a constantly evolving set of APIs, so covering everything you can do is a shot in the dark. By the time you read this book, you might find many more APIs and opportunities to integrate with Facebook. Facebook may have completely redone its API. Heck, just in the process of writing this book, Facebook removed its entire, original FBML (Facebook Markup Language, not to be confused with XFBML, which still, and will continue to exist) with not many guidelines on what would replace it. Such is the life of a social API developer!

Whatever you do, always make sure that you're checking the Facebook Developer docs to ensure that you're getting updated on anything I may miss. As Perl programmers are all too familiar with, "There's more than one way to do it." In this chapter, I cover just a few things that you can do with Facebook Platform and Graph API.

Working with Objects

At the heart of every Graph API call is an object (see Chapter 7). An object can be any number of things, such as

- Usernames
- User IDs
- Event IDs
- Photo IDs
- Page names
- Page IDs
- Group IDs
- Status message IDs
- Note IDs
- Check-in IDs
- Video IDs
- Application IDs
- Photo album IDs

Basically, any "thing" with metadata (meaning, it contains elements and properties) about it is an object. Most of those "things" have a Globally Unique Identifier (GUID) that is unique on Facebook's database referencing back to the "thing," what it is, and what fields are available to it. Some "things" can also be identified by a unique name, like a profile username or page username.

Accessing an object

To access an object, you simply make a Graph API call (see Chapter 7). You can make a Graph API call in your browser; if you want to, just test it out! A simple Graph API call referencing an object consists of the following items:

- **The protocol:** You can make very few Graph API calls without going through Secure Sockets Layer (SSL), so you should start every Graph API request with `https://`. This tells your browser to encrypt the request as it goes through, and it prevents people who might be sniffing your requests from knowing what your secret key and other private information are. It's also core to OAuth 2.0 (see Chapter 9).

- **The URL:** Every Graph API call should be sent to `graph.facebook.com`. This unique URL tells Facebook that you want to access information from the API, not the Web site. It also tells Facebook to return the data to you in JSON format, a format that is easy for parsing later on. (For more on JSON, see the next section.)

✔ **The object:** This is one of the elements I mention in the preceding section (reference Facebook's Developer documentation to know what types of objects are available to you when you read this). It can be an ID or a unique username for that object.

An example Graph API call to an object looks like what is shown in Figure 10-1.

Figure 10-1:
An example
object call
in Graph
API.

https://graph.facebook.com/dummiesbook
protocol   URL   object

Understanding data returned by objects

With every object call is a returned set of JSON data (see the following code). The data returned is basically a big dictionary of information about the object you are requesting. With a basic user object, you see the name, the profile URL, and location of the user.

```
{
    "id": "120809261289270",
    "name": "Facebook Application Development For Dummies",
    "picture": "http://profile.ak.fbcdn.net/hprofile-ak-snc4/27524_12080926128927
              0_4376_s.jpg",
    "link": "http://www.facebook.com/dummiesbook",
    "category": "Product/service",
    "website": "http://amzn.to/dummiesbook",
    "username": "dummiesbook",
    "company_overview": "Like this Page for important updates and information on
                the upcoming book, Facebook Application Development For Dummies!",
    "products": "Facebook Application Development For Dummies, by Jesse Stay",
    "likes": 428
}
```

Each object is returned in a format called JSON (pronounced *jay-sawn*). JSON stands for JavaScript Object Notation. JSON is a format that JavaScript understands well, and imported into a JavaScript function, JSON should immediately be interpreted as a JavaScript object. If you're a PHP developer, JSON should look a lot like an associative array with keys and values. If you're a Perl developer, JSON should look a lot like a `hashref`.

The JSON structure you get from Facebook starts with a beginning curly bracket and then has a series of keys and values, separated by commas. The structure closes with a closing curly bracket.

Getting more data with tokens

You only have access to a default set of data with the format listed in the section, "Accessing an Object" (also see Chapters 8 and 9). If you want to get access to additional data about an object, you need to gain permission from the user with OAuth. The OAuth workflow will return an `oauth_token` (see Chapter 9 for details). Append this as a parameter to your Graph API request, and you can now get more information about the object you are requesting. The following code shows a sample Graph API request with an `oauth_token` appended to the request. Just get an OAuth token and append this to your query in your browser to see what it looks like.

```
https://graph.facebook.com/dummiesbook?oauth_token=...
```

What if the information being requested isn't specific to a user? Some data, because of privacy reasons, still needs an OAuth token, but it may not be specific to a user. Examples of this include getting information about a Facebook Page, but you don't necessarily need admin-specific information about that page. You can get an application-specific token for your application by calling the following:

```
curl -F grant_type=client_credentials -F client_id=your_app_id client_
          secret=your_app_secret https://graph.facebook.com/oauth/
          access_token
```

Store the returned token in a configuration file, and you can access this token again if you ever need it.

Accessing Data in Objects

Accessing the data in an object can be as simple as just pulling it up in a browser window, or writing some JavaScript or PHP or other language that calls the object by making a GET request from your server or the browser client. Almost every language has some sort of Facebook library to allow this, so Google it, or look up what libraries are available for your language of choice.

As a worst-case scenario, making Graph API calls is as simple as knowing how to make a GET request from your preferred programming language, so even if it doesn't have methods for making Graph API calls, it should be trivial for most programmers to write their own. In the following sections, I show you how you can access a simple object's information in code using the standard languages JavaScript and PHP.

Accessing an object's information using JavaScript

In Chapter 7, I show you basic ways that you can integrate Facebook APIs on your Web site using JavaScript. In this section, I assume that you've already included the Facebook library `<script>` tags and that you've already called your `init` block with your app ID in it. Assuming that's the case, you just need to call the `FB.api` method to get your object. If not, I suggest you read Chapter 7, where I provide some samples you can use.

The `FB.api` call takes, at a minimum, the Graph API path followed by a list of parameters that you can use to get more specific in your object call. The basic parameters that `FB.api` takes are as follows:

- **Path (required):** This is just the path to your object (and connections — see "Accessing an Object's Connections with Introspection" later in the chapter for more). To get data about the "dummiesbook" Facebook Page, you just pass `/dummiesbook` to this part of your list.

- **Method (optional):** This defaults to GET, but can also be POST and DELETE. I cover this in the section, "Publishing to Facebook with Graph API," but for now you can just leave it blank or set it to GET.

- **Parameters (optional):** This is just an object with a named list of parameters that you want to pass to the object you're trying to get. I cover how to get parameters in the section, "Selectively Querying Information with Property Selection," but now you know this is possible. I also show you examples in that section.

- **Callback function (optional):** You can actually ignore all the preceding elements of the URL, except the path, and just pass this afterward if you like. You usually want to specify a callback function to handle the data in the object returned by Facebook. I show you how to do this in the following code:

```
FB.api('/dummiesbook',function(response) {
    alert("name: "+response.name+", id: "+response.id);
});
```

I start by showing you the basic call. To call your `dummiesbook` object, just make the following call:

```
FB.api('/dummiesbook',function(response) {});
```

That's it! You just told Facebook that you wanted the `dummiesbook` object. But how do you get the data from that object? The `function(response) {}` is the callback function that I talk about previously — this is where you're going to get the data for your object. Facebook places the returned JSON object in the `response` variable specified in your callback function. Now you just need to get that data. See the preceding code for how you do this.

You can call your returned JSON object anything you want. I call it `response` here because it's the response from Facebook. Really though, you can call it `bob`, `joe`, or even `dummy` — just remember when you need to access the data in the object to call it by that name!

In the preceding code, I take the returned `response` object, and to get at the data in the object, I just call the named item in the object with a period (`.`), followed by the name of the object. If I dealt with an array of items, I would iterate through the named items as a JavaScript array. Each named item in the JSON object is just another JavaScript variable that you treat as such.

Accessing an object's information using PHP

PHP works a lot like the JavaScript example in the preceding section. The format is just a little different, but the way that you access the data is very much the same.

Start with requiring your Facebook libraries and initializing your PHP with your application ID (see Chapter 7). Now you just need to make your API call. The following code shows how this works.

```
$response = $facebook->api('/dummiesbook');
echo "Name: ".$response['name']."<br />";
echo "ID: ".$response['id']."<br />";
```

In this code, I call the `api` method of the PHP Facebook libraries, which calls the `dummiesbook` object. The Facebook PHP libraries return an associative array, and I can call each element by its named value (in this case, `name` and `id`). If any of the values were a list, I would just loop through the list and retrieve the information as I iterated through the list.

Selectively Querying Information with Property Selection

In the olden days of Facebook, API developers had to use a query language called Facebook Query Language (FQL) to selectively query results. Selectively querying results from Facebook API allowed developers to reduce the bandwidth that was necessary when making calls to get large data sets. This way, Facebook was only returning the information that developers absolutely needed.

To this day, FQL is still available and is not rumored to be going away anytime soon. (I cover FQL in the section, "Retrieving Advanced Data with FQL.") However, you can selectively choose what you want returned to get the maximum bang for your buck using plain Graph API. Try this method first; then, if you need to get more specific (for example, joins), use FQL.

Using the IDs parameter to select more than one object

Selection in Graph API supports two ways to selectively choose information. The first is a way to select more than one object in a single request. You do this with the `ids` parameter appended to your Graph API call with a comma-separated list of the objects you want to have returned:

```
https://graph.facebook.com?ids=dummiesbook,stay
```

The URL GET request (that you can just paste into your Web browser for now) returns both Facebook Page objects for `dummiesbook` and `stay` in a JSON object that includes an array of two more JSON objects that include information about the two. The following code shows what this query would return:

```
{
    "dummiesbook": {
        "id": "120809261289270",
        "name": "Facebook Application Development For Dummies",
        "picture": "http://profile.ak.fbcdn.net/hprofile-ak-snc4/27524_12080926128
                9270_4376_s.jpg",
        "link": "http://www.facebook.com/dummiesbook",
        "category": "Product/service",
        "website": "http://amzn.to/dummiesbook",
        "username": "dummiesbook",
        "company_overview": "Like this Page for important updates and information
                on the upcoming book, Facebook Application Development For
                Dummies!",
        "products": "Facebook Application Development For Dummies, by Jesse Stay",
        "likes": 428
    },
    "stay": {
        "id": "12327140265",
        "name": "Jesse Stay",
        "picture": "http://profile.ak.fbcdn.net/hprofile-ak-
                snc4/50332_12327140265_882173_s.jpg",
        "link": "http://www.facebook.com/stay",
        "category": "Author",
        "website": "http://www.staynalive.com\nhttp://www.socialtoo.com\nhttp://
                www.facebookadvice.com\nhttp://page.facebookadvice.com\nhttp://
                page.fbmlessentials.com",
        "username": "stay",
        "location": {
            "city": "Salt Lake City",
            "state": "UT",
            "country": "United States",
            "zip": "84118"
        },
        "phone": "801-853-8339",
        "affiliation": "StayNAlive.com (Stay N' Alive Productions, LLC)",
        "birthday": "08/14/1977",
        "personal_info": "The \"Social\" Geek\n\nCo-Author, \"I'm on Facebook
                -- Now What???\" (Happy About)\nAuthor, \"FBML Essentials\"
                (O'Reilly)\nCurrently Authoring \"Facebook Application Development
                For Dummies\" (Wiley)\n\nI am a Social Media technologies expert.
                I specialize in integrating your software with Facebook, Bebo,
                Open Social, and other technologies that enable you as a business
                to better reach your customers in a viral manner, leading to more
                targeted ad and marketing positions, leading to faster adaptation
                of your brand through the social networks.\n\nIf you get a chance,
                try out my site, http://SocialToo.com, get a shortcut URL to
                your Facebook profile, along with many other useful tools that
                complement your experience on the Social Networks you belong to.",
        "personal_interests": "Facebook\nFacebook Graph API\nGoogle Friend
                Connect\nOrkut\nMyspace\nOpenSocial\nBebo",
        "likes": 1395
    }
}
```

The `ids` parameter can also return information about a URL. If you want to get the metadata about an Open Graph object on the Web (including Facebook ID), just specify a URL or URLs as the value for `ids`. Your request will look like this:

```
https://graph.facebook.com?ids=http://staynalive.com
```

Including `http://staynalive.com` as an `ids` value returns a JSON structure that includes the same types of JSON data about it that any other typical Facebook Page would return. Also, note that you can include a comma-separated list of URLs, or if you just have one, put the URL where you would normally put a username or ID. The following code shows the default data that would be returned for `StayNAlive.com`, my blog:

```
{
   "id": "111964528842411",
   "name": "Stay N\u2019 Alive - My View of the Real-Time Web \u2013 Tech and
            Rants From Jesse Stay, The \u201cSocial\u201d Geek",
   "picture": "http://profile.ak.fbcdn.net/hprofile-ak-snc4/27518_11196452884241
            1_6730_s.jpg",
   "link": "http://www.facebook.com/pages/Stay-N-Alive-My-View-of-the-
            Real-Time-Web-Tech-and-Rants-From-Jesse-Stay-The-Social-
            Geek/111964528842411",
   "category": "Personal blog",
   "website": "http://staynalive.com",
   "description": "My View of the Real-Time Web \u2013 Tech and Rants From Jesse
            Stay, The \u201cSocial\u201d Geek",
   "likes": 12
}
```

Using the fields parameter to return only certain fields

Like the `ids` parameter, you can also specify a `fields` parameter if the object or objects you're requesting only need to return a subset of data from the normal set of data they return. For example, if I want to just return the name and ID of the `dummiesbook` object, I would send

```
https://graph.facebook.com/dummiesbook?fields=name,id
```

Specifying just the name and ID returns a JSON object that only includes the name and ID for the `dummiesbook` object. The resulting JSON structure looks something like what is shown in the following code:

```
{
   "name": "Facebook Application Development For Dummies",
   "id": "120809261289270"
}
```

Using me to return the current user's info

Sometimes you don't know who is visiting your site from Facebook, and checking a cookie or access token is too much work. Assuming that the user is logged in, you can use the me selector to identify the currently logged-in user. The me selector goes right in the place of the object — it looks like this:

```
https://graph.facebook.com/me
```

You can also use the `fields` property and any connections with it to get specific information about the user. The me selector is a quick shortcut to find out information about the currently logged-in user.

Getting an Object's Main Picture

For any object with a profile graphic (for example, profiles, pages, events, and groups), you can call the `picture` selector to return the binary representation of that graphic. Then, by calling Graph API in an `<img>` tag, you can display that image for others to see. You can also download the image by just doing an HTTP GET on the URL.

To get the main profile graphic for `dummiesbook` and display it on a Web page, you would include an image tag like this:

```
<img src="https://graph.facebook.com/dummiesbook/picture" border="0"
          alt="Facebook Application Development For Dummies" width="50"
          height="50" />
```

Because you specified a width and a height, it will size the image down to those dimensions.

When you're calling the `picture` selector, you may also want to use the `type` property. By specifying `type`, you can tell Facebook to give you the prerendered size of the picture you want to display. The three sizes are as follows:

- ✔ `square`: Renders a 50 x 50 pixel version of the profile image. This is the "thumbnail" version of the image that users can select on Facebook.

- ✔ `small`: Renders a 50-pixel-wide version of the profile image, but dynamically adjusts the height of the image depending on scale.

✔ `large`: Renders an "about" 200-pixel-wide version of the profile image (Facebook says "about"; I'm not sure what that means) and dynamically scales the height by that measurement.

Facebook always stores two versions of a profile image: the main image, scaled depending on width, and the thumbnail image. The thumbnail image is the 50 x 50 pixel representation of the main image, which users can scale and choose by sliding around the main profile image. Users can select Edit Thumbnail when editing their profile picture to do this. When you are rendering a profile image in small format for a user and you don't want to worry about it being too high, or looking scrunched, use the square format (see Figure 10-2), which uses this thumbnail version of the image.

The following code shows how using the `type` property might look when used with the picture selector:

```
<img src="https://graph.facebook.com/dummiesbook/picture?type=square" border="0"
                    />
```

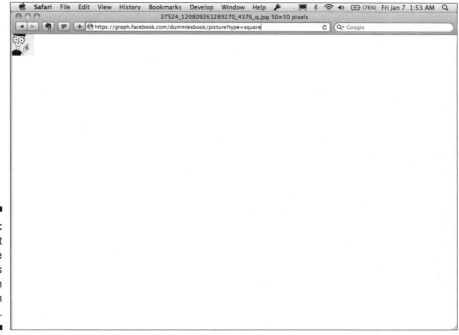

Figure 10-2:
This is what the square type looks like when rendered in the browser.

Accessing an Object's Connections with Introspection

Connections are the relationships between the objects in Graph API. You can find out what connections are available to each of your objects through a process called *introspection*.

Example connections include

- Friends
- Photos the user has uploaded
- The user's news feed
- Events a user is attending
- Groups a user is in
- Pages a user has liked
- Videos a user has uploaded
- Notes a user has written
- Books a user likes
- Music a user likes
- Places a user has checked in to

Objects by themselves are boring. What makes Facebook powerful and useful to you as a developer and marketer is the relationship among those objects. Facebook calls this the *social graph*. It's all the different ways that people connect with each other and share with each other, and you have access to all that, with the user's permission.

You can of course access connections if you already know what they are, but it's good practice to get the list of connections that are available for your objects. This keeps you from having to have a photographic memory and also protects you if Facebook ever changes its API.

A typical process of accessing an object's connections is as follows:

1. Introspecting the connections of an object through the `metadata=1` property to get the desired connection and the URL to call

2. Authorizing the user, if necessary

3. Calling the Graph API URL for the connection that you're trying to retrieve

4. Looping through each of the associated elements of that connection to get all the data returned

The following sections go through each step.

Step 1: Introspecting objects for connections

While you can always go to the Facebook Developer documentation to find out what relationships are available to the object you are trying to access, you can actually find this out on your own, through code.

To list an object's connections, simply add a `metadata=1` property to your Graph API call, and it will include a block that looks like the following code:

```
{
    "id": "120809261289270",
    "name": "Facebook Application Development For Dummies",
    "picture": "http://profile.ak.fbcdn.net/hprofile-ak-snc4/27524_12080926128927
            0_4376_s.jpg",
    "link": "http://www.facebook.com/dummiesbook",
    "category": "Product/service",
    "website": "http://amzn.to/dummiesbook",
    "username": "dummiesbook",
    "company_overview": "Like this Page for important updates and information on
            the upcoming book, Facebook Application Development For Dummies!",
    "products": "Facebook Application Development For Dummies, by Jesse Stay",
    "likes": 428,
    "metadata": {
        "connections": {
            "feed": "https://graph.facebook.com/dummiesbook/feed",
            "posts": "https://graph.facebook.com/dummiesbook/posts",
            "tagged": "https://graph.facebook.com/dummiesbook/tagged",
            "statuses": "https://graph.facebook.com/dummiesbook/statuses",
            "links": "https://graph.facebook.com/dummiesbook/links",
            "notes": "https://graph.facebook.com/dummiesbook/notes",
            "photos": "https://graph.facebook.com/dummiesbook/photos",
            "albums": "https://graph.facebook.com/dummiesbook/albums",
            "events": "https://graph.facebook.com/dummiesbook/events",
            "videos": "https://graph.facebook.com/dummiesbook/videos"
        },
        "fields": [
            {
                "name": "id",
                "description": "The Page's ID. Publicly available. A JSON string."
            },
```

```
        {
            "name": "name",
            "description": "The Page's name. Publicly available. A JSON string."
        },
        {

            "name": "category",
            "description": "The Page's category. Publicly available. A JSON
                string."
        },
        {

            "name": "likes",
            "description": "\\* The number of users who like the Page. Publicly
                available. A JSON number."
        }
    ]
    },
    "type": "page"
}
```

Your call looks like this:

```
https://graph.facebook.com/dummiesbook?metadata=1
```

Providing the `metadata` property returns a `metadata` object in your returned JSON structure, containing an additional `connections` object. Inside that object will be an array of key-value pairs that each reference a URL that you can call to find out about the connection you want to call. The following code shows what this structure looks like:

```
"metadata": {
    "connections": {
        "feed": "https://graph.facebook.com/dummiesbook/feed",
        "posts": "https://graph.facebook.com/dummiesbook/posts",
        "tagged": "https://graph.facebook.com/dummiesbook/tagged",
        "statuses": "https://graph.facebook.com/dummiesbook/statuses",
        "links": "https://graph.facebook.com/dummiesbook/links",
        "notes": "https://graph.facebook.com/dummiesbook/notes",
        "photos": "https://graph.facebook.com/dummiesbook/photos",
        „albums": „https://graph.facebook.com/dummiesbook/albums",
        „events": „https://graph.facebook.com/dummiesbook/events",
        "videos": "https://graph.facebook.com/dummiesbook/videos"
    },
    "fields": [
        {
            "name": "id",
            "description": "The Page's ID. Publicly available. A JSON string."
        },
        {
            "name": "name",
            "description": "The Page's name. Publicly available. A JSON string."
        },
```

```
        {
          "name": "category",
          "description": "The Page's category. Publicly available. A JSON
            string."
        },
        {
          "name": "likes",
          "description": "\\* The number of users who like the Page. Publicly
            available. A JSON number."
        }
      ]
    },
```

If you know the connection you want, you don't have to call the `meta-data=1` property. However, in the event that Facebook ever changes the connection URL, just verifying through this method can be a healthy way of ensuring that you're always calling the correct URL to access your connections.

Now you need to get the introspected connection URL. The following code shows how you would do this in JavaScript:

```
FB.api('/dummiesbook', { metadata: 1 }, function(response) {
   alert(response.metadata.connections.feed);
});
```

Step 2: Authorizing the user

After you discover the URL that you need to call to get the connection you desire, you need to authorize the user if you haven't done so already (see Chapter 9). Because I use JavaScript for the examples here, if you've used the JavaScript authentication process, you should pretty much be set.

Step 3: Calling the connection URL

Now it's time to do something with the URL that you retrieved in Step 1. In JavaScript, you need to parse out the `https://graph.facebook.com` part of the URL and get to just the path part. So, you do that and then make your call. The following code shows how to make your connection Graph API call in JavaScript:

```
FB.api('/dummiesbook', { metadata: 1 }, function(response) {
   if (response.metadata.connections.feed) {
   // This is just a shortcut way to get a path out of a URL in JavaScript
   var anchor = document.createElement('a');
   anchor.href=response.metadata.connections.feed;
   // now make an API call to get the feed connection
   FB.api(anchor.pathname, function(feed){
   // now do something with the feed
   });
   }
});
```

In this listing, I simply parse out the path of the URL and then call the Graph
API path via the `FB.api()` method. I pass the returned JSON response object
to the `response` variable, which you can do stuff with in Step 4.

Step 4: Looping through each connected object

After you have the list of connected objects, it's time to iterate through each
one. In most cases, the returned connection is usually just a list of objects
in the JSON structure. So in JavaScript, you would simply take the response
variable returned to your callback and do a `for()` loop on each item in the
array. The following code shows how you can do this:

```
FB.api('/dummiesbook', { metadata: 1 }, function(response) {
   if (response.metadata.connections.feed) {
   // This is just a shortcut way to get a path out of a URL in JavaScript
   var anchor = document.createElement('a');
   anchor.href=response.metadata.connections.feed;
   // now make an API call to get the feed connection
   FB.api(anchor.pathname, function(feed){
   for (var i=0; i<feed.length(); i++) {
   // output current feed object to the console
   console.debug(feed[i]);
   }
   });
   }
});
```

Then, getting at elements for each object in your loop is as simple as you
would any other object. You can just call `FB.api` on each individual object
in the loop and get data about those objects. For instance, to get the ID of the
feed item, you would call `feed[i].id`, as you see in the preceding code.

Paging through a List of Connected Objects

Sometimes Facebook has more objects returned than can fit on a single page of returned items. Facebook uses a technique called *paging* to let you page through each page of the full set of data.

Why does Facebook need to page data? Why can't it just return all the elements of the returned data in a single page? Having to page through data can add queries and time to your application. Unfortunately, it's one of the necessary steps to get a full set of data if you're looking at large sets of data. One example where you might want to page through data is a user's news feed. For many users, this can be tens of thousands of rows returned. That means memory consumed by your browser, which can often mean slowing your server down (or the user's browser if you're using JavaScript). It also means more bandwidth and processing time required by Facebook. The fact is, most queries just don't require the capability to pull the full set of data about connected objects. This is why Facebook implements paging.

You can get around this, however. FQL is one way, and you can try to make a query with FQL if for some reason you need to get at the full set of data in one query. Use at your own risk though, because with large sets of data, you're going to run into huge memory and processing problems, not to mention bandwidth going to and from Facebook!

If paging is available to your connection, you will get a `paging` parameter returned in the JSON object that you get back from Facebook. Inside the `paging` variable, you see both `previous` and `next` variables with associated values. These variables include parameters that tell Facebook which "page" of data to return to you. You have a few options available to you in each Graph API request that you make, and you don't need to reference this "paging" variable to use them. The `paging` variable looks something like this:

```
"paging": {
    "previous": "https://graph.facebook.com/dummiesbook/feed?limit=25&si
            nce=1298838987",
    "next": "https://graph.facebook.com/dummiesbook/
            feed?limit=25&until=1292487998"
```

To make a paging request, you can use these parameters:

- ✔ `limit`: This is the number of rows to return. If you only want to return three rows, specify 3 for the value.

    ```
    https://graph.facebook.com/jessestay/feed?limit=4&fields=id,name
    ```

✔ `offset`: This is where to start with the data returned. If you want to start on row 2, specify 2 here. If you want to start on row 18, specify 18 here.

```
https://graph.facebook.com/jessestay/feed?limit=4&fields=id,name&offset=2
```

✔ `since`: If you don't want to specify by row, you can specify by date which rows you want to have returned. This is a `strtotime`-formatted date that specifies the rows to return that were posted after the given date and time:

```
https://graph.facebook.com/dummiesbook/feed?since=yesterday
```

✔ `until`: If you need to just pull a snapshot in time of the rows you want to have returned, specify an `until` parameter. This returns all connected objects posted *before* the given date and time:

```
https://graph.facebook.com/dummiesbook/feed?since=yesterday&until=now
```

What is `strtotime`? This is a PHP function that accepts most English forms of dates. It can accept normal dates such as 5 January 2011 or English forms such as "next Saturday" or "last Tuesday." See `http://php.net/manual/en/function.strtotime.php` for more details on formats accepted by `strtotime`.

Now that you understand the parameters that Facebook supports for paging, the `paging` variable returned for your connection should make more sense. For example, at the time of this writing, pulling up my personal feed, the `next` variable contains this value:

```
https://graph.facebook.com/jessestay/feed?limit=25&until=2011-01-
        01T23%3A30%3A25%2B0000
```

Notice the `limit` parameter is 25 and the `since` parameter is sometime on January 1. This means that if I make the call to that given URL, it will pull the next 25 items in my news feed.

Using this variable, I should be able to go back as far as I need to get the news feed items I'm looking for. To go through the page after that, I just call the `next` variable on the following page of data.

Publishing to Facebook with Graph API

What if you want to post something to a user's news feed, publish a photo, or post a status update for a user?

It turns out that Facebook makes these tasks really easy. In fact, it's so easy that if you understand the things I discuss in the first half of the chapter, you can probably do it with little or no additional explanation from me.

POSTing data

Publishing to Facebook is as simple as making a POST request on your Graph API call instead of a GET request. Where it may get difficult for you is, because it is a POST request, you can't necessarily type it into a Web browser URL bar to make it work. That's okay, though, because you can still play with it using a tool like Curl to make your request from a command line.

 Curl is a command-line tool available for most operating systems that allows you to make HTTP requests. By passing the right parameters, you can make GET requests and POST requests, and it returns the data similar to what I show in simple GET requests from the browser so far — only on the command line. Curl can be a great tool for making test POST requests without writing any code. To initiate a POST request in Curl, just specify a parameter or two using the -F parameter.

Curl comes by default with most operating systems, but it does not come with Windows. To install Curl for Windows, go to `http://curl.haxx.se/dlwiz/?type=bin` and select your architecture (Win32 if you're on a 32-bit Windows system, or Win64 if you're on a 64-bit Windows system). Then follow the instructions.

I use Curl to make a post for the user on my wall (go ahead; try it for real with your own access token!). Here's the command:

```
curl -F 'access_token=...' -F 'message=Facebook Application Development For
            Dummies Rules!.' https://graph.facebook.com/dummiesbook/feed
```

Of course, replace the . . . with an access token that you retrieved from the user during your authentication process.

You can also make this call in JavaScript. To do it in JavaScript, just pass POST as the second parameter after the path, and then do something in the callback signifying that the message was published. The following code shows how you can do this (this assumes you have requested the publish_ stream permission from the user in your init block):

```
FB.api('/dummiesbook', 'POST', { message: 'Trying out an example in Facebook
            Application Development For Dummies!', function(response) {
    // do something now that it's been posted
}});
```

Using dialog boxes to prompt the user

While using POST to publish data on behalf of the user is great, Facebook recommends, wherever possible, to always prompt the user before making API calls, and especially when posting data on the user's behalf to Facebook. com. It is certainly just a guideline and won't get you banned, but it's common courtesy, and it may help your brand image by doing so.

Because of this, Facebook provides a series of dialog boxes that allow you to prompt the user in a simple, common, and Facebook-branded interface before publishing or acting on the user's behalf. This makes it easy for those who like to make life easier for the user.

Calling each dialog box

At its core, you can call each dialog box via a URL in the user's browser. Each URL brings up a page directly formatted for the environment that you are calling it in. Facebook supports the following display types (according to the Facebook Developer documentation):

- ✔ page (default): This formats a dialog box for a full-screen Web browser environment (see Figure 10-3). This works well in a Facebook.com-hosted app, for example.

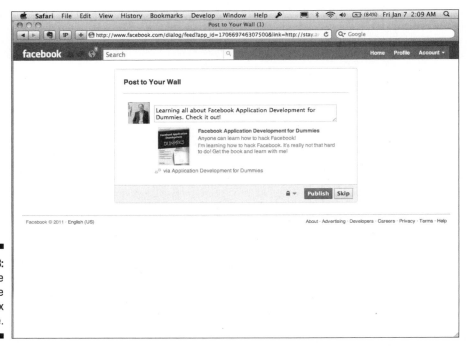

Figure 10-3:
Example
of a page
dialog box
type.

✔ popup: This formats a dialog box for a smaller pop-up window that rises above the browser (see Figure 10-4). This works great on third-party Web sites.

✔ iframe: This opens an iFrame-based lightbox that rises above the content of your page. To prevent click-jacking (a form of hacking), Facebook requires you to supply an access_token parameter in the URL for this.

✔ touch: This formats the dialog box for touch-based smartphone devices, like the iPhone, Android, or Windows Phone 7 (see Figure 10-5). It also works well for tablets with screens less than 7 inches in size.

✔ wap: This builds the dialog box for more primitive devices that don't support JavaScript.

The URL that you need to call to make your dialog box starts with

```
http://www.facebook.com/dialog/
```

Then, you just need to append the type of dialog box, followed by the parameters that you want to include to customize the experience. At a minimum, every dialog box needs the following parameters:

✔ app_id: The ID of your application that you set up in your application settings.

✔ redirect_uri: This is where to redirect the user after he clicks Submit in the dialog box.

✔ display: This is optional and defaults to page, but this is one of the types I mention previously.

The following code shows an example dialog box URL — just plug this into your browser and see!

```
http://www.facebook.com/dialog/feed?app_id=170669746307500&redirect_uri=http://
                    staynalive.com
```

Exploring types of dialog boxes

Three dialog box types are supported at the time of this writing:

✔ Feed dialog box

✔ Friends dialog box

✔ OAuth dialog box

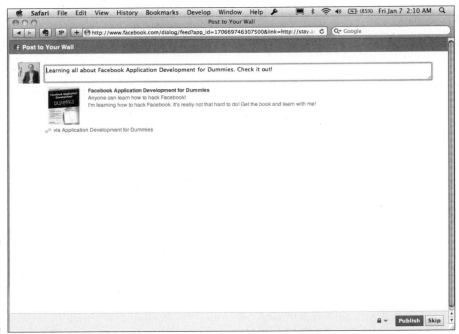

Figure 10-4:
Example of
a pop-up
dialog box
type.

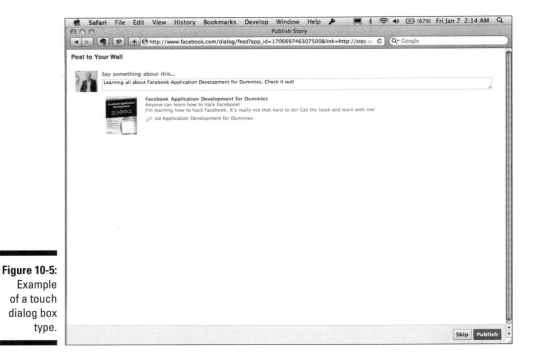

Figure 10-5:
Example
of a touch
dialog box
type.

The Feed dialog box

The Feed dialog box is a dialog box that prompts the user to publish to either her own feed or to someone else's feed. To create the dialog box, just post the following URL:

```
http://www.facebook.com/dialog/feed
```

Then, follow it with the default parameters that I list previously, and a series of additional parameters that you can use to tell it how to format the item you're publishing to the user's feed. Your call to Facebook will look something like this:

```
http://www.facebook.com/dialog/feed?app_id=170669746307500&link=http://stay.
         am/dummiesbook&picture=http://ecx.images-amazon.com/images/
         I/511oydQdwBL._SL500_AA300_.jpg&name=Facebook%20Application%20
         Development%20for%20Dummies&caption=Anyone%20can%20learn%20
         how%20to%20hack%20Facebook!&description=I'm%20learning%20how%20
         to%20hack%20Facebook.%20It's%20really%20not%20that%20hard%20
         to%20do!%20Get%20the%20book%20and%20learn%20with%20me!&%20
         message=Learning%20all%20about%20Facebook%20Application%20
         Development%20For%20Dummies.%20Check%20it%20out!&%20redirect_
         uri=http://staynalive.com
```

Here are the available parameters:

- ✔ from: This defaults to the current user ID. It is the ID or username of the user (or page) sending the update, and it must be the user's own profile ID or the ID of a Facebook Page for which the current user is an administrator.

- ✔ to: This defaults to the value of from. It is the ID or username of the user (or page) whose wall you are posting to.

- ✔ message: This is the message to prepopulate as the user's status when posting the message. At the time of this writing, Facebook's policy says that you can only set this if the user previously set this on your Web site or application (in other words, the user chose ahead of time to prepopulate this with a message that he chose). In every other case, you are supposed to leave this blank.

- ✔ link: If you're specifying a link to a third-party Web site or page, specify the URL for that page in this parameter.

- ✔ picture: If you want a specific picture to appear as the default image for this post, specify the URL for that picture in this parameter.

- ✔ source: If you want to attach a video or SWF file for the user's friends to play right in their news feed, specify the source URL for that file here. Keep in mind that if you specify a source, the picture URL will not be used.

✔ `name`: If you specify a link URL, this is the name of that link (the same as the text that would be between two <a> anchor tags). If this isn't included, only the URL will appear.

✔ `caption`: If you include a link URL, this is a small caption that appears below the link URL or name.

✔ `description`: This is the short paragraph that can appear below the caption and link. This is a great place to describe what the user is sharing.

✔ `properties`: You can include a list of properties underneath your description, which appear as a list of key-value pairs, with a key pointing to a piece of text or a link of some sort. This should be in JSON format, and the keys should be strings, followed by either a string value or another JSON object with both `text` and `href` keys to specify a link text and `href`.

✔ `actions`: These are links that appear next to the Comment and Like links in the post. These are a great way to easily encourage the user to click something in a native feel to Facebook. This parameter should have a JSON object for its value, and inside the JSON object, it should have both a `name` and a `link` key, representing the name of the action and where it links to.

In the return URL, you will also get a parameter called `post_id`, which you can use to then reference the ID of the post that you just published. This can allow you to track comments on the post, likes, and so on, in case you want to sync those to and from a Web site, for instance. Also note that if this isn't included in your `redirect_uri`, it means that the user clicked the Skip button.

Your resulting dialog box will look like what is shown in Figure 10-6.

The Friends dialog box

In addition to posting to a user's news feed, you can also prompt the user to friend someone. I like to use this in a list of other Facebook users of my apps and Web sites, where I want to give my users an opportunity to friend some of my other app users on Facebook.

For example, if I have an event Web site where people can RSVP for an event or party, I can display a list of all the user's friends who are attending, but why not also display a list of all the others who are attending who are not yet friends with the user? This way the people whom the user met at the party or event can be identified, and the user can keep that friendship going by friending them on Facebook. This dialog box isn't used quite enough, in my opinion.

Implementing the Friends dialog box is really simple. All you need is one parameter in addition to the default parameters I list in the previous "The Feed Dialog box" section. That additional parameter is the `id` parameter. This is the ID or username of the friend whom you are trying to initiate the friend request for.

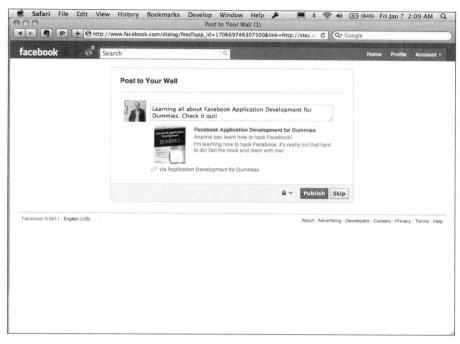

Figure 10-6:
The URL in
this figure
produces a
Feed dialog
box that
looks just
like this.

So, to friend me, just send the following URL to your browser — go ahead, try it! I'm not shy, and I'll probably accept your request, too:

```
http://www.facebook.com/dialog/friends/?id=jessestay&app_
        id=170669746307500&redirect_uri=http://staynalive.com
```

You can know that the user clicked Add Friend by an `action` parameter that gets added to the `redirect_uri`. If the parameter has a value of 1, that means the user clicked the Add Friend button. If the parameter has a value of 0, that means the user clicked Cancel.

Figure 10-7 shows what this dialog box looks like.

The OAuth dialog box

I cover this in Chapter 9. The OAuth dialog box initiates an OAuth dialog page or pop-up that logs the user in, and it returns an access token that you can use in your app (see Figure 10-8). This has a few different parameters than the defaults I mention under "Calling each dialog box" earlier in the chapter, so pay careful attention!

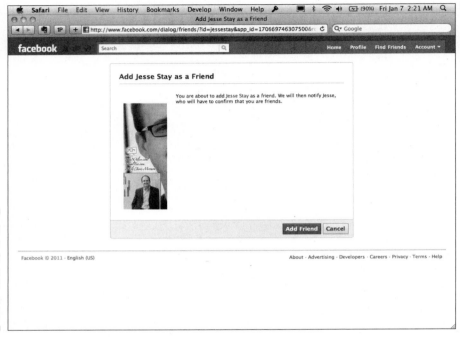

Figure 10-7:
The Friends
dialog
box — go
ahead, add
me as a
friend!

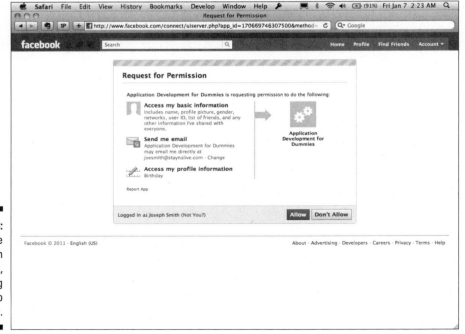

Figure 10-8:
Example
OAuth
dialog box,
prompting
the user to
authorize.

Implementing dialog boxes in JavaScript with FB.ui

Using the URL method from the "Calling each dialog box" section is a nice and simple way to prompt the user to publish to a feed, prompt a friend request, or initiate the login process using OAuth. You can also initiate this right on your Web site in the browser with JavaScript and the FB.ui method.

To make the FB.ui call, you just need to know the method type (feed, friends, or oauth at the time of this writing) and the properties I mention in the "Calling each dialog box" section. The successful post gets posted to a callback function that you can also specify. The following code shows an example feed method that does the same thing as the feed URL dialog box that I share in the section "The Feed dialog box," earlier in this chapter:

```
FB.ui(
 {
 method: 'feed',
 name: 'Facebook Application Development For Dummies',
 link: 'http://stay.am/dummiesbook',
 picture: 'https://graph.facebook.com/dummiesbook/picture',
 caption: 'Anyone can learn how to hack Facebook!',
 description: 'I'm learning how to hack Facebook. It's really not that hard to
           do! Get the book and learn with me!',
 message: 'Learning all about Facebook Application Development For Dummies.
           Check it out!'
 },
 function(response) {
 if (response && response.post_id) {
 alert('Post was published.');
 } else {
 alert('Post was not published.');
 }
 }
 );
```

Deleting Objects with Graph API

You have just about every type of data imaginable. You've created and published just about every type of object imaginable. Now how do you remove objects from a user's Facebook profile? How do you let the user undo what he or she just published? How do you "unlike" something that was just liked?

The answer is that you do it just like the GET and POST requests. While GET retrieves objects and relationships between objects, and POST creates and publishes new objects, the HTTP DELETE request deletes and removes objects from a user's profile.

Just like with POST, you can use Curl to send a DELETE command on behalf of the user, or you can just use the library of your choice (like JavaScript and `FB.api`), sending `DELETE` as the method type. If you were to do this with Curl, it would look like this:

```
curl -X 'DELETE' -F 'access_token=...' https://graph.facebook.com/ID
```

Of course, you would replace the `...` next to `access_token` with the user's access token and the `ID` in the Graph API URL with the ID of the object you want to delete.

Although in most cases, a `DELETE` actually deletes things, in some cases, such as a like when you send the `DELETE` for the likes of a post, it unlikes the post. You do this by sending the `DELETE` method to `https://graph.facebook.com/POST_ID/likes` (the `POST_ID` is the ID of the post).

Some libraries don't support the `DELETE` method. In such cases, you should use a `POST` method, and attach the `method=DELETE` parameter to the URI parameters, and it will do the same thing.

Retrieving Advanced Data with FQL

I show you under the "Selectively Querying Information with Property Selection" section how to select specific data using Graph API using the `fields` parameter. At times, you need to get even more detailed. It's in these cases that having a little FQL knowledge can be a big help.

FQL (Facebook Query Language) is a query language that's very similar to SQL, which allows you to use `select` and `where` statements to selectively choose data that you want to retrieve from Facebook. FQL supports joins (through subselects) as well. It's a very complex way of retrieving specific sets of data in an organized manner. It can also be a great way to save on bandwidth and keep out all the fluff that Graph API can sometimes give. You should weigh whether Graph API or FQL gives you better results.

Unlike Graph API, FQL must be called by a slightly different URL, and it supports both a return format in XML and in JSON. At the time of this writing, FQL is one of the few things that are left over from the old REST API that Facebook used before Graph API, so by the time you read this, Facebook might have already converted FQL to the newer Graph API format. The URL you must call to make a FQL query is as follows:

```
https://api.facebook.com/method/fql.query?query=QUERY
```

To specify whether your FQL response returns as XML or JSON, also include a `format` parameter in the URL and specify `XML` or `JSON` as the value.

Queries

FQL supports much of the traditional syntax of SQL. The general format of an FQL query looks like this:

```
SELECT fields FROM table WHERE condition
```

Keep the following points in mind about the FQL query format:

- ✔ The fields can be any number of fields allowed for the table that you specify.

- ✔ You may only specify one table, unlike SQL.

- ✔ The WHERE clause must reference an *indexable* field, which you can find in the Facebook Developer documentation.

- ✔ FQL also supports math operators, as well as AND, OR, NOT, ORDER BY, and LIMIT.

- ✔ FQL also supports basic functions like now(), strlen(), substr(), and strpos().

- ✔ FQL also supports a special function called me(), which represents the ID of the current, logged-in user.

If you already know SQL, FQL should be simple for you. If not, it might be worth spending some time in a good SQL book to understand the syntax and see how it works. If you can understand this, you'll be able to do some really advanced stuff with the Facebook API. You can find lots of hidden gems, some that aren't available in Graph API, in FQL.

Spend some time in Facebook's Developer documentation to find out more about FQL's syntax and to see how you can create your own queries.

Indexable fields

Each table has one or two (or more) indexable fields. You can find out what these are in the Facebook Developer documentation. You must include at least one of these indexable fields in your WHERE clause for your FQL statement to work. This sometimes limits what you can do, but this is intended to keep you using Facebook Platform the way that Facebook intends you to, and ensures Facebook can respond quickly to requests based on fields they have indexed in their own database.

Tables

After you're familiar with FQL's syntax, you should spend some time discovering what tables are available to you. You'll find some gems here. For instance, here are a few of my favorites — you won't get these, at least at the time of this writing, from simple Graph API calls:

- ✔ `insights`: Provides analytics information about applications, pages, and domains.

- ✔ `metrics`: Provides metrics info about your application.

- ✔ `permissions`: This provides a list of the permissions that a user has granted your application. It's useful to tell whether you should try a particular API call if the user hasn't granted permission to do so yet.

- ✔ `privacy`: This is a great way to find out about the privacy settings that a user has set.

- ✔ `standard_friend_info`: This can be used to tell whether two people are friends.

- ✔ `translation`: Provides information on translations — the native strings and the translated strings for those native strings.

- ✔ `friend_request`: This is a great way to find out who has requested friendship for the given user on Facebook. Use the Friends dialog box to allow the user to confirm friendship with these individuals.

These are just a few of the over 50 different tables that you can use. Can you find any more gems? Be sure to share your favorites and unique uses of FQL on this book's Facebook Page at `http://facebook.com/dummiesbook`.

Joining Data with Subqueries

Sometimes you need to combine tables to get the data you need. Facebook provides a great example in its Developer documentation that gets all the information about a user and his or her friends:

```
SELECT uid, name, pic_square FROM user WHERE uid = me() OR uid IN (SELECT uid2
         FROM friend WHERE uid1 = me())
```

This query returns, in XML or JSON format, an object including a list of IDs, names, and pictures for the currently logged-in user and his friends. Notice the subselect, which pulls a list of IDs from the friend table that have a friend as the currently logged-in user. You'll use this often in your FQL, so get used to subqueries and sometimes multiple subselects.

Testing Your Queries in the JavaScript Test Console

To test your FQL, Facebook provides a Test Console in which you can place your queries and see what they return. It was built to test old-style JavaScript REST API calls, but this is a great way to see what your query returns before formulating it into any sort of code.

To get to the FQL Test Console (see Figure 10-9), go to

```
developers.facebook.com/docs/reference/rest/fql.query
```

If that doesn't work, just search for "fql console" in the Developer documentation.

You can test this out. Just go to the preceding URL to get to the FQL Test Console. Then, in the Query box, place the following text that I show you in the preceding section:

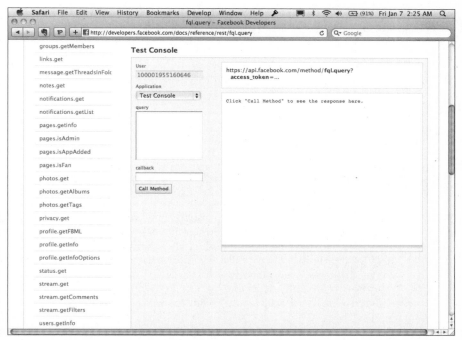

Figure 10-9:
The FQL
Test
Console can
help you
test your
FQL code.

```
SELECT uid, name, pic_square FROM user WHERE uid = me() OR uid IN (SELECT uid2
                    FROM friend WHERE uid1 = me())
```

Leave all the defaults in and click Call Method. After a short wait, you'll get a list of yourself and all your friends in the box on the right. It should look something like what is shown in Figure 10-10.

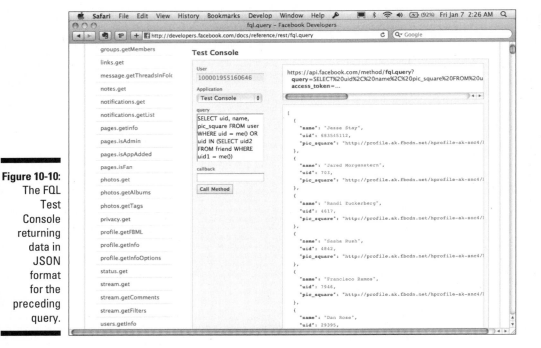

Figure 10-10: The FQL Test Console returning data in JSON format for the preceding query.

Making Queries with JavaScript

If you read the "Retrieving Advanced Data with FQL" section, you should know just about everything you need to know about creating queries in FQL. It's time to write some code. I show you JavaScript here, but your PHP, Python, Ruby, or C# library should look somewhat similar to this. In JavaScript, you can do this with FB.api() and specify fql.query as the method value and then a query. The following code shows you all you need to do to make the same query I list previously in JavaScript:

```
FB.api(
{
    method: 'fql.query',
    query: 'SELECT uid, name, pic_square FROM user WHERE uid = me() OR uid IN
                (SELECT uid2 FROM friend WHERE uid1 = me())'
},
function(response) {
    for (var i = 0; i < response.length; i++) {
      console.debug(response[i]);
    }
});
```

This example uses the `method` variable because it's an old-style REST API (at the time of this writing, Facebook had not yet converted FQL to Graph API). Specifying the query I use in this example returns a `response` variable to the function callback at the end. If you loop through the `response` variable, you can then do things with each element, each element being the logged-in user and her friends. Try it and see what happens!

Combining data sets

The more data you work with, and the more popular your application gets, the more likely you'll want to find ways to streamline the number of API calls you make back to Facebook. Not only does this reduce the time it takes to return data to the user (more calls means longer time), but it also saves you money if your hosting provider charges for bandwidth.

Because of this, Facebook has provided a `multiquery` method that you can use to combine FQL calls into a single API request, returning all the data as a combined JSON or XML object. The following code shows how you make this call in JavaScript. Again, you can use the `FB.api` call to do this.

```
FB.api(
{
    method: 'fql.multiquery',
    queries: {
      query1: 'SELECT name FROM user WHERE uid=me()',
      query2: 'SELECT checkin_id FROM checkin WHERE author_uid=me()'
    }
},
function(response) {
    // response includes the response for both queries - do something here
});
```

As you can see, to make a multiquery call, you need to specify a list of key-value pairs in a `queries` block. I call mine `query1` and `query2`, but you can name each one anything you want, and they'll be called that in the response with their corresponding result set. You can have as many queries as you like in the `queries` block.

Facebook then returns the response for each query in a combined JSON or XML block, with each result set as an object value to the corresponding keys that you set in the preceding code.

Chapter 11

Getting Updated with Facebook's Real-Time API

In This Chapter

▶ Accessing data in real time

▶ Exploring PubsubHubbub and RSS Cloud

▶ Staying updated with real-time objects

*F*acebook is a living, breathing network. Just as soon as you retrieve information about a user, that information may very well have changed within a minute after retrieval. For this reason, Facebook has provided an application programming interface (API) to notify you when the data you have collected about a user changes. Facebook encourages developers who store data about users to use this API to always keep that information as up to date as possible.

Nowadays, just about everywhere you go, you can consume data in *real time,* or as it occurs. Just set up a search for *earthquake* in your favorite Twitter client to understand what I mean. Sites such as Twitter allow you to post and consume data, giving you a glimpse into the world without actually having to be there. At the time of this writing, sites that allow you to see data as it happens include (but are far from limited to) the following:

- ✔ Facebook
- ✔ Twitter
- ✔ Google Reader
- ✔ Google Search
- ✔ Microsoft Bing
- ✔ Quora

You may have watched as riots in Iran happened, and you could read it directly from the people who were experiencing it as it happened. You may have seen posts from friends during a recent earthquake. I have seen posts from people in plane crashes, just minutes after the crash, and others rushing to help just minutes later.

Where I live, an entire mountainside caught on fire and an entire city rallied together on social media sites, communicating in real time where the shelters were and where the city needed help. Having this data available to us in real time brings the world together in ways that we have never imagined!

You can see "real time" in action right in your own Facebook stream. To get an idea of what I'm talking about, just go to your Facebook home screen and click the Most Recent link. You'll see a new view of your news feed, and when you click it or refresh the page, it updates in real time. You then see your friends' updates, when they happen, as they happen.

Now, start a conversation with someone — it can be either in the comments or in a direct message to that individual. Watch as the person responds — you'll get notifications that appear in the lower-left corner of your screen as those things happen. Or, if you sent a direct message to the individual, you may see it in a little chat window in the lower-right corner of the screen. All this is happening through real-time technologies!

Getting into Real-Time APIs

You have many ways of accessing data in real time. The technologies have evolved a lot over the years to make this a simpler operation.

In the earlier days of the Web, the way you retrieved data quickly was to constantly "poll" data that you needed from sites. This involved a simple cron job (scheduling software for Linux and Unix-based systems) or similar scheduler to regularly run the script (or a regular loop that sleeps every so often), and the script constantly called a URL to get the information it needed. This process is similar to you calling `https://graph.facebook.com/dummiesbook` regularly to see whether you find any new information about the Facebook Page.

This approach had pros and cons. The few pros were as follows:

- ✔ **It was simple to write.** You write the script as though it's going to be run once, and simply schedule it to run regularly and you're done. You had no other methods to call to subscribe to another service, no Web servers to run, and so on.

- ✔ **You could run the script fewer times, resulting in batch processing of data.** This could be a pro or con depending on your viewpoint, but it allows you to process lots of data at a time, which may give your script a greater bird's-eye view of what's going on. Technically, assuming that you always have data, this could also mean slightly lower bandwidth costs.

However, the old way had many cons, listed as follows:

- **It was costly to your servers.** Having to constantly repoll when most of those polling times no data was being returned costs bandwidth on your servers. At the same time, CPU cycles were being used each time, meaning fewer processes were available for other things going on within your server.

- **It was costly to the API provider's servers.** While you think that the constant polling is expensive on your servers, think about what it must be like for the API provider's servers. The provider had hundreds to thousands of applications all polling its servers simultaneously, causing an exponential cost on its own server bandwidth and CPU cycles.

- **Data retrieval was slow.** Because you never know when the data is going to change, it may change between polls, meaning that your users aren't getting data as it happens. You can poll faster, and spread that across more servers, but then you run into the cost issue again, and even then your data isn't 100 percent real time.

- **It resulted in stale data.** While data retrieval is slow, the data on your servers is getting stale. It's old data, and it isn't fair to your users to be retrieving information about them from another service they are updating when your service can't keep up with that data. What if your user has an embarrassing post that needs to be taken off the Web? If your service is slow to update, it can cause unneeded embarrassment for that user.

The old way is still in use by many sites today. However, as more and more real-time APIs become available, the old way is very quickly becoming the lazy way. You can find much faster, cheaper, and more efficient ways of being completely up to date with data about your users, and you should use those instead.

For example, Twitter provides you with a stream that you can subscribe to that feeds all the data you can consume through a pipe of information. Other sites use technologies such as "Web hooks," where you give the service a URL that it can ping with information, and it pings that URL with information when it becomes available. Facebook uses a form of Web hooks (which is also close to what PubsubHubbub, discussed later, does).

Like the old way, the new way has pros and cons as well. I start with the cons:

- **If you're getting a lot of real-time data, it too can be expensive!** Google, for instance, gets Facebook's real-time stream of all public data. They call it "The Firehose" and indeed it is! Imagine having to handle all that data, up to petabytes of it. What do you do with it? Where do you store it? How do you handle the bandwidth for so much data? Most people are probably not ready for the Firehose (only available to very select partners of Facebook).

✔ **You need a fast Web server to handle the requests.** Your responses to the requests by the API containing new data should be as quick as possible. If you get a lot of requests that can bog down your Web server, you need to be sure that your script is quick and that your Web server can handle responding quickly. In most cases, this won't be too big of an issue.

✔ **It takes a little longer to write a real-time script.** Because you have to write it for a Web server, you probably need a model, a view, and a controller script all working together to receive the request, do something with it, update the data in a database, and then generate a response that the real-time API sending you updates can understand to know that you got it. While it isn't a huge amount of effort, this is a little more complicated than just creating a quick script that you can attach to a scheduler.

The new real-time way has these pros, though:

✔ **You get the data as it updates.** You don't wait for data, and the user can see the data the minute it updates.

✔ **Your data is always fresh.** You don't have to worry about deleted posts or edited information polluting your database. Your database will always have the most current version of the user's data, and will respect his or her wishes.

✔ **Data retrieval is less expensive.** Because you aren't in need to poll regularly, you only get the data as it gets updated. On users who don't have a lot of updates, this can significantly reduce the number of calls that you have to make to an API to update the user's data, and also reduces CPU time and memory used as a result.

Finding the Hubbub about PubsubHubbub

At the time of this writing, one of the more popular real-time updating services is a protocol called PubsubHubbub. As funny as the name sounds, it's actually quite an efficient way of subscribing to real-time updates, with the capability to insert a "hub" in the middle so that the content provider doesn't have to do all the heavy work if it doesn't want to.

A typical PubsubHubbub workflow involves a subscriber, a hub, and a publisher. It works like this (see Figure 11-1):

1. The subscriber does a typical RSS or Atom request to the publisher's feed.

The publisher's feed includes an item in the feed, directing the subscriber to a hub for that feed where it can subscribe to get future updates.

2. The subscriber notifies the hub, via the specified URL, that it wants to get updates from the publisher.

   The subscriber sends the hub a URL that the hub can notify the subscriber with when it has new updates.

3. When the publisher has new updates, it notifies the hub that it has new updates. The hub then requests those updates, and the publisher sends those updates to the hub.

4. The hub then posts the new update to the subscriber via the URL that the subscriber sent to the hub in Step 2.

   If multiple subscribers exist, the hub posts to all the subscribers.

The goal of PubsubHubbub is to provide a means for publishers to reduce the load on their servers through one or multiple hubs through which subscribers can subscribe.

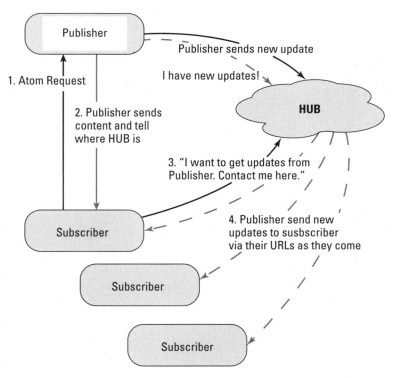

Figure 11-1:
The general workflow of a Pubsub-Hubbub request looks like this.

Differentiating RSS Cloud

A similar protocol to PubsubHubbub (see the preceding section) is a protocol native to RSS, called RSS Cloud. RSS Cloud works very similarly to PubsubHubbub, but rather than contain the content of the update in the request back to the subscriber, RSS Cloud just sends a notification to the subscriber, letting the end subscriber know that an update occurred. The subscriber would then have to make a request to the publisher to get the updated content. (See Figure 11-2.)

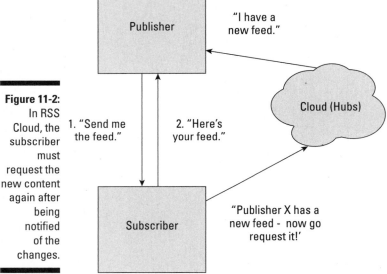

Figure 11-2:
In RSS Cloud, the subscriber must request the new content again after being notified of the changes.

In comparison to Facebook's real-time APIs, RSS Cloud is the most closely related in that Facebook does not include the content of the update in its response to the subscriber. Facebook only notifies the subscriber, and the subscriber has to then request the update from Facebook.

Fundamentally, Facebook's real-time methods are also different in that Facebook does not use RSS or Atom (a protocol similar to RSS) to send updates. Facebook is most closely related to a Web hooks–type model and relies on the developer knowing the URLs to subscribe to ahead of time, rather than being included in a feed. All feed data is returned in JSON format, rather than Atom or RSS, like PubsubHubbub and RSS Cloud provide.

Staying Updated via Real-Time Objects on Facebook

Facebook has its own real-time features. To understand these features, you need two things:

- ✔ **A callback URL:** This is the Web address that Facebook will notify each time it finds new data about the objects you are subscribing to.
- ✔ **A subscription:** You can have multiple subscriptions, and this is where you tell Facebook what data you want to be notified about and where on your Web server Facebook should be notifying.

The following sections show you how this process works.

Creating your callback URL

Facebook requires you to have a script somewhere on your Web server that can handle the requests it sends. Facebook can send two types of requests:

- ✔ **GET request:** Gets sent to your Web servers when Facebook is creating the subscription you set up under the section "Creating your subscription," later in this chapter.
- ✔ **POST request:** Notifies your Web server that new information is available about an object.

To create your callback URL, you need to set up a subscription responder. This simple script detects that a GET request was sent to your Web server, reads the information that Facebook sends to it, verifies it, and sends some information back to Facebook.

Here's the data Facebook sends:

- ✔ `hub.mode`: This will always be "subscribe."
- ✔ `hub.challenge`: This is a random string of text that I show you what to do with in a second.
- ✔ `hub.verify_token`: This is (hopefully) the token that you sent to Facebook previously in the `verify_token` parameter.

You need to read each of these parameters. In PHP, you would read them with a call similar to the following:

```
$hub_mode = $_GET["hub_mode"];
$hub_challenge = $_GET["hub_challenge"];
$hub_verify_token = $_GET["hub_verify_token"];
```

PHP automatically converts parameters with dots in them to underscores, so `hub.mode` would be read as `hub_mode`. This explains the underscores in the preceding code.

After you understand the preceding variables, you need to verify the data that Facebook just sent you. The main thing that you need to check is the `verify.token` value. Make sure it is exactly the same as the `verify_token` parameter you sent to Facebook in your subscription request. If they are the same, just return the `hub.challenge` value as the only thing in the body of the response.

A sample PHP request for the entire process looks like this:

```php
<?php
$hub_mode = $_GET["hub_mode"];
$hub_challenge = $_GET["hub_challenge"];
$hub_verify_token = $_GET["hub_verify_token"];

if ($hub_verify_token == "foo") {
    echo $hub_challenge;
}
?>
```

With this in place, you should have no problem subscribing to objects on Facebook.

Creating your subscription

To add a subscription, you need to know the object that you want to subscribe to and you need an access token. (You can create one in Chapter 9, if you haven't already.)

First, you should understand the objects that are available to you. This list changes, so check Facebook's Developer documentation as you refer to this list. At the time of this writing, these objects were available to retrieve real-time data:

- ✔ `user`: You can get updates on all user object properties except `verified`. For connections, you can get updates on `feed`, `friends`, `activities`, `interests`, `music`, `books`, `movies`, `television`, `likes`, and `checkins`.

- ✔ `permissions`: This is important. Anytime a user adds or revokes permissions for how your application can access his data, this subscription will get notifications of the updates.

✔ page: This sends your application or Web site updates when changes occur to the public properties of a Facebook Page.

Making a POST request

Now you need to make a POST request with the appropriate attributes added to the URL. Here's an example POST request, using curl to do the request:

```
curl https://graph.facebook.com/<app-id>/subscriptions -F "access_token=..."
           -F "object=user" -F "fields=name,picture,feed" -F "callback_
                 url=http://staynalive.com/callback" -F "verify_token=foo"
```

As you can see, you can pass several fields to your POST request:

✔ object: This is the type of object (listed previously) that you want to subscribe to. This monitors all objects of the type you specify.

✔ fields: This is a comma-separated list of the fields or connections you want to monitor that are associated to that object across everyone using your application.

✔ callback_url: This is the URL that Facebook will notify when it has new updates for you.

✔ verify_token: A component of the PubsubHubbub spec, this is a string that you create (it can be anything) that Facebook will use to verify your identity. This is mostly for security.

You can't subscribe to just a single user's updates. With Facebook, it's all your application's users or nothing, so when you subscribe to the user object, you get the updates for every user who ever authenticated through your application. The same goes for permissions and page objects.

If you want to just update a subscription, you can do that with the same POST request, just adding the new information as you need.

Listing your subscriptions

At times, you need to know what objects you already subscribe to. You can list your subscriptions by making a GET request to

```
https://graph.facebook.com/APPLICATION_ID/subscriptions?access_token=...
```

Of course, you want to replace APPLICATION_ID with the application ID from your application settings, and access_token should be that access token you got earlier.

Anywhere I say, "GET request," you can also do this in your browser URL bar. Type it into your browser, and you'll see what gets returned. All this data you can read and parse in your preferred language!

```
[
{
  "object": "user",
  "callback_url": "http://www.staynalive.com/subscription_callback",
  "fields": ["email", "friends", "name", "picture"],
  "active": true
},
{
  "object": "permissions",
  "callback_url": "http://www.staynalive.com/subscription_callback",
  "fields": ["email", "read_stream"],
"active": true
},
{
  "object": "errors",
  "callback_url": "http://www.staynalive.com/subscription_callback",
  "fields": ["canvas"],
  "active": true
}
]
```

Knowing what items you are subscribed to can help you understand whether you need to resubscribe.

Deleting a subscription

Deleting a subscription is quite simple. If you send a DELETE request to `https://graph.facebook.com/<app-id>/subscriptions`, it will delete all your subscriptions. If you only want to delete one object's subscription, also pass the object type for which you want to delete your subscription.

Setting up the notification processor

After you're subscribed, you need to do something with the notifications that Facebook sends to you. Facebook is going to send you a generic POST request, letting you know that something has changed with a specific object type. It is then your responsibility to do something to get that new object and do something with it.

So, consider that you've subscribed to the user object type. Whenever new user data is available, you'll get a POST request with the body containing something that looks like the following code:

```
{
"object": "user",
"entry":
[
  {
    "uid": 4,
    "changed_fields":
    [
      "locale",
      "picture"
    ],
    "time": 212325
  },
  {
    "uid": 40,
    "changed_fields":
    [
      "name"
    ],
    "time": 192212
  }
]
}
```

To process the code above, your script on the Web server will need to do the following:

1. Detect that the above GET parameters do not exist.
2. Look to see that this is a POST request.
3. Read the body of the request to get this information.
4. Parse the information from a JSON format into a more readable format, such as an array or associative array.

After you have this information, you need to make a Graph API request to Facebook to get the updated information and update your database or user interface to reflect the information, and you're done!

Like the rest of Graph API, you'll find that even real-time subscriptions and notifications are really easy in Facebook Platform. It's simply a matter of understanding the subscription model and then understanding when you need to make or read a GET, POST, or DELETE request and know what to do with it.

As always, check the Developer documentation for updates, because this is one section that will frequently change.

Chapter 12

Searching with Facebook's Search API

*F*acebook is a new form of search engine optimization (SEO). The Web itself is being indexed by people, and it's becoming more and more important for Web sites to integrate the proper Open Graph tags and strategies necessary to rank high in search results on Facebook.com.

Right off the bat, every user has a big search box at the top of every Facebook Page on the site. Users can very quickly receive relevant pages, people, and status updates that are being sorted by what their friends are interested in, just by typing in a keyword or two.

Facebook also provides a tool for developers, marketers, and data analysts to see information that users are posting and sharing online. With privacy in mind, Facebook has given you access to every post and item in its database that users want you to see. You can access all of this through Facebook's Search API.

In this chapter, I talk about all the different ways you can access data from Facebook's database. You can use simple Graph API object calls (see Chapter 7) to access individual objects in the database. Or you can find many objects at once by making Search API requests (Search API is actually just a subset of Graph API), which I cover in the next section. Lastly, if Search API isn't returning what you need, you can use more advanced joins and FQL statements (see Chapter 10) to access multiple levels of items in Facebook's database at once.

Searching with Graph API

Facebook allows developers to use simple Graph API calls, with `search` as the object, to make their queries in the Facebook database (I talk in much more detail about Graph API in Chapters 7 and 10).

Here is what a typical search query looks like:

```
https://graph.facebook.com/search?q=dummies
```

No matter what you're searching for, every search query you make using Graph API relies on some basic elements. The elements you need are as follows:

- ✔ **The main graph API URL:** This is just `https://graph.facebook.com`, just like all Graph API calls.

- ✔ `search`**:** This is your object. It is the path of your Graph API call, so the full URL would be `https://graph.facebook.com/search`.

- ✔ **A keyword or phrase to search for:** This goes in your query parameters, and is specified via the `q` query parameter. If I want to search for "dummies books," I would specify `https://graph.facebook.com/search?q=dummies+books`. This would search all public status updates on Facebook for "dummies books." Go ahead; try it in your browser to see for yourself!

- ✔ **The type of objects among which you're trying to search:** If you want to only search for people, or only search for Facebook Pages, you can specify an object type as a query parameter. This is done with the `type` query parameter. A `type` search query in Graph API would look like this:

```
https://graph.facebook.com/search?q=dummies&type=page
```

Knowing what you can search for

Facebook allows you to search different types of objects, including the following:

- ✔ All public posts
- ✔ People
- ✔ Pages
- ✔ Events
- ✔ Groups
- ✔ Places
- ✔ Check-ins

In addition, you can also search through just an individual's news feed, among the posts of that individual's friends.

You can specify what you're searching for by using the `type` query parameter in your URI string. The different types you specify are

- ✓ **Public posts:** `post`: Queries all public posts on Facebook.
- ✓ **People:** `user`: Queries for all users and people on Facebook with a name that matches the specified query terms.
- ✓ **Pages:** `page`: Queries for all pages on Facebook with a name that matches the specified query terms.

  Querying the `page` type can be a great strategy to find out which pages are using your trademark on Facebook. Show this list to your legal team!

- ✓ **Events:** `event`: Queries the names of all events for your specified search terms.
- ✓ **Groups:** `group`: Queries the names of all groups for your specified search terms.
- ✓ **Places:** `place`: Queries the names of all places for your specified search terms.
- ✓ **Check-ins:** `checkin`: With a user-level access token (required), this queries the given user (identified by the access token) for recent places that he or she has checked into.

Searching places

Places are unique, because you can specify coordinates around which you want to search. For example, if I want to find all bookstores within five miles of my city, I just need to identify the GPS coordinates of my city and then place a GET request for the URL:

```
https://graph.facebook.com/search?q=book+store&type=place&center=37.76,122.427&d
               istance=5&access_token=...
```

As you can see, searching for places takes a few extra parameters to allow you to search effectively. In addition to the `q` and `type=place` parameters, you need

- ✓ `center`: These are the *x* and *y* GPS coordinates to the location around which you want to search.

  You can use a site like `http://itouchmap.com/latlong.html` to convert an address to latitude/longitude *x,y* coordinates. You can also find many APIs and libraries for various languages that can help you do this.

> ✔ `distance`: This is the number of miles from the center from which you want to search.
>
> ✔ `access_token`: Unlike the other search types, places needs an application-level access token to be able to make queries on places.

Breaking the preceding example apart, I specify any Facebook place within five miles of the coordinates 37.76 latitude, 122.427 longitude. You've just built a simple local search engine for places!

Searching a user's home (news) feed

In addition to searching on a general basis, you can also search a user's own home feed (the news feed) for data among the things that user's friends are sharing.

To search the user's home feed, add `home` as the connection type for the `me` object (meaning the current, logged-in user) and add the `q` parameter to specify what to search. You will also need the appropriate access token, and data will only be available based on the permissions allowed to that access token. So, if I want to search the logged-in user's page for anything related to Facebook, I just specify

```
https://graph.facebook.com/me/home?q=facebook&access_token=...
```

At the moment, you can only search the current, logged-in user's home feed. Specifying another user's username or ID as the object in place of `me` will not work. It is unclear whether Facebook will change this anytime soon.

Understanding the return format of search results

For Search API calls, results are returned, just like any Graph API request. You make a simple GET request (you can even do this in your browser), and Facebook returns a JSON object with a list of feed items, places, groups, pages, or other types, depending on the type of your query. At the end of the search results, you will have a `paging` variable, with all the information you need to go find the next page of results if your current result set doesn't return enough information.

Accessing search results from Graph API via code

To make a search request, you can make the request and access the results from that request very similarly to how you would any other Graph API call in the language you choose. Just specify /search as the path (or /me/ home), and then add on the parameters as a GET request, and the data will be returned in an easily parseable format in most cases.

Making a PHP request

To access these results in PHP, use the api() call after initializing your $facebook object and requiring the Facebook libraries. Your Search API request in PHP looks like this:

```
$search_results = $facebook->api('/search','get',array('q' => 'dummies', 'type'
          => 'post'));

foreach ($search_results as $result) {
   // do something with the result
}
```

This makes a simple call, just like the "dummies" search example you typed into your browser earlier in the chapter. The resulting status updates get put into a $search_results multidimensional array, and you can iterate through each result to then do something with those search results. Also note that you can also use the final paging variable if you have one, to go through more than just the one page of results returned.

Making a JavaScript request

JavaScript is handled much the same as a PHP request. You initialize your JavaScript, as always, and then make an FB.api() call to the /search or / me/home path to make your call (your user must be logged in and authorized to access /me/home!):

```
FB.api('/search', {q: 'dummies', type: 'post'},
function(response) {
   for (var i=0; i<response.data.length; i++) {
    // do something with response.data[i], iterating through the returned JSON
             object
   }
})
```

With this API call, the returned JSON response gets put in the response. data variable in the callback function that you specify. Iterate through that and work with the search results, and you're done!

Searching with FQL

Facebook Graph API and Search API are certainly the easiest ways to search for specific information about things on Facebook, but you also have an alternative way if you want to get more precise. Depending on what you're looking for, you may find that this allows you to get even more specific. Because

Facebook Query Language (FQL) provides an SQL-like syntax toward queries, you can't neglect it as an option in doing your search queries on Facebook.

As I was writing this, I kept wondering, "The Graph API search seems very limited! Why can't I do things like search in individual users' streams, or search through just certain types of objects like links or photos?" If you search through Facebook's Developer forum, you see that this is also a common question there. Facebook actually does make this possible, with a catch. The catch is that you can't specify keywords if you're searching the stream, and you have to specify a filter. The stream_filters table is what makes this possible.

Working with filters

Facebook has been a little finicky over the years about using filters in its user interface. At times, filters have been prominently visible, and at other times, Facebook has completely removed the filters. Recently, shortly before this writing, Facebook added filters again. If Facebook's user interface is the same when you read this, the filters will be in the upper-right corner, where you can click the down arrow next to Recent Items.

All this time, however, Facebook has always supported filters on the back end. Filters are new and different ways to categorize your Facebook news feed.

Each filter provides a different view into your news feed and filters out the rest of the stuff. It's a great way to retrieve a list of "just photos" or "just certain friends" or "just links."

Facebook stores all the unique keys for each user's filters in the stream_filters table available through FQL.

You can find out the different types of stream filters available to you (or another user) by going to the FQL console and typing the following:

```
select filter_key,name,rank,icon_url,is_visible,type,value from stream_filter
          where uid=me()
```

Different types of filters returned from that query include

- ✔ **Friend lists:** Specifying a specific friend list that you or the user created returns all the updates from the friends in that friend list.
- ✔ **Photos:** Specifying a specific photos filter lists just the updates with photos in them.
- ✔ **Status updates:** This type of filter returns just the status updates of the user's friends (no links, photos, or anything else).

- ✔ **Links:** This type of filter returns just the links that the user's friends shared.

- ✔ **The main news feed with everything:** This is the firehose for the user — it's every status update, link, photo, or other type of update shared by the user's friends.

- ✔ **Check-ins:** This returns just the check-ins from the user's friends.

- ✔ **Applications:** This is a useful one. If you just want to return updates that your application or Web site has published to a user's feed, or to the user's friends, you can use this filter to return only the updates from your or another application's updates to the user's feed.

- ✔ **Pages:** This returns just the updates from Facebook Pages in the user's news feed.

- ✔ **Videos:** This returns only the videos in the user's news feed.

- ✔ **Notes:** This returns just the notes in the user's news feed.

- ✔ **Groups:** This returns only the group updates in a user's news feed.

You can see the different types in the Type column for the table in the preceding query. Different users and objects may have different types, so it's important to run this query to see what's available to you. Also note that things like notes, groups, and links all get lumped into the `application` type.

Note the `filter_key` value for the stream filter you want to use, and then continue on to the next section.

After you know what type of stream filter you want, you just need to make your query on the user's stream to get the fields that you want. To make this query, go to the FQL Test Console and try out this query:

```
select message from stream where filter_key="nf"
```

This query returns all status updates (via the Message column) in the currently logged-in user's news feed. Change `nf` to any of the other `filter_key` values that you discovered previously to see other ways of filtering this data.

Querying other tables

The `stream` and `stream_filters` tables aren't the only options that you have in FQL. You can search Facebook Pages (by name), groups, photos, and more. Go to the Facebook Developer documentation, and reference Chapter 10 for more information on how to do this.

After you know the correct FQL statements that you need to make, you can place them in the appropriate API call for your preferred development language. In Chapter 10, I cover different ways that you can do this.

Understanding Facebook Privacy and Facebook Search

As you're writing your search queries, it's important to understand a little about how Facebook privacy settings work with search. Keep in mind that every query you make depends on people making their status updates, links, and other items on their news feeds available to the world.

Unfortunately, that isn't the default on Facebook.

So, while you'll still get a lot of updates from a basic Graph API search, it will only be a minute portion of all the updates on Facebook that actually match your search terms. As of this writing, the only way to search more private status updates is to use FQL, obtain `read_stream` permission from that user, and know the users whose feeds you're trying to search through. When you do that, use Facebook's real-time APIs to deliver your new updates from those users, and query each update in your own code to see whether the update matches what you're looking for.

Beyond that, you're stuck with public updates to respect the privacy of Facebook users. That can still have its uses, though, and I think you can find some creative ways to approach it.

Chapter 13

Integrating Facebook into a Mobile Experience

In This Chapter

▶ Programming iOS

▶ Programming Android

▶ Using Facebook Places API

*I*f I picked one technology that could possibly be more powerful than social networking in terms of scale of audience, and capability to spread quickly, it would be mobile networking. The fact is, mobile networking is growing while desktop usage is shrinking. Almost every human being on earth has a mobile phone. Facebook realizes this and has created some amazing libraries and tools to enable you as a developer to integrate Facebook very easily into a mobile experience. In fact, at the time of this writing, Facebook is rumored to be doing some work of its own on a Facebook-powered (or -themed) phone. When you read this, you could actually own one of these mythical devices. If so, say hello from the future!

This chapter explores a few facets of the Facebook mobile experience. In it, I cover why I think mobile networking is powerful through some simple stats on the usage of mobile devices. I also go in detail how you can integrate Facebook into an iOS or Android experience, and I even show you how to build your app entirely from HTML and JavaScript on a mobile device using Facebook Platform. After you read this chapter you should be able to produce a Facebook app or integrated Web site on just about any device out there.

Motivating You with Just a Few Mobile Stats

If you thought Facebook was a force to be reckoned with, wait until you see mobile. You really can't grasp the power of mobile without seeing some stats first. Here are a few of my favorites:

- ✔ **When compared to the world population, mobile devices comprise over 70 percent of the world population.** This means that there's a good chance a good majority of the world's 6.4 (approaching 7) billion people are on a mobile device of some sort! This is astonishing! It means that you can now write software for mobile and pretty much guarantee that your audience will be able to use it. Just before I wrote this, the sales of mobile phones actually exceeded those of desktops. See why you need to have a mobile strategy?

- ✔ **Half a billion people accessed mobile Web in 2009.** Not only are people using their mobile phones, but they're also actually accessing the Web through their phones. In fact, over a year before I wrote this, one-sixth of the world was accessing mobile Web through a mobile device. This is probably exponentially higher as you read this, and probably why you should have a mobile version of your Web site ready.

- ✔ **Seventy percent of Egyptian Internet users use only a mobile phone. Fifty-nine percent of Indian Internet users use only a mobile phone. Twenty-five percent of the United States Internet users use only a mobile phone.** These are some of my favorite numbers. These numbers represent those people who have completely ditched their desktops and moved entirely to a mobile phone to access the Internet. A time could come when writing for a traditional Web browser on the desktop just won't make sense any more. All your development could be for mobile devices in the future — this is an area that you need to pay attention to!

- ✔ **In 2011, over 85 percent of new handsets sold will be able to access the mobile Web.** Not only can people access SMS, make phone calls, or access apps, but in the same year I write this, almost the entire world's population should have access to phones that are able to access the Web through a browser. That opens all sorts of possibilities, and you can now feel okay embracing those possibilities.

- ✔ **One in five mobile subscribers has 3G or greater access.** One-fifth of users can access video and higher-bandwidth items on their phones because they have faster Web access. Getting any app ideas now?

- ✔ **Mobile advertising and marketing was between $1.4 billion and $7.5 billion in 2009.** Not only are these numbers significant, but there is also money behind them, too. Marketers and businessmen should take note here, as the future of money is in these mobile devices!

Now that you see the power of mobile, it's time to show you how you can integrate Facebook into a mobile experience. I focus on iOS and Android here because that is what Facebook provides officially, but you can defer to the developer docs for your preferred phone's SDK if you want to develop for other operating systems.

Programming the iOS Facebook SDK

The iOS SDK is a software development kit for accessing Facebook Platform. At the time I write this, iOS is one of the most popular development platforms in the world. With Apple's operating system for such devices as the iPhone, the iPad, and the iPod touch, iOS had first mover's advantage for developers to build amazing apps on mobile devices. Approaching 10 billion app downloads as I write this, and an average of 60 apps downloaded for every device sold, it's an enticing platform for any mobile app developer.

I've asked Stephan Heilner, one of the best iOS developers I know, to write about Facebook integration on iOS devices. This way, you can get the information from someone who spends his hours full-time working in iOS. The following section on iOS development is in Stephan's own words.

This section might be a little more advanced for some readers. Although I always suggest finding out about more advanced topics like mobile development, you might be able to skip this if your programming expertise isn't up to par.

To integrate Facebook into an iOS environment, you need to prepare a little. Here are the steps to take to integrate Facebook into your iOS app:

1. **Install Xcode.** Before you begin development with the Facebook iOS SDK, you will need to install Xcode. Xcode is Apple's IDE (Integrated Development Environment) for editing and creating iOS (the operating system that runs the iPhone and iPad) and Mac applications. You can do this by going to `developer.apple.com/technologies/tools/xcode.html` and clicking the Free Download button, followed by the iOS Dev Center button, and logging in with your Apple ID. Then click on the latest Xcode and iOS SDK link under Downloads.

2. **Download the Facebook iOS SDK.** After installing Xcode, go to `github.com/facebook/facebook-ios-sdk` and click the Download button. (Select the `Download .tar.gz` option.) After it is downloaded, unzip the archive (typically named something like `facebook-ios-sdk`) into a directory that you can remember.

Sample project

To keep this example simple, create a new project in Xcode. To do this, open Xcode and select File⇨New Project. Then select Navigation-based Application. Now, save your project as `DummiesBook` (click Choose, and type a name in the directory of your choice) and click Save.

Xcode should have created the new project now. It will have created several classes for you (see Figure 13-1).

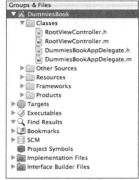

Figure 13-1:
Your Xcode
project
creates
several
classes for
you when
you
create it.

In my projects, I like to simplify the name of the `AppDelegate` class.
This is the class where all your Facebook access will occur — to find
out more about the specifics of what this file will do, I recommend
Wiley's *iPhone Development For Dummies*. To do this, double-click on the
`DummiesBookAppDelegate.h` class (you might have to expand the Classes
folder) and right-click (or Ctrl-click) the interface name. (See Figure 13-2.)
Select Refactor on the menu, and then type **AppDelegate** in the name to
change it to. Click the Preview button and then the Apply button. It should
have now renamed that file and the class name to `AppDelegate`.

Figure 13-2:
Simplifying
the App-
Delegate
class.

Including the iOS source files in your project

To use the iOS Facebook SDK, the source files you downloaded must be brought into the app project. This can be done in a number of different ways, but the easiest way is to just drag the contents of the src folder for the SDK (such as ~/facebook-ios-sdk/src) into the app Xcode project. In order to do this, do the following:

1. **Open Finder and go to the** facebook-ios-sdk **folder that was created when you unzipped the tar file (the one with** .tar.gz **at the end of it).**

2. **Change the name of the** src **folder to** facebook-sdk.

3. **Drag the** facebook-sdk **folder into your Xcode project. Make sure that you select the Copy Items into Destination Group's Folder (if Needed) check box and click the Add button. (See Figure 13-3.)**

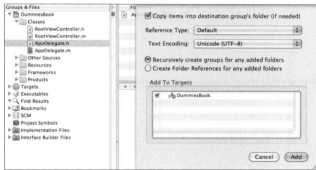

Figure 13-3: Including the FBConnect folder in your Xcode project.

For some initial setup, you need to add your Facebook app ID to the project's .plist file. This file handles the configuration for your application. It should be created automatically for the application when it was created in Xcode. It will be located in the Resources group, in a file named DummiesBook-Info. plist. To do this, double-click on the DummiesBook-Info.plist file to open it in Xcode, and follow these steps:

1. **Create a new row in your project's** .plist **file named** URL types.

   To do this, go to the last row in your .plist file and press Enter. A new row should appear, prompting you to enter a key and a value. For the key, add URL types.

2. **Click the arrow to the left of** `URL types`.

   After you expand Item 0, you see `URL identifier` as the key.

3. **Click the right side of** `URL identifier` **and a drop-down menu opens.**

4. **Select URL Schemes instead of the default** `URL identifier` **selection, and continue to drill down by clicking the arrows on the left of each item until it shows Item 0 (I only had to do this once).**

5. **For the value of Item 0, add** `fb[YOUR APP ID]`.

   Note that you should replace *YOUR APP ID* with your own information. If your app ID was `12345`, you'd enter **fb12345**.

Your finished plist settings should look like Figure 13-4.

Application requires iPhone enviror	☑
Main nib file base name	MainWindow
▼ URL types	(1 item)
▼ Item 0	(1 item)
▼ URL Schemes	(1 item)
Item 0	fb170669746307500

AppDelegate

I'm going to include an instance of the Facebook object in the `AppDelegate` class. This makes it so you can start making calls to Facebook's API from your iOS application. To do this, open `AppDelegate.h`. Under the `#import` section, add the following:

```
#import "Facebook.h"
```

You want `AppDelegate` to implement the `FBSessionDelegate` protocol to handle the Facebook callbacks. After `UIApplicationDelegate`, add `FBSessionDelegate` in your interface declaration. The full line of code will look like this when you're done — notice the `FBSessionDelegate` after the `UIApplicationDelegate` call:

```
@interface AppDelegate : NSObject <UIApplicationDelegate, FBSessionDelegate> {
```

Then in your `AppDelegate.h` interface file, declare the `facebook` object (and instance of the Facebook class) in your `AppDelegate`:

```
Facebook *facebook;
```

You also need to make your `facebook` object a property:

```
@property (nonatomic, retain) Facebook *facebook;
```

When all this is put together, your code in `AppDelegate.h` should look like this:

```
//
//  DummiesBookAppDelegate.h
//  DummiesBook
//
//  Created by Jesse Stay on 3/8/11.
//  Copyright __MyCompanyName__ 2011. All rights reserved.
//

#import <UIKit/UIKit.h>
#import "Facebook.h"

@interface AppDelegate : NSObject <UIApplicationDelegate, FBSessionDelegate> {

    UIWindow *window;
    UINavigationController *navigationController;
            Facebook *facebook;
}

@property (nonatomic, retain) IBOutlet UIWindow *window;
@property (nonatomic, retain) IBOutlet UINavigationController
            *navigationController;
@property (nonatomic, retain) Facebook *facebook;
```

Now, in your `AppDelegate.m` class (click on it to open it), import the `Facebook.h` header file from Facebook's iOS SDK just like you did in your AppDelegate.h file. This will go just below the import of `RootViewController.h`:

```
#import "Facebook.h"
```

Then synthesize your Facebook object so that you have accessor methods. Place the following below the `navigationController synthesize` line in your `AppDelegate.m` file:

```
@synthesize facebook;
```

iOS is picky about memory allocation and won't just clean up memory for you as the app exits (causing crashes). Because of this, you need to release any object that you allocate memory for. To do this, release the `facebook` object in the `(void)dealloc` method of the `AppDelegate.m` file. You can place the following line just above the `[navigationController release];` line in the `(void)dealloc` method way down at the bottom:

```
[facebook release];
```

Within the body of the `application:didFinishLaunchingWithOptions:` method in `AppDelegate.m`, create an instance of the Facebook class using your app ID in place of `YOUR_APP_ID` (available from your application settings). This should go just under the method declaration, under `// Override point for customization after application launch.`:

```
facebook = [[Facebook alloc] initWithAppId:@"YOUR_APP_ID"];
```

This instance is used to invoke SSO (Single Sign On) as well as the Graph API and Platform dialog boxes from within the app. After the instance is created, call the `authorize` method, which both signs in the user and prompts the user to authorize the app. To call this method, just place the following code on the line after the `facebook` instance created in the preceding example (within `AppDelegate.m`):

```
NSArray *permissions = [NSArray arrayWithObjects:@"publish_stream", @"offline_
          access", nil];
[facebook authorize:permissions delegate:self];
```

Facebook Graph API supports all kinds of different things, but for the sake of this example, I request authorization from the user for posting to his or her wall, and for offline access. As a rule of thumb, *only* request authorization for what you need.

Finally, add the `application:handleOpenURL:` method to the `AppDelegate.m` file with a call to the `facebook` instance created in the preceding two examples. This can go anywhere in your `AppDelegate.m` file (I put it just above the memory management lines):

```
- (BOOL)application:(UIApplication *)application handleOpenURL:(NSURL *)url {
    return [facebook handleOpenURL:url];
}
```

This method is called by iOS when the Facebook app redirects to the app during the SSO process. The call to `Facebook::handleOpenURL:` provides the app with the user's credentials. When all this is put together, your final `AppDelegate.m` file should look something like this:

```
//
//  DummiesBookAppDelegate.m
//  DummiesBook
//
//  Created by Jesse Stay on 3/8/11.
//  Copyright __MyCompanyName__ 2011. All rights reserved.
//

#import "AppDelegate.h"
#import "RootViewController.h"
```

```
#import "Facebook.h"


@implementation AppDelegate

@synthesize window;
@synthesize navigationController;
@synthesize facebook;


#pragma mark -
#pragma mark Application lifecycle

- (BOOL)application:(UIApplication *)application didFinishLaunchingWithOptions:(
            NSDictionary *)launchOptions {

    // Override point for customization after application launch.
    facebook = [[Facebook alloc] initWithAppId:@"170669746307500"];
    NSArray *permissions = [NSArray arrayWithObjects:@"publish_stream",
            @"offline_access", nil];
    [facebook authorize:permissions delegate:self];

    // Add the navigation controller's view to the window and display.
    [window addSubview:navigationController.view];
    [window makeKeyAndVisible];

    return YES;
}


- (void)applicationWillResignActive:(UIApplication *)application {
    /*
    Sent when the application is about to move from active to inactive state.
            This can occur for certain types of temporary interruptions (such
            as an incoming phone call or SMS message) or when the user quits
            the application and it begins the transition to the background
            state.
    Use this method to pause ongoing tasks, disable timers, and throttle down
            OpenGL ES frame rates. Games should use this method to pause the
            game.
    */
}


- (void)applicationDidEnterBackground:(UIApplication *)application {
    /*
    Use this method to release shared resources, save user data, invalidate
            timers, and store enough application state information to restore
            your application to its current state in case it is terminated
            later.
```

```
        If your application supports background execution, called instead of
                applicationWillTerminate: when the user quits.
        */
}


- (void)applicationWillEnterForeground:(UIApplication *)application {
    /*
    Called as part of  transition from the background to the inactive state:
            here you can undo many of the changes made on entering the
            background.
    */
}


- (void)applicationDidBecomeActive:(UIApplication *)application {
    /*
    Restart any tasks that were paused (or not yet started) while the
            application was inactive. If the application was previously in the
            background, optionally refresh the user interface.
    */
}


- (void)applicationWillTerminate:(UIApplication *)application {
    /*
    Called when the application is about to terminate.
    See also applicationDidEnterBackground:.
    */
}

- (BOOL)application:(UIApplication *)application handleOpenURL:(NSURL *)url {
    return [facebook handleOpenURL:url];
}

#pragma mark -
#pragma mark Memory management

- (void)applicationDidReceiveMemoryWarning:(UIApplication *)application {
    /*
    Free up as much memory as possible by purging cached data objects that can
            be recreated (or reloaded from disk) later.
    */
}


- (void)dealloc {
    [facebook release];
    [navigationController release];
    [window release];
    [super dealloc];
}

@end
```

Running the app

Now that you have the `AppDelegate` all set up, run the application in the Simulator by clicking the Build and Run button on the top menu. The application should start and prompt you to log in to grant access to your Facebook application. (See Figure 13-5.)

Figure 13-5: Your application prompts you to log in after you start it.

 You may run into an issue here where you click Build and Run, and the application just quickly opens and closes. If this is the case, you may have to modify one of your Interface builder files. To do this, expand your `Resources` folder, and right-click on `MainWindow.xib`. In the drop-down menu, select Open As, and then Source Code File. Do a search on the content for *DummiesBookAppDelegate*. Everywhere you see this, change *DummiesBookAppDelegate* to just *AppDelegate*. Save your changes, and when you're done you should be able to click Build and Run and your application will run fine.

Because you don't want to have to prompt the user to log in every time, it's a good idea to store the access token in the NSUserDefaults object. To do this, implement the fbDidLogin method and the fbDidLogout methods into the AppDelegate.m file (insert it anywhere):

```
- (void)fbDidLogin {
   [[NSUserDefaults standardUserDefaults] setObject:facebook.accessToken
          forKey:@"FACEBOOK_ACCESS_TOKEN"];
}

- (void)fbDidLogout {
   [[NSUserDefaults standardUserDefaults] removeObjectForKey:@"FACEBOOK_ACCESS_
          TOKEN"];
}
```

With the access key stored in NSUserDefaults, you can post directly to Facebook without forcing the user to create a login session every time she uses the app. In most cases, the user will already be logged in to Facebook through the Facebook iOS app, so nagging her to log in to create an access token each time could be frustrating.

Now that you've stored the access token, create a helper method in AppDelegate.m to load the accessToken from NSUserDefaults if it doesn't already exist. This allows you to ensure the user isn't already logged in, and you won't be logging her in every single time she goes into the application. Refer to the following code, which should go above your didFinish-LaunchingWithOptions method somewhere:

```
- (NSString *)facebookAccessToken {

   if (facebook.accessToken) {
      return facebook.accessToken;
   }

   NSString *accessToken = [[NSUserDefaults standardUserDefaults]
          objectForKey:@"FACEBOOK_ACCESS_TOKEN"];
   if (accessToken) {
      facebook.accessToken = accessToken;
   }

   return facebook.accessToken;
}
```

Now you can check to see whether the access token exists before you request the user again for authorization in the application:didFinish LaunchingWithOptions method. See the following code:

```
- (BOOL)application:(UIApplication *)application didFinishLaunchingWithOptions:(
          NSDictionary *)launchOptions {

  // Override point for customization after application launch.

  // Add the navigation controller's view to the window and display.
  [window addSubview:navigationController.view];
  [window makeKeyAndVisible];

  facebook = [[Facebook alloc] initWithAppId:@"170669746307500"];
  if (![self facebookAccessToken]) {
    NSArray *permissions = [NSArray arrayWithObjects:@"publish_stream",
            @"offline_access", nil];
    [facebook authorize:permissions delegate:self];
  }

  return YES;
}
```

Programming the Android Facebook SDK

By the time you read this, Android will likely be the largest smartphone OS in the world. Because it is open source, with the help of Google, Android can run on any device in many different forms. Best of all, every update by the community gets submitted back to the main OS, making Android a quickly developing platform to build apps. That's why it makes sense to integrate Facebook into Android, and in fact, you can already find Android devices as I write this that integrate Facebook very deeply into the mobile experience.

I've asked Ray Hunter, one of the best Android developers I know, to show you how you can integrate a Facebook experience into an Android app.

Downloading the Facebook Android API

Android integration with Facebook begins with using Facebook's mobile API. Its API is stored on GitHub, which is an online GIT repository. First, I show you how to download the Facebook API from GitHub. You need to have a GIT client to download the project from GitHub (you can find some good clients at `http://en.wikipedia.org/wiki/Git_(software)#Portability`). After you have the client installed, you need to run the following command, which will download the Facebook Android SDK (as a clone) onto your hard drive:

```
got clone git://github.com/facebook/facebook-android-sdk.git
```

When run, that command creates a new project directory named `facebook-android-sdk`. This directory contains the Facebook Android API that you will be using with your Android application. You now need to add this project to Eclipse (the editor Google recommends you write Android apps in — you can download it at `http://eclipse.org`) so that you can reference the project as a library. Here are the steps to add the project to Eclipse (see Figure 13-6 for the final result):

1. **Create a new Android project in Eclipse (choose File⇨New⇨ Android Project).**

2. **Enter the project name.**

3. **Select Create Project from Existing Source.**

4. **Browse for the location of the project (you need to browse to the project that was downloaded with GIT and select the** `facebook` **subfolder in the** `facebook-android-sdk` **directory).**

5. **Click Finish.**

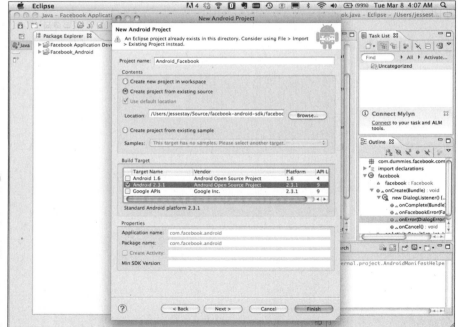

Figure 13-6:
Creating your Android project from the Facebook Android SDK.

Creating your Android project with Facebook API

Now that you have added the Facebook Android API to Eclipse, you are ready to create a new Android project that will use the API to connect to Facebook. This allows you to reference the API. Here are the steps to create your Android project and reference the API (see Figure 13-7 for the final result):

1. **Create a new Android project in Eclipse (choose File➪New➪ Android Project).**

2. **Enter the project name.**

3. **Select Build Target: Android 2.3.1.**

4. **Enter the project package name (I chose** `com.dummies.facebook`**).**

5. **Enter the activity name (I put** `com.dummies.facebook` **in here as well).**

6. **Click Finish.**

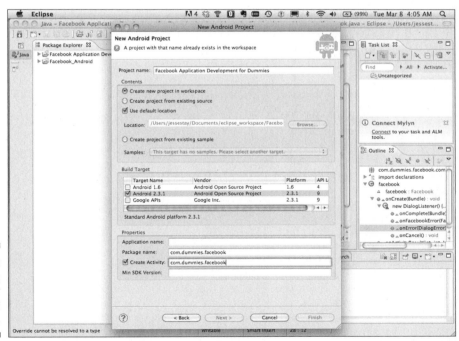

Figure 13-7:
Creating your Android project.

Now that you have created your new Android project, you can link the Facebook Android API to your project. Here are the steps to set that up (see Figure 13-8 for the final result):

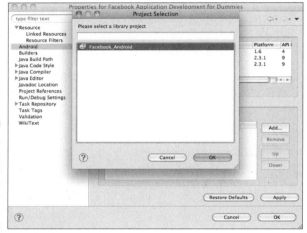

1. **In the Package Explorer in Eclipse, select the project.**

2. **Right-click the project name.**

3. **Select Properties from the list.**

4. **Select Android from the list on the left.**

5. **Under the Library section, click Add (this opens a selection box containing a list of Android library projects).**

6. **Select the Facebook Android API project that you added to Eclipse.**

7. **Click OK twice.**

After you add the library, you will see the referenced library as a resource under your project (see Figure 13-9). This will be a linked resource in Eclipse and will allow you to browse the source code from your project.

Now that your project is created and configured to use the Facebook Android API, you need to do a couple of more tasks for your integration into Facebook. First, you need to configure your Developer App's Mobile and Devices section on Facebook with a developer's key. You can get this key by generating the key with keytool or by using one that you might have already generated. In the .android directory within your home directory, find a file named debug.keystore. That is the file that can generate the key for your application. Here is the command to do that in your Android directory. On a Mac you can enter this in a terminal. On a Windows machine you can enter it in a Command Prompt, and will need to download an `openssl` client from `http://www.openssl.org/related/binaries.html`:

```
openssl sha1 -binary debug.keystore | openssl base64
```

If you don't find a `debug.keystore` file, create one with the following command into your command prompt (or Console app on the Mac):

```
keytool -exportcert -alias androiddebugkey -keystore ~/.android/debug.keystore |
              openssl sha1 -binary | openssl base64
```

After you run this command, you need to copy some output to your Facebook Developers App Mobile and Devices section under Android Key Hash. (See Figure 13-10.)

For the second task, you need to make sure that your Android application is set up to make Internet connections. This is accomplished by adding a user permission to your Android manifest XML file (this file, called `AndroidManifest.xml`, sets all the configuration settings for your Android app). Add the following code to your manifest file, right above the first `<application>` tag:

```
<uses-permission android:name="android.permission.INTERNET"></uses-permission>
```

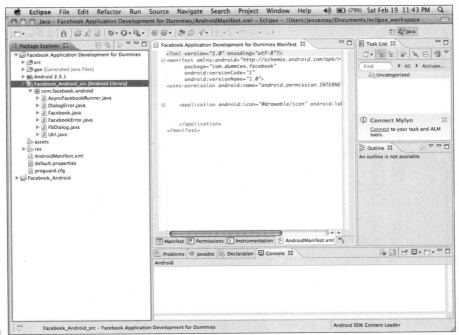

Figure 13-9:
Your
referenced
library.

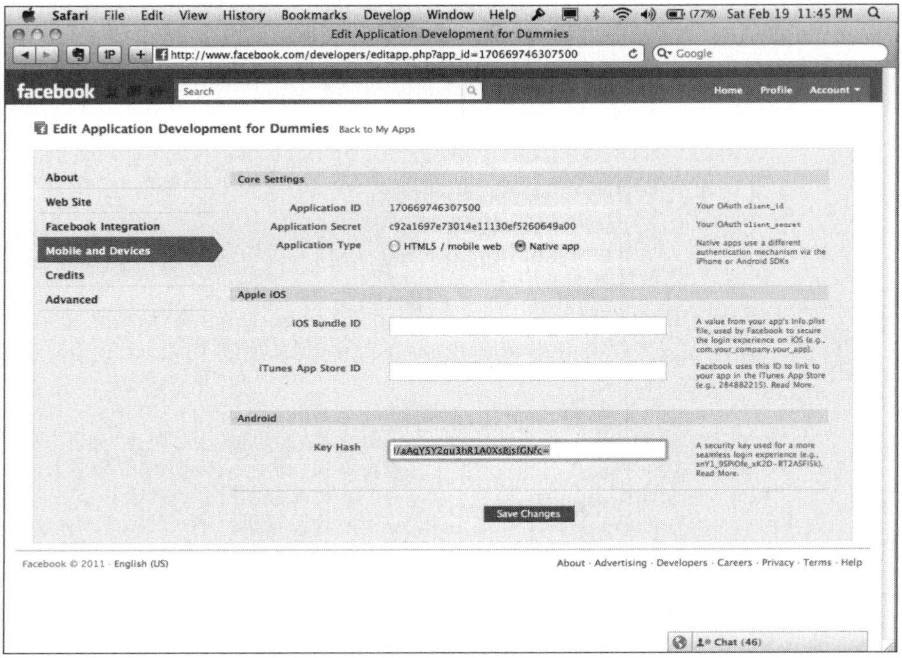

Figure 13-10:
When you get your Android key hash, place it in your Facebook application settings under Mobile and Devices.

After you add this code to your Android manifest XML file, you are ready to add some sample code from Facebook to demonstrate how its API works. Open the `Activity` class that was generated for your Android application (mine was called `facebook.java`). This class should have one method in it named `onCreate`. You can replace the `onCreate` method in the `Activity` class with the following method and the class variable `facebook`:

```
Facebook facebook = new Facebook("APP_ID_HERE");

@Override
  public void onCreate(Bundle savedInstanceState)
  {
    super.onCreate(savedInstanceState);
    setContentView(R.layout.main);

    facebook.authorize(this, new DialogListener() {
      @Override
      public void onComplete(Bundle values)
      {}

      @Override
      public void onFacebookError(FacebookError error)
      {}
```

```
        @Override
        public void onError(DialogError e)
        {}

        @Override
        public void onCancel()
        {}
    });
}
```

Next, you can add the following method to your class, right after the `onCreate` method you created in the preceding example:

```
@Override
  public void onActivityResult(int requestCode, int resultCode, Intent data)
  {
    super.onActivityResult(requestCode, resultCode, data);
    facebook.authorizeCallback(requestCode, resultCode, data);
  }
```

For the last item, replace the *APP_ID_HERE* placeholder with your actual App ID from the application that you created on Facebook. If you select the application under the Developer app, you can find the App ID to use. After you update your code with the preceding sample code, you are ready to test. You can right-click your project and select Debug➪Android Application.

Your resulting code will look like this:

```
package com.dummies.facebook.com.dummies;

import android.app.Activity;
import android.os.Bundle;
import android.content.Intent;
import com.facebook.android.*;
import com.facebook.android.Facebook.*;

public class facebook extends Activity {
    /** Called when the activity is first created. */
    Facebook facebook = new Facebook("170669746307500");

    @Override
      public void onCreate(Bundle savedInstanceState)
      {
        super.onCreate(savedInstanceState);
        setContentView(R.layout.main);

        facebook.authorize(this, new DialogListener() {
```

```
    @Override
    public void onComplete(Bundle values)
    {}

    @Override
    public void onFacebookError(FacebookError error)
    {}

    @Override
    public void onError(DialogError e)
    {}

    @Override
    public void onCancel()
    {}
    });
  }

@Override
  public void onActivityResult(int requestCode, int resultCode, Intent data)
  {
    super.onActivityResult(requestCode, resultCode, data);
    facebook.authorizeCallback(requestCode, resultCode, data);
  }
}
```

When you run your new application in the Android emulator (see Figure 13-11), a Facebook dialog box prompts you to log in. After you log in, you are prompted to allow your application access to your Facebook account.

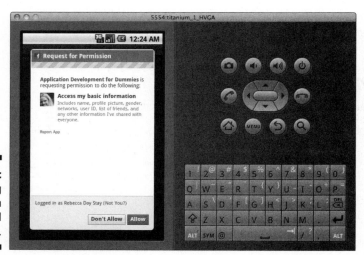

Figure 13-11:
Running the app in the Android emulator.

After you log in to your Facebook account and authorize access for your application, you are able to access the user account information. You can now start accessing the Facebook API methods.

Some methods you might want to familiarize yourself with in order to provide more Facebook functionality into your application are as follows:

- `facebook.request`: This is how you synchronously call Graph API methods. For instance, to get the current user's information, call

```
facebook.request("/me")
```

- `facebook.dialog`: This launches a dialog box. See the section in Chapter 10 on the types of dialog boxes that are available. For instance, to launch the Feed dialog box and prompt the user to post to his news feed, use the following code (per Facebook's documentation):

```
facebook.dialog(this,"feed",

    new DialogListener() {
        @Override
        public void onComplete(Bundle values) {}

        @Override
        public void onFacebookError(FacebookError error) {}

        @Override
        public void onError(DialogError e) {}

        @Override
        public void onCancel() {}
    }
);
```

Programming with Facebook, Mobile, and HTML

The most standard way that you can write your code once and have it work across multiple devices is by using HTML5. In fact, you can even use platform environments like Appcelerator's Titanium to build your application in simple HTML and JavaScript and have the platform compile to native iOS or Android code. Whatever way you choose to develop your mobile app using HTML, you'll find that integration with Facebook on mobile devices is similar to the way that you build any traditional Web app with Facebook.

To get started, you need to know some basic things that may make this experience just slightly different than a traditional Web app:

✔ FB.ui does not seem to work well on mobile devices. Instead, redirect to a dialog box URL.

✔ For dialog boxes, use the "wap" or "touch" display types to indicate that you want to format the experience for a mobile device.

✔ Be sure that you're formatting the rest of your user experience to be the exact height and width of the device you're building for. Frameworks like Titanium can make this process fairly simple.

To build the basics of your Web application, you need some simple scaffolding to initialize your Facebook JavaScript SDK libraries and allow you to make calls to get data about the user. That simple code looks like this:

```html
<html>
    <head>
      <title>Sample HTML App</title>
    </head>
    <body>
      <div id="fb-root"></div>
      <script src="http://connect.facebook.net/en_US/all.js" />
      <script>
        FB.init({
            appId:'APP_ID_GOES_HERE', cookie:true,
            status:true, xfbml:true
        });
      </script>
      <fb:login-button onlogin="login()" autologoutlink="true">Login through
            Facebook</fb:login-button>
    </body>
</html>
```

This HTML just renders a simple Facebook Login button. Create a login() function to handle the callback when a user clicks the Login button. This function would look something like this, and should be placed right above the last </body> tag:

```
<script>
   function login() {
   window.location.href="http://www.facebook.com/dialog/oauth?client_id=YOUR_
            APP_ID&redirect_uri=YOUR_URL&display=touch";
   }
</script>
```

When the user clicks the Facebook Login button, Facebook initiates the login() callback that you specified in the onlogin attribute of your `fb:login-button` call. This call redirects the mobile device's browser to the OAuth dialog box URL for touch devices. You need to specify the URL to then redirect to as the *YOUR_URL* field and *YOUR_APP_ID* in the App ID field so that when the user is finished logging in, Facebook knows where to take the user.

After the user is logged in (keep in mind that you can use `FB.getSession` to determine whether the user is logged in), you can now make Facebook API calls. Here, I do a simple share, so all you need to do is redirect the user to the proper share dialog box for your device. You can just do something like this, placing it anywhere in your HTML document:

```
<a href="http://www.facebook.com/dialog/feed?app_id=YOUR_APP_ID&redirect_
            uri=YOUR_URL&display=touch">Click to post to Facebook</a>
```

This sends the user to the dialog box for sharing back to Facebook. Make sure the `redirect_uri` value is the same URL in your Web site settings for your application (the application you specified in the `YOUR_APP_ID` field above).

Keep in mind that dialog boxes don't require you to previously have logged the user in. If the user isn't logged in, Facebook will automatically prompt him to log in. Facebook takes care of everything for you in that case. Therefore, you really don't need any of the fancy login stuff that you used previously unless you want to make other API calls like `FB.api()` to get other user information.

After you authenticate the user, you can really do anything you want. Try making some `FB.api()` calls to get information about the user. Print out a list of the user's friends. Refer to Chapter 10 to find out what API calls are available. Everything else should work as normal on a mobile device. Now do you see the advantages of HTML?

Using the Facebook Places API

In Chapters 10 and 12, I show you in detail how to access Facebook Places through Graph API. Refer to them to find out how you can integrate this into a mobile environment. The mobile app that you build may be one of the most interesting uses of this API. Imagine being able to check into Facebook, for instance, with the mobile experience that you build. All major mobile SDKs support the same Graph API calls that I mention in Chapters 10 and 12.

Chapter 14

Testing Your Application

● ●

In This Chapter

▶ Checking out the development tools

▶ Understanding the approaches to creating test accounts

▶ Assigning test users and "friending" test accounts

▶ Removing test accounts

● ●

As you develop your application, Facebook provides several tools that can help you develop and test your application. I suggest that you become familiar with these because they can save you a lot of time and headaches if you ever need to test a problem accessing the Facebook APIs from your application.

This chapter explores these tools and takes you through the process of creating test environments, conducting tests on your in-progress application, and deleting old test accounts.

Facebook's API Test Console

Available at `http://developers.facebook.com/tools/console`, the API Test Console can tell you your login status and allow you to place basic API calls and HTML/FBML that you can test. Any error produced is then generated in an error console in a convenient location that you can watch as you test.

Your API Test Console consists of the following components (see Figure 14-1):

▶ **Login/Authorization:** This area consists of three buttons — a normal Facebook Login button, a Disconnect button, and a Logout button. The Facebook Login button is used to log in to Facebook and authorize your application for use in your testing. The Disconnect button disconnects your application from being authorized on Facebook but keeps you logged in to Facebook while you're testing your application. The Logout button completely logs you out of Facebook and disconnects your application for the user. These three connect phases are important to consider as you develop your application.

✔ **Login/Authorization status:** This is the current status of your logged-in user. If you aren't logged in or disconnected, it will say `notConnected`. If you're logged in, it will say `Connected`.

✔ **Text area:** This is where you enter your API test calls. They can either be FBML tags or JavaScript calls to the Facebook JavaScript SDK within HTML `<script/>` tags.

✔ **Run button:** Clicking this button runs the application that is in the text area box.

✔ **Examples:** This little button provides you with several examples of how to use the API. If you're unsure how a particular API call works, check out the examples here, because there is a good chance your case may be provided.

✔ **Output area:** This area below the Test Console is where your HTML gets output. Any FBML tags that are parsed appear here, along with any output from JavaScript.

✔ **Log area:** This is your error log, and it shows you a stack trace of everything that is loaded and logged during the run process. Click the little triangles and you can see an output of what is being logged and debugged during the run process.

Figure 14-1:
API Test
Console
components.

You may want to play with Facebook's API Test Console and the examples it provides just to get a feel for the Facebook JavaScript SDK and/or FBML. This is a good playground, especially if you don't have many resources for hosting or other places to store your code. I try to use this in my demos throughout the book so that you can also play with it and try your own adaptations to the code.

Facebook's URL Linter

Did you know that you can turn your Web site into a Facebook Page? I won't get into many details here (I cover this thoroughly in Chapter 6), but by using a protocol of simple meta tags that you put in the header of your HTML, you can identify your Web site to Facebook as a Page on Facebook's network. When you implement these tags, you can run your Web site by Facebook via its URL Linter (`http://developers.facebook.com/tools/lint/`) and Facebook can tell you what it knows about your Web site based on those tags.

So, for instance, I run my own blog at `http://staynalive.com`. I have added these meta tags to my blog in the header to identify it as a Web site (I could also identify it as a blog), show what URL I want Facebook to link it to, and provide other metadata such as images, my phone number, my e-mail address, and more:

```
<meta property="fb:page_id" content="12327140265" />
<meta property="fb:app_id" content="293151070252" />
<meta property="og:title" content="Stay N' Alive" />
<meta property="og:type" content="Web site" />
<meta property="og:url" content="http://staynalive.com" />
<meta property="og:phone_number" content="801-853-8339" />
<meta property="fb:admins" content="683545112" />
<meta property="og:description" content="My View of the Real-Time Web - Tech and
            Rants From Jesse Stay, The 'Social' Geek" />
<meta property="og:email" content="jesse@staynalive.com" />
<meta property="og:site_name" content="Stay N' Alive" />
<meta property="og:image" content="http://staynalive.com/wp-content/themes/
            staynalive/images/Logo-20080519-113612.png" />
```

Imagine someone shares my blog on Facebook and it isn't showing right. Maybe the main image isn't showing properly, or it isn't bringing in the proper description text. My HTML code above looks correct, and follows Facebook's Open Graph Protocol standards. Why isn't it working? That's where the URL Linter can help.

If I pass `http://staynalive.com` by the Facebook URL Linter, it gives me all kinds of information that it just retrieved from those meta tags, telling me what it was able to parse based on the Open Graph Protocol (see Figure 14-2). It also gives me sample HTML that I can copy and paste to put a Like button on my site and the URL in the Facebook Graph API that I can use to pull all kinds of information about my Web site that Facebook has collected (or will collect) via the API. Through the URL Linter, Facebook shows me what it is seeing and what it is reading from my site. If anything looks wrong, I can adjust my meta tags and see, based on what the URL Linter sees, what I need to fix.

There is a bug at the time I write this where Facebook appears to be reading traditional title and description tags over the data I pass to my Open Graph Protocol meta tags. In these cases, the URL Linter shows that it's reading the Open Graph Protocol tags, but when users share your site on Facebook, Facebook reads the traditional title and description tags. You can get around this by removing your title and description tags completely (blank values won't cut it), and relying on the Open Graph Protocol tags. The other option is to just rely on the traditional title and description tags. I share this just in case it happens to you.

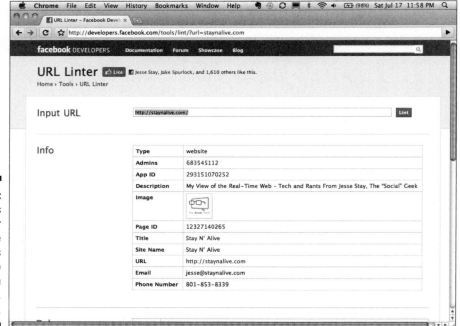

Figure 14-2: Facebook's URL Linter shows the data it is able to extract from StayNAlive. com.

Creating Test Accounts

I suppose as long as you're building a Facebook application, you're going to want to have some test accounts set up. With these accounts, you can test the application without worrying about friends seeing that testing or without worrying about anything going wrong that could affect your personal Facebook account. The problem is that Facebook, through policy, won't allow people to create fake accounts. It wants every profile on its network to be real and authentic, and it will suspend accounts that violate this rule. So how do you test your application?

Facebook frowns big-time on fake accounts! Always be sure that if you need an account to test with, you identify it as a test account. If you ever use a fake name or create a fake profile, if Facebook catches you (which it often does), your account *will* be suspended!

There are currently two ways to set up test accounts on Facebook. Both have their own environments and restrictions. The first is the old way, and probably will go away soon. The second is a more automated way that requires a little programming knowledge to get set up. It's well worth it though, as you can create bulk accounts, relationships between those accounts, and more to set up a true test environment. I recommend getting to know the second approach.

First approach: Manually creating test accounts

The first solution lies in an exception to the rule, where Facebook has laid out a method of identifying certain user accounts as "fake" and for development testing. These accounts cannot be seen by normal user accounts and vice versa. This enables you to test your application without other friends potentially seeing what you're testing. Here's how you set up a manual test account:

1. **Create a new Facebook account, and populate it with dummy data for your test account.**

   Remember your login credentials!

2. **Go to your real account's profile URL (you may need to log out and log back in to get this, or you can search for it in Facebook).**

   Request to be friends with your real account from your test account.

3. **Log out and then log back in as your real Facebook account.**

4. **Accept the friend request you just made from the test account.**

5. **Go to** `http://facebook.com/developers`, **authorize the application if you haven't already, and go to your application (I go through the setup process in Chapter 2).**

6. **In your application settings, under Developers on the main page, type in the name of your new test account and press Enter after it has been highlighted.**

   Your new test account is now a developer of your application! Now you need to identify it as a test account.

7. **Log out of your real account, and log in to the test account.**

8. **While logged in to your test account, visit** `www.facebook.com/developers/become_test_account.php`.

   You are prompted to confirm that you are sure. Accept, and now your account is identified as a test account on the Facebook Platform Developer Test Accounts Network. You may now test your application in confidence. (See Figure 14-3.)

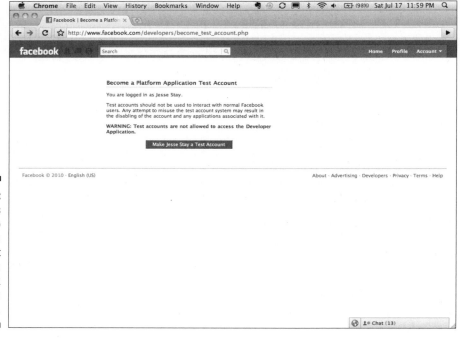

Figure 14-3:
Facebook's prompt to become a test account when you use the link shown in Step 8.

In the manual test account example, when you identify a Facebook account as a test account, Facebook identifies this by adding your account to the Facebook Platform Developer Test Accounts Network (yeah, long name, I know). This is what distinguishes your manually generated test accounts from the normal accounts. That's basically the only difference for manually generated test accounts. If you ever make a mistake, or need to turn a test account into a normal account, just go to your Network Settings page for that account and remove the network affiliation.

Manually generated test accounts generally can't see real accounts and real accounts generally can't see these manually generated test accounts. There is no expiration on manually generated test accounts (note that isn't the case for the second approach of automated test accounts), so be sure to set up your own test environment and rely on those test accounts to test your application as often as you like. With these manually generated test accounts, you can have a great environment to test your applications in without worry of others seeing the activity.

Keep in mind that the above differences and restrictions are applicable to manually generated test accounts only! For automated test accounts, which I talk about next, there are a few more restrictions and differences that I share.

Applications have to be created by real Facebook accounts. If you created the application with your manually generated test account, after you identify it as a test account, you will no longer be able to administer the application or access the Developer application from that test account. Make sure that you always have a real Facebook account as a developer of the application. If you do this, you don't necessarily have to use the application from that real account, but this way, you can still administer and edit the application settings after you turn the account you'll be testing with into a test account.

Second approach: Creating automated test accounts

If you're going to create a test environment, this is the approach you should be using. As I mentioned, the first approach I describe will likely eventually go away (I shared it so you know it's possible, especially since Facebook has removed its own documentation for the process). Automated test accounts allow you to create, with simple code or tools like Curl, multiple test accounts that are all related to each other. With automated test accounts, you can truly test your applications in a test environment completely separated from your real Facebook environment.

You can actually use simple Graph API requests to create your test accounts. Like all Graph API calls, you can use GET, POST, and even DELETE to accomplish the various tasks associated with testing your application with groups of users. As always, refer back to the Facebook Developer documentation to be sure that none of this has changed since I wrote this.

To create a test account, you just need to make a simple POST request to `https://graph.facebook.com/app_id/accounts/test-users`. This calls the test-users connection of the associated account's connection for your application. Of course, you would replace `app_id` with the ID of your application taken from your application settings. You also need to pass the following settings to your POST request:

✔ `installed`: This is a true or false value intended to indicate whether you want the test user you create to have already authorized the application. It defaults to `true`.

✔ `permissions`: This is a comma-separated list of the permissions you want this user to have granted your application. You might want to create different users with different permission levels just to be sure that your app operates in different permission settings. You can find out all about the various permissions that are available in Chapters 8 and 9.

✔ `oauth_token`: This is the application token I show you how to get in Chapters 8 and 9. You do not need a user token to access this — just the one granted to your app (which hopefully you wrote down or stored somewhere). This is just the token of the app used to create the user. It does not need to be the same token used for the application ID in the URL. The application ID in the URL is just the application that this user is authorizing.

I'll create a simple test account using the method I shared previously. You can either write your own code to do this in a script somewhere, or you can just use plain old Curl to create your test accounts. For this exercise, I use Curl. Type the following into your terminal (assuming that you've installed Curl as I explain in Chapter 10):

```
curl -F 'installed=true' -F 'permissions=read_stream' -F 'oauth_token=OAUTH_
          TOKEN_GOES_HERE' https://graph.facebook.com/APP_ID_GOES_HERE/
          accounts/test-users
```

You'll get back a response from Facebook that looks like this:

```
{"id":"100002096155790",
"access_token":"8665218278|2.j6GKAkeebcty33i9gkbEfw__.3600.1298628000-
          100002096155790|Mqm2h8hyat26fp_fw0FLQAzQHv8",
"login_url":"https:\/\/www.facebook.com\/platform\/test_account_login.php?user_
          id=100002096155790&n=g6REBZHeq2rnw8E"}
```

The returned values include the following information:

- ✔ id: This is the ID for your test account. Use this in future requests to build friend relationships, test retrieving information about your user, and so on.

- ✔ access_token: This is the access token for your user. Keep in mind that it was given the same permissions that you told it to grant previously.

- ✔ login_url: If you ever want to log in as your user on the Facebook.com Web site, you can use this URL to log in to the Facebook interface as your user. This can be helpful to interact with your application as the test user.

You can only add 100 test accounts per application. If you ever exceed this number, you'll receive an error code 2900 from Facebook stating that you've created too many users. It looks like this:

```
Error code: 2900 (Too many test accounts)
```

Assigning a test user to another application

You can also assign your test user to another application if you don't want to bother creating a new user. This user might already have all the friend relationships you need to test your app properly, so you don't need to re-create all of that. To assign a user to another application, you just need to append the following parameters to your previous POST request:

- ✔ uid: This is the user ID of the account that you're trying to reassign.

- ✔ owner_access_token: This is the application access token of the application that created the user. Note that you still need to pass an oauth_token parameter for the new application's access token.

The application ID passed to the URL should be the new application ID you are transferring the user to. The oauth_token parameter should reflect the application token for the new application. Here's how your Curl statement would look:

```
curl -F 'installed=true' -F 'permissions=read_stream' -F 'uid=100002096155790' -F
        'owner_access_token=ORIGINAL_OAUTH_TOKEN' -F 'oauth_token=OAUTH_
        TOKEN_GOES_HERE' https://graph.facebook.com/APP_ID_GOES_HERE/
        accounts/test-users
```

As you can see, the creation and assign calls are similar.

Getting the list of test accounts for your application

This is the easiest part. Getting a list of all the test accounts available to your application is simply a matter of sending a GET request to your previous URL (`https://graph.facebook.com/YOUR_APP_ID/accounts/test-users?oauth_token=OAUTH_TOKEN_FOR_GIVEN_APP`).

Note that, in contrast to the creation of test accounts, the retrieval of test accounts must be done with the `oauth_token` being the `oauth_token` that has authorization to access these accounts on behalf of the specified application ID. Therefore, you can't try to get the test accounts from an application that you don't own. You can, however, create test accounts that have authorized an application you don't own.

To try retrieval of a user, paste the following into your browser, replacing the appropriate fields with your own application ID and `oauth_token` for that application:

```
https://graph.facebook.com/YOUR_APP_ID/accounts/test-users?oauth_token=OAUTH_
            TOKEN_FOR_GIVEN_APP
```

Your browser should return something that looks like this:

```
{
   "data": [
      {
         "id": "100002096155790",
         "access_token": "8665218278|2.24eqHA_7onzIGjsXjYNLNQ__.3600.1298631600-
               100002096155790|I1C0jIsGgwCWW71_1GZ_B8FkLB8",
         "login_url": "https://www.facebook.com/platform/test_account_login.
               php?user_id=100002096155790&n=g6REBZHeq2rnw8E"
      }
   ]
}
```

You could have multiple objects in the `data` array, so be sure to iterate through if you're doing this in your own code.

Friending your test accounts

Now that you know how to create and access your test accounts, create friendships between these accounts. This is important because you often want to see how your application renders a user with lots of friends (again, with a maximum of 100 users per application).

The method that you use to create friendships between your test accounts is interesting because it implements something not heavily documented. Basically, you're automating the friending process. To do this, you have to

1. Send a friend request from test user 1 to test user 2.

2. Send a friend request from test user 2 to test user 1.

Approaching it in this manner basically accepts the friend request that test user 1 sent in the first step. To send a friend request, send a POST call to

```
https://graph.facebook.com/TEST_USER_ID_1/friends/TEST_USER_ID_2
```

Then, to accept the request, just repeat that process but interchange TEST_USER_ID_1 with TEST_USER_ID_2 (remember to switch TEST_USER_ID with your users' actual user IDs):

```
https://graph.facebook.com/TEST_USER_ID_2/friends/TEST_USER_ID_1
```

Here's how you would do it in a Curl statement. For the first request:

```
curl -F 'oauth_token=8665218278|2.j6GKAkeebcty33i9gkbEfw__.3600.1298628000-
         100002096155790|Mqm2h8hyat26fp_fw0FLQAzQHv8' https://graph.
         facebook.com/100002096155790/friends/100002080705788
```

Note that the oauth_token I use (required) is the access_token returned for the first user in the friend request. Now you need to accept that friend request. Just do the opposite, passing in the access_token returned for the second user this time in the oauth_token field:

```
curl -F 'oauth_token=8665218278|2.FNPiJZv7HWc59VUP1i141g__.3600.1298631600-
         100002080705788|PDHOhjsJg9ipKH5qRh8v-EtbmKo' https://graph.
         facebook.com/100002080705788/friends/100002096155790
```

If both examples were successful, you should get a true response back from Facebook. Also, be sure to replace the oauth_token and user id values with your own, because my examples will probably be expired IDs by the time you try this.

You can do this as many times as you want, and you can even write your own scripts to do this, so this should allow you to create many friends for each of your users.

Deleting test accounts

You can also delete test accounts, and this is easier than everything else. To delete a test user (note this only works on test users), just send a DELETE request to

```
https://graph.facebook.com/TEST_USER_ID
```

Your DELETE request will need an `oauth_token` that has permission to delete the user (the application `oauth_token` that created the user). Here's the Curl request:

```
curl -X DELETE -F 'oauth_token=APPLICATION_OAUTH_TOKEN' https://graph.facebook.
          com/100002096155790
```

If your request was successful, Facebook should return `true`.

Test account restrictions

Keep in mind a few restrictions as you create, update, and manipulate your test accounts. Remember that these apply to automated test accounts, not the manual test accounts I listed previously. According to Facebook (`http://developers.facebook.com/docs/test_users`):

- ✔ "Test users can interact with other test users only and not with real users on site."

- ✔ "Test users cannot fan a public Page or create public content on them like writing on a Page's wall. A test user can, however, view and interact with the application tab on the Page if they are associated with that app."

- ✔ "They can be accessed and used by any developer of the associated application."

- ✔ "They only have test privileges on the associated application. This implies that they can use the app in live mode or sandbox mode but cannot edit any technical settings or access insights for that application."

- ✔ "A test user is always a test user and cannot be converted to a normal user account."

That's it! Now you can create your own unit tests, scripts, and tools to create your own test users. With the things I list, you can now build a fully integrated test environment for your applications using Graph API.

Part V

Turning Your Facebook Application into a Legitimate Business

The 5th Wave   By Rich Tennant

"Yeah, this should help me with my business. It's got 'FelonHelper,' 'Goonicator,' 'You Outlookin' at Me?'..."

In this part . . .

With more than 600 million active users, half of those logging in at least once daily, it's no wonder that businesses are flocking to Facebook to build word about their brands, increase page views, and improve sales. Facebook is a force to be reckoned with!

You probably bought this book because you have intentions of building a business, or perhaps you just want to improve your existing business plan. You can't do this fully effectively through Facebook without knowing at least some of the principles that I explore in this book.

Earlier chapters describe some of the benefits that Facebook can provide for your business. However, I can still show you a few things that I think will make Facebook even more valuable for your business. That's what the chapters in Part V are all about.

Chapter 15

Helping Your Business and Brand Benefit from Facebook

*F*acebook is chock-full of information about users and the relationships between those users. That relationship graph is called "the social graph," and your goal is to place your brand or message on top of all the connections that link the nodes (users) within that graph.

Because you can retrieve so much information about users on Facebook and their friends, you can customize a message that works perfectly for those users so that they are more likely to share your message with their friends. In this chapter, I show you basic tools that, without any code, you can use to insert your branding and message into the hands, and the relationships, of your users. These tools use the user data that users share about themselves, at an anonymous level, and allow you to both track more information about who is visiting your Web site and target your message to them in ways that you've never been able.

Measuring Data with Facebook Insights

You can start a business strategy by knowing a little about the users who visit your site. Many sites use analytics tools like Google Analytics or Omniture to track visitor data. The problem with these tools is that they rely on an IP address to learn who is visiting. An IP address is quite useful at tracking things around the Web, but the problem is that each of those IP addresses is just a "thing." IP addresses don't equate to people or real personalities — they equate to computers.

An IP address is just a numerical ID, like 64.54.82.182, that's assigned to each computer on the Internet. The servers that provide Web sites have IP addresses, and the users' computers, which consume those Web sites, also have IP addresses.

That's where Facebook Insights, shown in Figure 15-1, comes in. Facebook provides its own analytics tool for any Webmaster or page owner, called Insights, that you can integrate into your Web site to understand more about what specific demographics are visiting your Web site.

Insights provides a slew of information about your visitors who are Facebook users. Facebook takes the data provided by the users visiting your Web site or Facebook Page and combines it into a cumulative set of information about the users who are visiting your site. Information, at least as I write this, available by Insights includes the following:

- **Gender:** Facebook shows the number of each gender, separated by age range, who are visiting your Web site or page in a given set of time.

- **Age:** Facebook takes the genders and splits them into age ranges so that you can tell the percentage of people in a given age range who are visiting your Web site. This is data that no IP address can provide!

- **Country:** While you can get this from an IP address, this is the country that a person has listed he lives in, not where he currently is when he visits your Web site. Therefore, this can be very useful information in understanding the nationality of your visitors.

- **Language:** This is the native language of the individuals who are visiting your Web site or page. This depends on the locale that they set in Facebook and the language that they are reading Facebook in. Therefore, this is likely to be the most native language for that individual. (Don't be surprised if you see some "English (Pirate)" in there!)

- **Likes:** This is the number of people who have liked your Web site or page in a given period of time. It requires you to have a Like button on your Web site. This also shows the percent that it increased or decreased compared to the previous equivalent time period.

    In addition to this number, Facebook also provides a line graph, showing the number of daily likes during that time period. This can be useful to tell whether something you did on your Web site increased the number of likes. Remember, for every like, you can send those users a message through the Admin Page link next to your Like buttons!

- **City:** These are the cities that the users who are visiting your Web site or page have listed they are living in. This is not the city that they are in when they actually visit your site.

✔ **Shares:** These are the number of times that your Web site has been shared by users on Facebook over the specified time frame. Also included is the amount of change (up or down) since the previous, equivalent time period. Facebook also includes a line graph over the period of time that shows the number of shares per day.

In the section, "Discovering what people are sharing on your site," I show you how you can tell who is sharing your Web site (at least among your friends).

✔ **Feedback per share:** These are the number of comments, on average, per share that show up on your Web site. This is important, because the more comments and likes those shares have, the more likely they are to appear in their friends' news feeds. You want this number to be as high as possible, so be sure to track this and the response of this number, based on things you change on your Web site.

All this information is available for each individual page on your Web site. Facebook includes a list of the top liked and shared pages on your Web site, so you can click through to those, or you can enter the URL to any page on your Web site in the field provided and see the stats for that page.

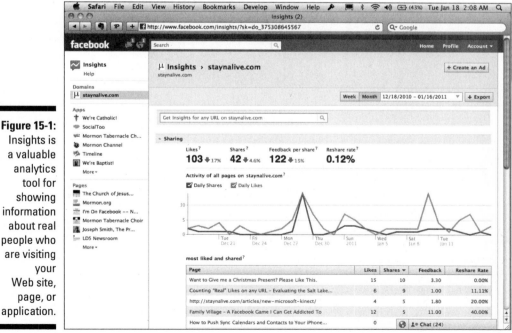

Figure 15-1: Insights is a valuable analytics tool for showing information about real people who are visiting your Web site, page, or application.

Accessing Facebook Insights for your site

You can access Facebook Insights for your site in two ways. The first, and probably simplest, way to access Insights for your domain or page is to go to `http://facebook.com/insights` (see Figure 15-2). If your Web site or page is set up, it will appear here. Just click the site or page name to get to the Insights for that domain or page.

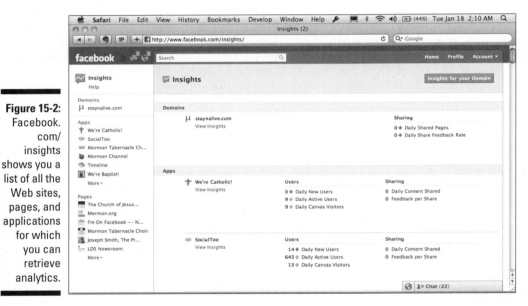

Figure 15-2: Facebook.com/insights shows you a list of all the Web sites, pages, and applications for which you can retrieve analytics.

The other way is to go to the actual page on `Facebook.com` and click See All under the Insights box on the left. (See Figure 15-3.) This is a little tricky if you're on your Web site — you need to add a Like button to do this for your Web site. After you've added a Like button, be sure that the `fb:admins` `<meta>` tag in your HTML head is set to point to your Facebook ID as one of the IDs, and an Admin Page link will appear next to the like.

Figure 15-3: Clicking See All under Insights on any page will also reveal the Insights Dashboard.

You can use one other trick to get to the page for your Web site where you can send updates to fans, look at the insights, and so on. To do so, just go to the Graph API page for your domain. You do this by typing **https://graph. facebook.com/http://*path-to-domain***, replacing *path-to-domain* with your own path. On that page, you can get the Facebook ID for your Web site. After you have that, go to `http://facebook.com/profile.php?id=...` and replace the `...` with the new ID that you found. You'll be taken straight to the admin page for your Web site or URL through this method. (See Figure 15-4.)

Figure 15-4:
Having an
fb:admins
meta tag
on your site
enables the
Admin Page
link that
looks like
this.

> Like StayNAlive.com on Facebook!:   Jesse Stay, Debbie Rivera and 1,316 others like
> this. Unlike · Admin Page

Three types of Facebook insights are available to you:

✔ **Websites:** This is for any URL on the Web that has integrated Open Graph Protocol.

✔ **Pages:** This is for any Facebook page that you set up on `Facebook.com` (like `http://facebook.com/dummiesbook`).

✔ **Applications:** This is for your applications. You can get valuable analytics and information about each of your applications and the way your users are using your application through these insights.

The layout of Web site insights

When you are on the Insights page for your Web site, you see two sections: Sharing and Demographics. Then, above those sections is a place to enter any URL from your site and get insights for that page. Above that is a place to select a date range for the insights that you are trying to gather. (See Figure 15-5.)

Sharing

In this section, you see three rows:

✔ **Period difference:** This is the positive or negative change (in percentage) from the preceding period. You'll see the difference in Likes, Shares, Feedback per Share, and Reshare Rate. You can see the number of each, followed by the positive or negative change (next to a green arrow denoting an increase and a red arrow denoting a decrease).

✔ **Line graph for daily shares and daily likes:** This is just a line graph that shows, over time, the number of likes each day and the number of shares each day. Daily Shares is shown in blue, and Daily Likes is shown in green.

✔ **Most liked and shared URLs on your site:** This is just a list, sorted by the most likes and the most shares, of the most popular URLs on your site.

Demographics

The Demographics section shows all the different types of people who are visiting your site, using Facebook data to determine that information. Demographics is split into two sections:

✔ **Gender and age:** This is a double bar graph, the upper bars representing the percent of females in each age group. The age groups are 13–17, 18–24, 25–34, 35–44, 45–54, and 55+. The bottom bars represent the percent of males in each of those age ranges. Next to the Male and Female labels is the total percentage of males versus females visiting your site. This is great data for determining how you should be targeting your content. If your site has been visited by mostly female visitors, you should target your content more toward females.

✔ **Location data:** This is split into three columns: Countries, Cities, and Language. Each respective column is sorted by the total number of Facebook users from those locations or languages who have visited your Web site.

The layout of page insights

Page insights are split into two different sections, and you can click into each to get more data from each section. The two sections are Users and Interactions. (See Figure 15-6.)

Users

This is a lot like the earlier "Sharing" section. With it, you get the number of New Likes, Lifetime Likes, and Monthly Active Users, followed by a line graph that includes Daily Active Users, Weekly Active Users, and Monthly Active Users. These numbers are just the average number of people who actively visit your page and interact with it. Facebook defines this as "1-day, 7-day, and 30-day counts of users who have engaged with your page, viewed your page, or consumed content generated by your page."

Figure 15-5:
The Insights page for a Web site.

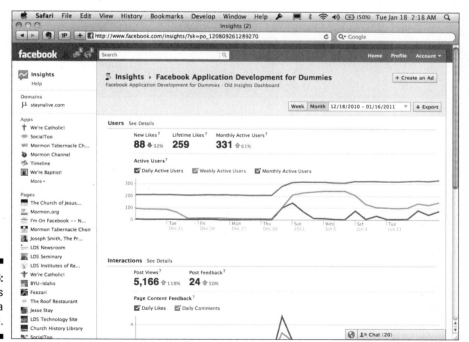

Figure 15-6:
The Insights page for a page.

When you click See Details for the Users section, you're taken to a completely new page, this one with nine rows of information. (See Figure 15-7.) Those rows include:

- ✓ **Change over time:** This is the same as the preceding page, with the New Likes, Lifetime Likes, and Monthly Active Users increase or decrease over time.

- ✓ **Active Users:** This is the same line graph as the preceding page.

- ✓ **Daily Active Users Breakdown:** Here's where it gets interesting. You can pull up the total unique page views, total post viewers, total people who liked a post, total people who commented on a post, and total daily wall posts broken down by day in a nice line graph.

- ✓ **New Likes:** These are the total new likes and unlikes for the page, on a day-to-day basis for the page, broken down into a line graph.

- ✓ **Gender and Age:** This is just like the Gender and Age graph for the previous Web site insights. It shows you how many male and female visitors came to your page, broken down by age.

- ✓ **Location:** This is the same as the data for your Web site insights — it breaks down your users by country, city, and language.

- ✓ **Page Views:** This is a line graph of the total page views, by day, as well as the total unique page views, by day (measured by logged-in users).

- ✓ **Breakdown of Page Views:** This is how you can tell which tabs your visitors are seeing on your page, as well as how many sources outside Facebook.com are leading users to your Facebook page.

- ✓ **Media Consumption:** This breaks down, by day, the total number of different types of media that your visitors to your page are consuming. Media types include video, audio, and photos.

Interactions

Interactions are just the types of interactions that occur on your page. These are usually likes and comments. This section includes the total increase or decrease in views over the period selected (and total overall for the period), as well as the total increase or decrease in comments or likes per post over the given time period (and total overall for the period). It also includes a bar graph that shows the total likes and comments on a day-to-day basis over the given time period. (See Figure 15-8.)

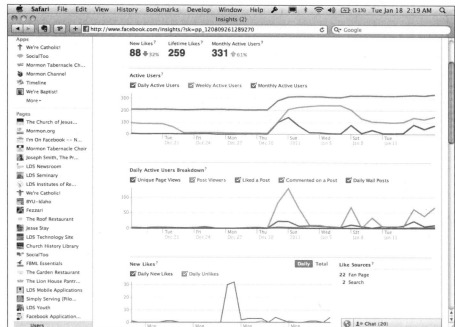

Figure 15-7:
The Users
detail page
for page
insights.

Clicking See Details reveals a new page for interactions. The resulting page includes the following information:

- ✓ **Total Views and Feedback, and gain/loss:** This is the total views and feedback for the page (comments and likes) over the given time period, including how much gain or loss occurred over the previous similar time period.

- ✓ **Daily Story Feedback:** This is a line graph showing likes, comments, and unsubscribes for each individual post you post on your page, on a day-to-day basis.

- ✓ **Data for the most popular posts:** This is a list, sorted by the highest percentage of feedback (likes and comments per view) of the posts that you share during the given time period. Use this to get an idea of what types of posts can be most interesting for your fans, and how you can improve your posts to have more clicks, likes, and comments.

- ✓ **Daily Page Activity:** This is the activity, on a day-to-day basis, that shows mentions, posts to your page, reviews on the page, wall posts, and videos shared on the page. This is cumulative, including posts by your fans.

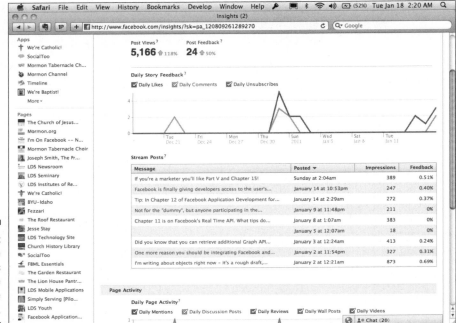

Figure 15-8:
The
Interactions
detail page
for page
insights.

The layout of application insights

Application insights are built to provide additional details that you need about an application. Information like installs (people authorizing your app), Canvas response time, and amount of content shared from your app are all things that you discover from these types of insights. (See Figure 15-9.)

The application insights provide three sections of information:

- ✔ **Users:** Information about your application's users, installs, and how many people are accessing your application regularly.

- ✔ **Sharing:** Information about how many people are sharing your application.

- ✔ **Performance:** Information about how well your application is responding. This is important to ensure that users aren't getting errors from Facebook, and that your servers are responding in a timely manner.

Users

The Users section has information about total New Installs, Lifetime Installed Users, and Monthly Active Users over the given time frame (minus the Lifetime number), along with positive or negative change from the previous equivalent time period. In addition, you're given a line graph of day-to-day Daily Active Users, Weekly Active Users, and Monthly Active Users. (See Figure 15-10.)

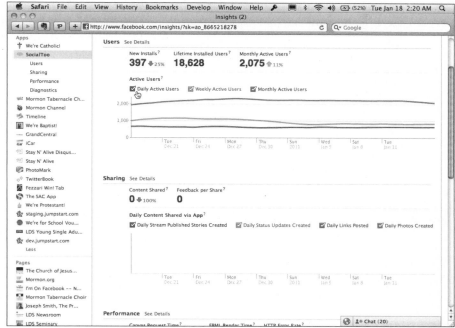

Clicking the See Details link reveals one of the most detailed insights pages so far. Some of the highlights of that page include the following:

✔ **Daily New Users:** These are the total new users who have authenticated with your application, as well as the total number of uninstalls, meaning the users who have deauthorized your application from accessing their data on Facebook. You want as few uninstalls as possible and as many installs as possible.

✔ **Demographic Information:** These are your typical bar graphs that show percentages of male or female users, and country, city, and language information about the people who are using your application.

✔ **Daily Canvas Visitors:** You can get a count of page views, and visitors to your Canvas Pages, on a day-to-day basis from this line graph.

✔ **Referral Sources:** You have two columns for this. One shows you where users are coming from within Facebook, and the other shows you where users are coming from outside of Facebook. Keep a good eye on this section — it could be a great way to know when someone else is talking about you so that you can respond appropriately.

✔ **Daily New Bookmarks:** When users bookmark your application, your application appears prominently in the left column. You want users to be bookmarking your application within Facebook, so the higher the number, the better you will do. This is just a graph that shows the daily number of new and deleted bookmarks on a day-to-day basis.

✔ **Daily Permissions Granted:** This may be an interesting chart for you. It shows the types and total permissions per day that users are granting your application.

✔ **Daily Blocks:** These are the total number of people who are blocking and unblocking your application on a day-to-day basis. People can block your application by clicking the *x* next to your application in their news feed and selecting Hide All By, or opting to ignore in their application requests page.

TIP

If you want to see your graph a little better, mouse over the upper-right corner of any graph in Insights. A drop-down box appears, allowing you to print, but more importantly, make your graph full-screen. Clicking the icon to make your graph full-screen expands the graph, making it easier to see large data sets that are bunched closely together, such as Daily Permissions Granted.

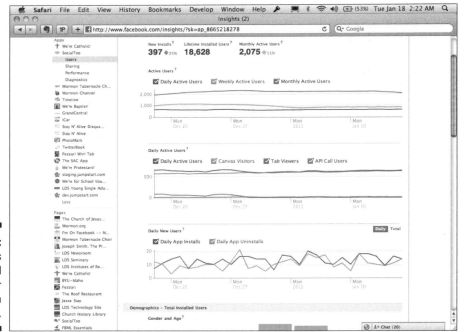

Figure 15-10:
The Users detail page for application insights.

Sharing

The Sharing section is all about the things that users have shared through your application. This would be done through a POST to the feed, or by doing a `stream.publish FB.ui` call in JavaScript. This section shows you how many items have been shared, as well as how many people are commenting and liking those shares. If this section has low numbers, you need to prompt your users to share more to their walls within your application. (See Figure 15-11.)

Clicking See Details reveals a new page, with additional information on it. This page tells you the following information:

- ✓ **Number of people hiding your shares:** This section tells you, on a per-day basis, how many people are clicking the *x* in the upper-right corner of the posts shared, opting to hide your shares.

- ✓ **Number of requests, and how many are accepting them or ignoring them:** This tells you how successful your application requests are on the requests page when your users send requests or invitations to other users.

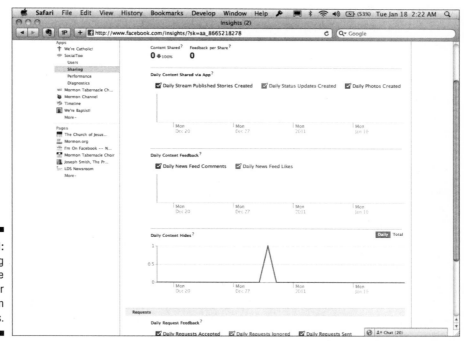

Figure 15-11:
The Sharing detail page for application insights.

Performance

Performance is all about how well your application is responding. If you have problems in this section, you probably have a problem on your server or you need to optimize your code so that it responds faster. The main section here includes Canvas Request Time, FBML Render Time, and the HTTP error rate for your application. (See Figure 15-12.) Clicking See Details takes you to a page that includes the following:

✔ **Daily Canvas Views:** These are the number of times that people are visiting your Canvas Pages on Facebook.com.

✔ **Average Canvas Request Time:** This is the average time it takes for your Canvas Pages on Facebook.com to load. You want this to be fast; otherwise, users will see errors.

✔ **Average FBML Render Time:** This is the average amount of time that it takes FBML to render in your application.

✔ **HTTP Errors Returned:** These are the number of HTTP errors (server errors) that your application is returning. If you're seeing a lot of these, you may want to contact your administrator or check your server error logs for errors and get them fixed.

✔ **Daily API Calls:** These are the total API calls per day. Keep in mind that each API call is bandwidth consumed, costing you money. Therefore, you want this number to be as low as possible.

✔ **Average API Request Time:** This is the average amount of time that it takes to make an API call. This can be because Facebook is being slow or because your servers are taking too long sending and receiving the request to and from Facebook.

✔ **API Errors Returned:** These are the number of errors returned by Facebook's API. If you're sending a request the wrong way, you'll see a lot of these, for instance.

Facebook will not tell you who has installed your application. You will have a number (Lifetime Installed Users), but that is it. For this reason, be sure to add each new user to your database when she first authorizes your application. You can also set it so that when she deauthorizes your application, it notifies a URL that you set in your application settings, and you can remove her from your database (or set a flag disabling her) at that point. This will allow you to accurately track who is currently using your application or Web site at any given time.

Facebook seems to add to Insights over time. When you read this, you might have access to even more information. I suggest looking at your insights to see what information is available to you right now.

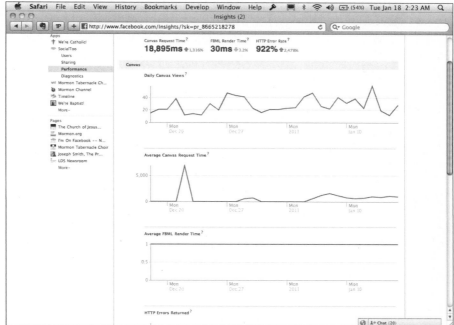

Figure 15-12:
The
Performance
detail
page for
application
insights.

Integrating Facebook Insights into your site

You can add Insights to your Web site pretty easily. Insights is automatically added to every Facebook Page and application, so if you set up a page or application, you shouldn't have to do anything else to get Insights going.

For a Web site, just follow these steps:

1. **Go to** `http://facebook.com/insights` **and click the big green Insights for Your Domain button in the upper-right corner. (See Figure 15-13.)**

   Keep in mind that this may change by the time you read this — you may have to search a bit if you can't find it. Ask on this book's Facebook Page if you can't find it anywhere.

2. **In the resulting dialog pop-over, in the Domain field, enter your Web site's address.**

3. **Next to Link With, select the option that says [You] next to it, probably with your name in it.**

   A `<meta>` tag will appear below, specifying the `fb:admins` for the site.

4. **Copy the tag that appears, and put it between the `<head>` tags in your Web site. (See Figure 15-14.)**

5. **After the `<meta>` tag is in place, click the Check Domain button.**

   If all is well, your Web site will be added under the Domains section, and you can begin collecting insights for your domain. If you previously had a Like button or other similar social plugin on your Web site, you probably already have data there — go check and see!

TIP

Your Web site may also have an application associated with it. This is required if your Web site is going to be making any Graph API calls, for instance. It is not required if all you need to do is add social plugins. If you've created an application for your Web site, you will have Insights in both the Application section and the Web Site section. You will also still need to set up Insights for your Web site, even if you already have an application set up for it.

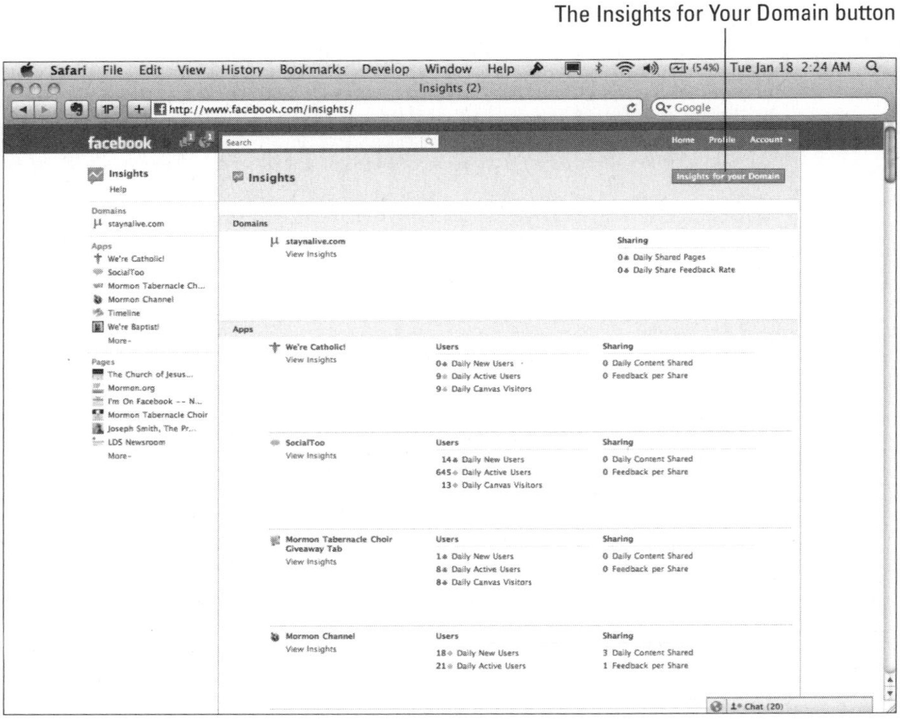

The Insights for Your Domain button

Figure 15-13:
Click the
Insights
for Your
Domain
button.

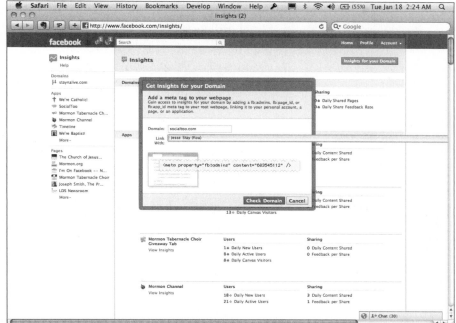

Figure 15-14: Filling in the appropriate information should produce a <meta> tag that you can copy and paste into your Web site.

Discovering What People Are Sharing on Your Site

This is a fun little trick I like to try with my clients. It works especially well if you have a lot of friends, but you will probably see some results as well if you pick a popular site.

Using social plugins, you can find out who, among your friends, has been sharing content from your Web site to Facebook. (See Figure 15-15.) Follow these steps:

1. **Go to** `developers.facebook.com/plugins`.

   This is the main page for all the available social plugins.

2. **Click the Activity Feed plugin, and type any domain in the Domain field.**

   Try a more popular domain, like `Google.com`, to start.

3. **Click any other field to force the preview on the right to refresh.**

   See all the friends who show up?

4. **In the Height field, increase the size to about 700.**

5. **Click any other field, and the preview on the right will refresh again.**

   You can now see a lot more of your friends' activity.

If you ever try to show a boss, client, or friend the power of integrating Facebook into a Web site, be sure to show this to that person. This shows that, whether these friends like it or not, people are out there sharing their content, and they could be doing something with that.

Figure 15-15:
Here are all my friends who have shared items on Amazon.com.

Targeting Your Creations with Facebook Advertising

Before Facebook, you had basically one option in advertising on the Web: ads that show up when you search, put there by advertisers that specify given keywords hoping that they'll catch people in the act of searching for something relevant to what they're advertising. (See Figure 15-16.) Advertising companies got really smart at this, and they could produce ads that were quite relevant to the things you were searching for. However, no matter how they tried, they were still guessing, based on your IP address, search activity, and other factors, what ads you might most be interested in. They still didn't know who you were.

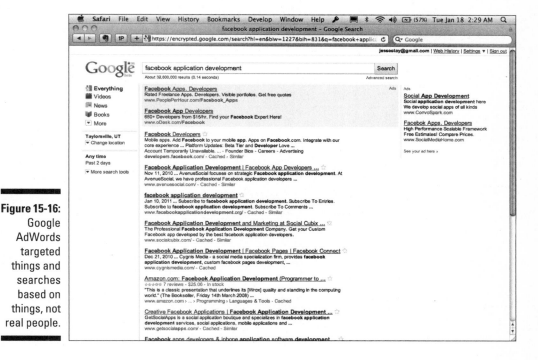

Figure 15-16:
Google AdWords targeted things and searches based on things, not real people.

When Facebook began making inroads, it brought in a new element to advertising, something perhaps made popular before by Myspace. Facebook made it possible for advertisers to target individuals based on the types of things available in the user's profile, not just an IP address. This way, ads were being generated based on real information about the individual, which the individual was providing — the person's interests, age, gender, and location could all go into a targeted ad.

Facebook took this one step further. Facebook made it possible for any user of its Web site to create ads that target specific demographics and interests of users.

To show you the power of this, I take you through just the motions of creating an ad. This can be useful not only in advertising but also in knowing who the audience might be for your application or Web site on Facebook. Try this:

1. **Go to** `facebook.com/ads`**.**

   This is where you should always go to create your ads.

2. **Click the Create an Ad button.**

   When I wrote this, it was a big, green button in the upper-right corner of the page. (See Figure 15-17.)

The Create an Ad button

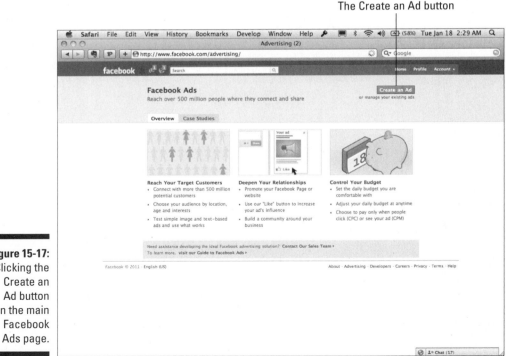

Figure 15-17:
Clicking the
Create an
Ad button
on the main
Facebook
Ads page.

3. Go to the Targeting section.

On some accounts, for some reason, Facebook makes you fill out a form before you get to this section. If you don't see the option to enter a country and demographic information, fill in the information as though you were creating a fake ad. Don't worry, you won't be charged anything for doing this.

4. After you're in the Targeting section, play around with the demographics.

Facebook has had this almost as long as I can remember. You can specify all kinds of information to customize who and how many users your ad appears to. Change the age range. Change the gender. Add a like or interest. (See Figure 15-18.)

5. Look at the Estimated Reach.

Notice how that number changes with every change you make on the form? This is approximately how many people on Facebook match the criteria that you've set. Consider that your app just targets people who like *Star Wars.* Type in **Star Wars** in the Likes & Interests field, and notice how that number changes. If that number is too small, it may not be worth targeting Facebook or integrating with Facebook, but then again, a small number may be just right for your needs, and your niche may hit just that perfect number of users.

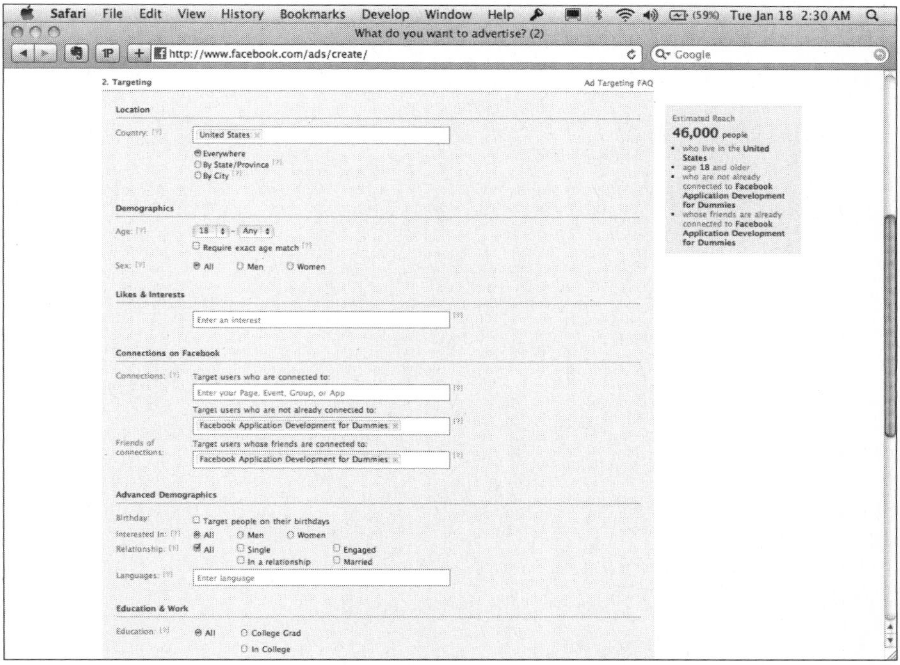

Figure 15-18: The Targeting section shows you an estimated number of people who match your demographic criteria.

As you can see, your ads can target a very finite number of users. You can get as targeted as one user or millions of users.

Try this: Target your spouse or significant other on his or her birthday by finding something that you know only he or she is interested in. Then prepare a birthday message for this person in the form of an ad. Set a high click-through rate on it to guarantee that your ad trumps the others, and then ask the person not to click it (that could get expensive!). You can thank me later.

Creating your ad

To create your ad, you need to be on the Ad Creation page (see Figure 15-19). You need to fill out the fields on this page to create your ad.

All the fields here might change, so feel free to ask on this book's Facebook Page if you have any questions about this process.

Start by filling out the form fields. At the time of this writing, you need to fill out three sections.

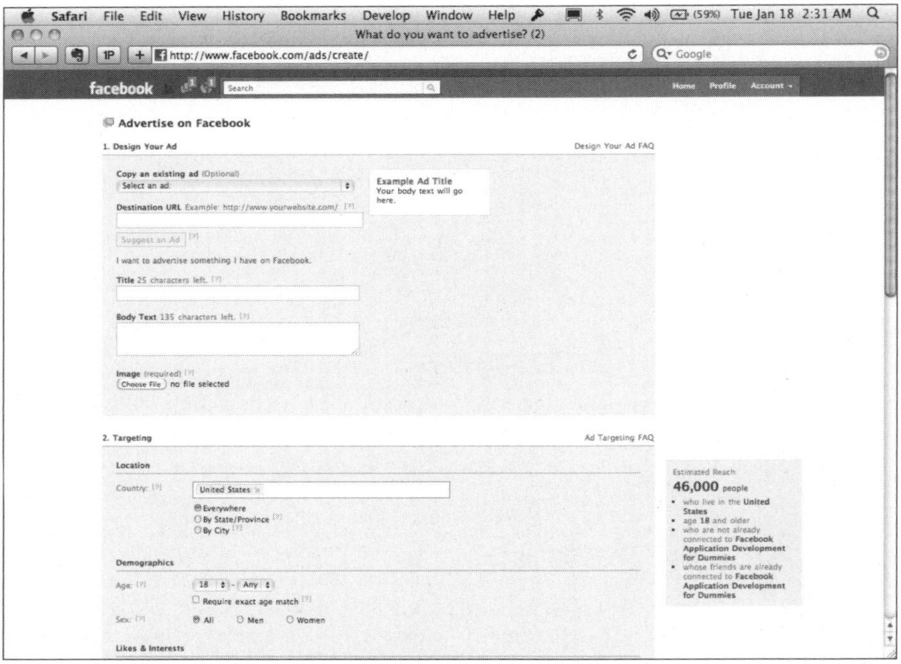

Figure 15-19:
The ad creation form.

Design your ad

Fill out the following fields in this section:

- ✔ **Copy an Existing Ad:** If you've previously created an ad, select one from this list to copy from. If it's a new idea or campaign, you can create something new by filling in the additional fields.

- ✔ **Destination URL:** This is where the ad will link. Keep in mind that Facebook users tend to prefer to stay on Facebook. You'll do better here linking to a Facebook Page that they can like, giving you a continued relationship with that individual, whom you can send future messages to.

- ✔ **Title:** This is the title of the ad. At no more than 25 characters, it appears above the body text in the ad, below the main image.

- ✔ **Body Text:** This is a 135-character description where you can sell your ad to customers.

- ✔ **Image:** This is the main image for the ad. Pick something that grabs the attention of your users or customers.

Targeting

This is one of the most powerful pieces of Facebook. All sorts of fields are available for you to fine-tune whom your ad appears to. Keep in mind that these fields have changed a few times over the life of Facebook, so they may not be exactly as I describe here:

- ✔ **Country:** You can get as specific as a state or province or even a city, and you can specify more than one location. If you're just trying to target a local deal to people in your city, remove United States, type in your city and state, and select it from the drop-down box.

- ✔ **Age:** Facebook allows users age 13 and up to join, so you can select anywhere between 13 years old and up to target your ad. If you're selling kids' toys, you may want to specify 13–18 here. If you're targeting baby boomers, adjust for the appropriate age range.

- ✔ **Sex:** You can target men, women, or both.

- ✔ **Likes & Interests:** This matches to any Facebook Page from the Interests section of the profiles on Facebook. You see a drop-down box appear as you type in the interest. If it's in that drop-down box, you can select it.

- ✔ **Target Users Who Are Connected To:** You can specify any page, event, group, or application here, and it will target users who are fans or members or users of those applicable objects.

- ✔ **Target Users Who Are Not Already Connected To:** If you want to target everyone but a specific page on Facebook (maybe you want to target just the friends of fans of *Facebook Application Development For Dummies*, but not the fans of *Facebook Application Development For Dummies*), specify that here.

- **Target Users Whose Friends Are Connected To:** This is a powerful field. If you enter **Facebook Application Development For Dummies** here, it will target all the friends of those who have clicked the Like button on this book's Facebook Page.

You can only target the friends of people who have liked pages that you administer. Facebook will not let you target the friends of your competitors, for instance.

- **Target People on Their Birthdays:** This can be a fun one if you want to get very personalized. You can specify a special deal or just a message for people interested in a specific thing or page on their birthday. Or maybe you just want to wish those who are fans of your page a happy birthday — do that here!

- **Interested In:** This can be All, Men, or Women.

- **Relationship:** Facebook provides the options All, Single, Engaged, In a Relationship, and Married.

- **Languages:** If you want to target a specific language (or more), you can specify it here. This is a great place to make versions of your ad in different languages.

- **Education:** Facebook gives you the options All, College Grad, In College, and In High School.

- **Workplaces:** I've seen this used in very creative ways. For instance, I've seen people who are looking for jobs create ads that target people at the places they're looking for work by creating ads solely targeted toward them. You can specify any company or organization here in this field.

Campaigns, pricing, and scheduling

In this section, you either want to create a new campaign or select from an existing campaign. If you click the Create a New Campaign link, you'll be given the option to specify the name of your campaign, the budget, and how much you want Facebook to spend for you per day, or over the lifetime of your ad.

After you specify a name and budget, specify what days and for how long you want your campaign to run. Do this in shorter increments to test the success of your ads and various things that make your ads successful (or not).

Finally, you can set the pricing of your ad. Facebook automatically suggests a default bid for your ad. You can go with this, or you can also choose to pay by impressions, pay by clicks, and set your own maximum bid for the ad. If you want to guarantee that your ad always appears for your audience, set the maximum bid high. If you're more on a budget, set it lower. You also want to experiment with this to ensure that you don't spend more than you need.

When you're done filling out your ad, click Place Order to start it now, or you can review what it looks like by clicking Review Ad. You might want to just see what it looks like first and review the fields that you filled out just to be sure that it is exactly what you think it should be.

Filling out a sample ad

It's time to create a real ad. I'm biased, so I have you create an ad just for this book. Follow these steps:

1. **Select the URL to link to.**

   In the Design Your Ad section, enter **http://facebook.com/dummiesbook** as the destination URL.

2. **Enter your title.**

   Next to Title, enter **Facebook Development**.

3. **Specify a body text.**

   For the body text, enter **Anyone can develop a Facebook app. Learn for yourself with Facebook Application Development For Dummies!** (Include the exclamation mark.)

4. **Upload the image.**

   If you go to `http://stay.am/dummiescover`, you can download the cover image for this book. Download that, and click the Choose File button to upload the image.

5. **Target the ad.**

   Now you need to decide who will see the ad. Because those who have liked this book's Facebook Page probably have friends who will like the book, I keep this simple. Leave all the defaults, but next to Target Users Who Are Not Already Connected To, type **Facebook Application Development For Dummies**. Then, next to Target Users Whose Friends Are Connected To, type **Facebook Application Development For**

Dummies. You need to choose a page that you own for this, because Facebook only allows you to choose friends of pages that you are an administrator of. This ensures that all the fans of the page's friends are targeted, but not the fans of the page itself. As I write this, I show approximately 46,000 users who potentially could see this. You can target this further if you like.

6. **Set your budget.**

    Click the Create a New Campaign link, and enter **Dummies Book** as your campaign name. Specify your budget. I selected $50 and then Lifetime Budget in the drop-down list. This ensures that I only spend $50 over the entire lifetime of the ads.

7. **Set a schedule for your ad.**

    Choose any time period that's convenient here. I select Pay for Clicks (CPC, the default) for the type of ad pricing and go with the default price that Facebook suggests.

8. **Click Place Order and give your payment information.**

    Enter your payment information (you can also use ad credits here if you have them), and your ad will go live! (See Figure 15-20.)

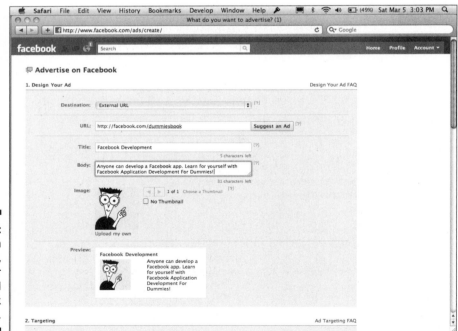

Figure 15-20: When you're done, your For Dummies ad should look like this.

Tips for good advertising on Facebook

There is no exact formula for advertising on Facebook. You have to try it out and see what works best for you. However, a few tips can guide you along the way as you create your ad campaign. Here are a few suggestions:

- ✔ **Experiment.** This is the most important thing you can do. Try different things. Try different audiences. Try different prices. Try CPM instead of CPC. Try multiple ads targeting different audiences. Keep a log, comparing your different experiments, and see which ones are the most fruitful for your campaign. It's good to set a short time limit until you hit that sweet spot for your campaign. Then choose a longer time limit and use the more successful ads in your new campaign.

- ✔ **Target your competitors' audience.** Remember, you can't explicitly target your competitors' audience. However, you can find people who have an interest that's similar to your competitors. Try to find keywords in the Interests field that match what your competitors' audience would like and target them. When you do, you can create ads that try to sway people away from your competitor and to your own Facebook Page.

- ✔ **Don't overspend.** Use experimentation to come up with a sweet spot for spending. Determine what price gets you just the number of clicks that you need to accomplish what you want, without going over. Graph your results, determine where the peak is, and go by this.

- ✔ **Do multiple ads per campaign.** Don't just stick with one generic ad. Make multiple ads, each targeting a different audience. If one audience that likes your brand likes chocolate, create an ad for chocolate lovers that points back to your Facebook Page. People are much more likely to click an ad that contains something they are interested in than an ad that is just generic for lots of different types of people. This is the power of Facebook — embrace that!

- ✔ **Use the free as much as the paid.** This is important. While creating an ad is a very easy way to get your message to a very specific audience, you may be able to be just as effective by targeting your own audience. Use your Facebook Page to create targeted posts that target specific languages and locations. Create specific posts with calls to action that people are likely to comment on and share with their friends. Build apps that allow your customers to share with their friends. You'll do much better if you can get your message in the hands of friend-to-friend communication than in direct brand-to-consumer communication. Sometimes "free" can be the most effective means of communication for you — don't jump into building ads until you're sure that they can help beyond doing all you can with free tools.

Selling Your Creations with Facebook Credits

One tool that should get more and more valuable as more users use it is a product called Facebook Credits. Credits are a currency of sorts, which Facebook sells to users to make purchases within games and applications on Facebook. As I write this, the cost is 10 cents per credit, the minimum credit purchase being 15 credits for $1.50. You can buy more credits either in the applications that use credits, or if you go into your account settings and choose Payments, you can buy them there as well. (See Figure 15-21.) Credits will get more and more popular as more applications and Web sites implement them across Facebook and the Web. Just before I wrote this, Walmart and other stores started selling Facebook Credits gift cards in stores. Facebook Credits could become as popular as PayPal and other forms of online payment, so consider applying yourself to the program. In fact, Facebook has started placing restrictions on games within Facebook, asking developers of games to use Facebook Credits as the main form of payment within their apps.

Figure 15-21:
You can add Facebook Credits in your account settings on Facebook.

Building Credits into your application

Building a payment solution into your application is as simple as calling an FB.ui dialog box call — with a few complexities you need to take care of first. To accept payments through Facebook Credits, you first set up your company and a callback script location in your application settings. I show you that in Chapter 2.

After you set up your company and your callback script location in your application settings, you need to set up some code on your server that understands how to process what Facebook sends to you. This is called your *callback script,* and it's how Facebook tells your application that it has received a payment request and when the user has paid you through Facebook Credits.

After your callback script is created and ready to process payments, you need to call FB.ui, using the pay dialog box as your method type in your JavaScript dialog box code (see the next example). The basic parameters you need to send are:

- ✔ **credits_purchase.** This defaults to False. You can enable the capability to purchase credits within your application. By sending this with a true value, it tells Facebook to make a credits_purchase request, which provides a dialog box for the user to purchase new credits.

- ✔ **order_info.** This is a value intended to identify the product you're trying to sell in some way or another. You can send the actual product name and price as a JavaScript object, or you can just pass an id string of the product you want to look up, and do some additional lookups on that ID in your database from the callback script to get the product name and price information. What's important is that your callback script has all the information it needs to return back a product name and price to Facebook when it gets called for the first time.

  When you make the pay dialog box JavaScript call, Facebook sends the order_info variable to your callback script, and you can process the information accordingly to identify your item. The structure of the order_info variable goes straight through to your callback script, so how you structure it is up to you. order_info is only required if credits_purchase is False.

- ✔ **dev_purchase_params.** This is a JSON object you can pass to Facebook that allows you to send special information with your request. For instance, sending {"shortcut":"offer"} initiates an offer dialog box, allowing the users to select from a list of Facebook-provided offers they can pick from (like, "try out Netflix for 125 free credits"). I don't go into too much detail on this parameter here, but know you can go to http://developers.facebook.com/docs/creditsapi to find out more about the additional things you can do with dev_purchase_params.

At the time of this writing, Credits work only in iFrame apps on `Facebook.com`. Be sure you load your app in a tab, or an `apps.facebook.com` Canvas Page!

Here I show you a simple `pay` prompt. This is just the tip of the iceberg as to what you can do with credits, so refer to `http://developers.facebook.com/docs/creditsapi` to find out more. Here's how you initiate a simple `pay` dialog box in JavaScript:

```html
<html>
    <body>
        <h1>Order Something</h1>
        <div id="fb-root"></div>
        <script src="http://connect.facebook.net/en_US/all.js"></script>
        <a href="#" onclick="order_something(); return false;">Order
            something...</a>

        <script>
        FB.init({appId: 170669746307500, status: true, cookie: true});

        function order_something() {

                var order_info = 'PRODUCT_ID';

                // calling the API ...
                FB.ui({
                        method: 'pay',
                        order_info: order_info,
                        purchase_type: 'item'
                },
                function(data) {
                        console.debug(data);
                });


        }
        </script>
    </body>
</html>
```

Calling the dialog box sends the product ID to Facebook in the `order_info` variable. Facebook then calls your callback script, which should contain in the POST variables passed to it a variable called `method`. In that variable, look for the `payments_get_items` value.

Then you need to parse the signed request (remember, you're in a Canvas Page or iFrame environment). The entire signed request, parsed, will look like this:

```
array (
  'algorithm' => 'HMAC-SHA256',
  'credits' =>
  array (
    'buyer' => 683545112,
    'receiver' => 683545112,
    'order_id' => 187499737951937,
    'order_info' => '"someID12345"',
    'test_mode' => 1,
  ),
  'expires' => 1299657600,
  'issued_at' => 1299570372,
  'oauth_token' => 'OAUTH_TOKEN',
  'user' =>
  array (
    'country' => 'us',
    'locale' => 'en_US',
    'age' =>
    array (
      'min' => 21,
    ),
  ),
  'user_id' => '683545112',
)
```

Within your parsed signed request will be the credits variable with an associative array of values. In that array, look for the get_info key, which should have the product ID you include in your dialog box call. You should now read that, look it up in your database, and return the title, description, price, product URL, and image URL as the variables item_title, item_description, price, product_url, and image_url. Here's what that code looks like in PHP:

```php
<?php
$app_id = '170669746307500';
$secret = 'APP_SECRET_GOES_HERE';

include_once 'facebook.php';

$facebook = new Facebook(array(
        'appId'         => $app_id,
        'secret'        => $secret,
));

$data = array('content' => array());
$request = $facebook->getSignedRequest();

if ($request == null) {
  // handle an unauthenticated request here
```

```
        }

        $payload = $request['credits'];

        // retrieve all params passed in
        $func = $_REQUEST['method'];
        // this is Facebook's id for the order
        $order_id = $payload['order_id'];

        if ($func == 'payments_status_update') {
                // When the user clicks "Buy Something", this block runs
                if ($payload['status'] == 'placed') {
                        $data['content']['status'] = 'settled';
                }
                $data['content']['order_id'] = $order_id;
        } else if ($func == 'payments_get_items') {
                // When the user clicks your link, "Order something..." this block runs

                // remove escape characters
                $order_info = stripcslashes($payload['order_info']);
                $item = json_decode($order_info, true);

                // do some database look up here on the id that was just passed in
                        order_info
                // run something like SELECT * FROM table WHERE product_id='$item';
                // now assume we have the data from the database.
                $item = array();
                $item['price'] = 2;
                $item['product_url'] = 'http://facebook.com/dummies';
                $item['image_url'] = 'http://platform.ak.fbcdn.net/www/app_full_
                        proxy.php?app=4949752878&v=1&size=o&cksum=e2e790b093bc8
                        716dfa3702d900dea87&src=http%3A%2F%2Fecx.images-amazon.
                        com%2Fimages%2FI%2F51nymRpKBqL._SL500_AA300_.jpg';
                $item['title'] = 'Something';
                $item['description'] = 'This something is worth everything to
                        everybody!';
                $data['content'] = array($item);
        }

        // this just tells Facebook to what method we were just responding
        $data['method'] = $func;

        // send data back to Facebook
        echo json_encode($data);
```

Be sure to replace *APP_SECRET_GOES_HERE* with the secret key from your application settings. The data Facebook will obtain from this code (that you return in a JSON-encoded format) will look like:

```
array (
  'content' =>
  array (
    0 =>
    array (
      'price' => 2,
      'product_url' => 'http://facebook.com/dummies',
      'image_url' => 'http://platform.ak.fbcdn.net/www/app_full_proxy.php?app=49
              49752878&v=1&size=o&cksum=e2e790b093bc8716dfa3702d900dea87&src=htt
              p%3A%2F%2Fecx.images-amazon.com%2Fimages%2FI%2F51nymRpKBqL._SL500_
              AA300_.jpg',
      'title' => 'Something',
      'description' => 'This something is worth everything to everybody!',
    ),
  ),
  'method' => 'payments_get_items',
)
```

When Facebook gets back this JSON structure from your callback script, the user will be prompted to confirm the payment with a pop-up dialog box (in this example, it will be through a Buy Something button). When she does, this sets off a series of requests back and forth to your callback script (via the PHP code). In the first request, a request will be sent to your callback script, sending the value in the `method` POST variable, `payments_status_update`. Then, in the signed request is a variable called `status`, which should have the value, `placed`. You also get the order number and information about the item. Assuming that is the case, your callback script should return back a structure that looks like this (in the body of the response):

```
array (
  'content' =>
  array (
    'status' => 'settled',
    'order_id' => 187499737951937,
  ),
  'method' => 'payments_status_update',
)
```

In your callback script you verify that the status is "placed," which Facebook sent to you. If so, you know the order was placed, and you can update your database of the transaction, and send back Facebook another response with the `status=settled` variable, as I show in the preceding example. If all went well, Facebook will respond back saying it got your request with another `payments_status_update` request, and a status of `settled`. You then respond with a blank status like this:

```
array (
  'content' =>
  array (
    'order_id' => 187499737951937,
  ),
  'method' => 'payments_status_update',
)
```

There are many more things you can do with Credits, and I don't cover everything here since it is such a new feature to Facebook and is likely to change as you read this. Check out the Developer documentation on Facebook for up-to-date information.

 Be sure you add your Facebook user ID to the list of test users in your application settings for Credits. By doing so, you can work in test mode, and your credits account will never be charged. If you don't, each test you make will charge real credits from your account, which could get expensive for you!

Understanding the rules surrounding Credits

As with anything you do on Facebook Platform, it's important you find out the rules. Where transactions involving money are involved, it's important you understand what you can and can't do with Credits as you plan your application. You can get all the details and rules surrounding Facebook Credits at `http://developers.facebook.com/policy/credits/`. Here are the highlights:

- ✔ **Credits must be the sole method of payment within games on Facebook Platform.** This is not the case for traditional applications. This doesn't mean you can't use some other form of virtual currency in your game. It just means to pay for that virtual currency, you must use credits to do it.

- ✔ **Credits cannot be used in exchange for tangible goods or items.** Credits are for purchasing virtual goods only.

- ✔ **You can't trade credits with any third party.** Don't allow your users to trade their credits with other people.

- ✔ **You can't exchange credits for cash.** Don't offer any users the option to "cash out" their credits. Once they're credits, they're always credits.

Getting People to Your Stores and Venues with Facebook Places

You know a few ways that you can access information about Facebook's location service, Places, via Graph API (see Chapter 10). You can pull information about single places. You can search for check-ins that users have visited. You can search for detailed information about who has checked in to a specific place.

You don't, however, have to use Graph API to get value from Places. The following sections discuss a few things that you can do with Places that will get more customers into your venues and stores and get them purchasing every time they visit. Not only that, but their friends will also see their check-ins and hopefully be enticed to come visit as well.

Using Facebook Deals

Facebook Deals is an advertising service that, like Facebook ads, allows business owners to target ads to specific individuals. The difference is that Deals allows business owners to target people at the actual location where they are. As I write this, Deals is also free, although Facebook says this is a limited-time offer.

Currently, anyone on a mobile phone can either open the Facebook app or visit `touch.facebook.com` and check in to the location where he or she is. Deals allows businesses to target "deals," or advertisements, to people who check in to specific locations, or to be aware of deals if they are checking in at a location nearby where the deal is taking place. This is a great way to entice customers to come into your store during a given time frame. Not only that, but as customers check in on Facebook, their friends see it too. (See Figure 15-22.)

Figure 15-22:
A Facebook deal on your mobile phone looks like this (image taken from Facebook's Developer blog).

As I write this, you can create four types of deals:

- ✔ **Individual deals:** These are deals targeted toward individual customers. These deals can be things like giving a percent off of a product for the first 100 customers who check in to your store, maybe giving something away free, or just offering a coupon to customers as they check in on Facebook.

- ✔ **Friend deals:** These deals require the customer to tag a certain number of friends in the customer checks in. The end goal is to get customers to bring their friends with them to the store. You can offer a coupon or something free if your customers tag five friends on Facebook when they check in on Facebook. This has three benefits:

   - The user has motivation to check in on Facebook.

   - The user's friends who are tagged get a notification that they were tagged, and those friends' friends also see the tag.

   - All the customer's friends see that the customer just checked in to your venue. See the power of deals yet?

- ✔ **Loyalty deals:** Think of this as the loyalty card of Facebook. You can set this so that on every x number of times the customer visits and checks in to your store or venue on Facebook, he gets a "check" on his virtual Facebook loyalty card for your store. After he reaches your limit, you offer him the deal. This gets the customer coming back more than once, and because his check-in is seen by his friends, each time he checks in, his friends also see that he likes your store.

- ✔ **Charity deals:** If you just want to give back, you can use this to say, "For every check-in, we'll donate x amount of dollars to this charity." You can set a maximum amount that you're willing to donate. This encourages customers and visitors of your locations to check in just because it's the right thing to do, and they can feel good about doing it as a result.

The process of setting up a deal is as follows:

1. **Go to the Places page for the place that users will check in.**

   A good way to find this is to check in to the place when you're there (via your mobile phone), look at your Facebook profile, and click the link to the place in your Facebook profile.

   You can use a trick to find the Places page for your venue. Remember the Search API in Chapter 12? You can use the Places search type to search for places that match your venue. So, if I'm looking for a Borders location, I type **https://graph.facebook.com/search?q=books&type= place&center=37.76,-122.427&distance=1000&oauth_token=ACCESS_ TOKEN** into my browser, and it will return all venue pages for Borders. Pick the right one, and continue on to the next step.

2. **Claim your Facebook Page.**

   If you haven't already, click the Is This Your Business link in the lower-left corner of the page. You need to fill out a form asking you to prove that you own the place (it usually requires you to either have an e-mail address denoting that you work at the place or provide official papers). After you fill out the form, you have to wait for Facebook to approve your request. This usually takes about a week, and you get an e-mail when it's done. So sit back, relax, and go build a Facebook application while you wait!

3. **Click Edit Page.**

   After you claim the place, you should see an Edit Page link in the left column. Click that link, and you're taken to the Page Administration screen, which should look a lot like a traditional Facebook Page Administration area (because your place is actually now a Facebook Page).

4. **Click the Deals link on the left.**

   This is the last option at the bottom as I write this. You're taken to a screen that tells you about Facebook Deals.

5. **Click Create a Deal for This Page on the ensuing page.**

   Now you should be at the form to create your deal!

6. **Pick your deal type, and create the deal. (See Figure 15-23.)**

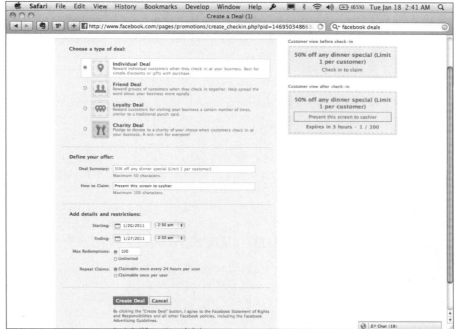

Figure 15-23: The Create a Deal page looks like this (available from your page settings).

Now you just need to fill out the form. Choose which of the deals I list previously that you want to go with, select the wording that you want to appear in your deal when customers check in, and select the time frame in which you want it to appear. You're done!

At the moment, Facebook Deals is so easy and so convenient (and as I write this, free!) that I don't know why every store isn't currently using Deals.

Building strategies for using Places with Graph API

Deals is certainly one of the easiest (and at least for the time being, cheapest) ways for you to leverage Facebook Places to gain customers and get them talking about your brand and business with their friends. You can use some other great strategies that involve a little integration with Facebook Graph API to make happen. Here are some ideas:

✔ **Track check-ins.** You can use Graph API to know who has been checking in to your location. You may want to set an e-mail notification to go out every time a new customer checks in. Maybe your CEO wants to send that person a thank you message (but be careful — you don't want to sound spammy!).

✔ **Point out your loyal customers.** You could build an application as a tab on your Facebook Page or another Web site that shows thumbnail images of the customers who are checking in, and maybe what they are saying. Show this prominently in your store or venue. If you have multiple stores or locations, show all of them so that customers know that other people are checking in elsewhere.

✔ **Give deals on your Facebook page to people who check in.** Because you know that a user has previously checked in to your venue, you can provide special discounts on your Facebook Page, or even your Web site, by tracking his Facebook ID and checking to see whether he has checked in before. Then, present him with a special deal — maybe he gets a discount if he buys something in your online store or has ever stopped in to one of your physical locations.

Tips for using Facebook Places

Your main goal for Facebook Places should be to get people checking in on Facebook so that as many of their friends as possible see that they're visiting your location. Here are a few ideas you can implement:

✔ **Show people where they can check in.** Place stickers, signs, and other markers where you want people to check in. A university actually tried this, placing signs around campus to get students to check in around campus. The school's hope was that students' younger friends would see the check-ins and want to attend the university. Students loved it and checked in often. You can do the same types of things with your stores and locations to spread word about your location.

✔ **Use Deals.** Make sure that you're using Facebook Deals to entice users to check in with discounts, promotions, and loyalty rewards.

✔ **Use Graph API.** Find ways to use check-ins from your customers on your company Web site so that you reward those visiting your Web site who have also visited your physical locations.

✔ **Announce it over the loudspeaker.** Have a loudspeaker? Spread the word over the loudspeaker every so often that customers can check in on Facebook. Or maybe you're a band hosting a concert — ask your fans to check in on Facebook.

✔ **Put it on your receipts.** Make sure that your Facebook Page for the venue is on the receipts, and that your receipts encourage customers to check in. Remember that every check-in starts a conversation. Every conversation lets others on Facebook know they were there, and those friends will also come and visit your location.

Chapter 16

Preparing for the Worst: What Every Facebook Application Developer Should Know

*F*acebook application development is a whirlwind journey of ups and downs, API changes, and platform terms updates. If you haven't experienced this yet, it will hit you eventually. If your software development relies heavily on other systems' APIs, you are always subject to their whim: When Facebook goes down, you are affected; when Twitter slows down, you are affected; when a Terms of Service agreement changes, you are affected.

It's important to prepare for this journey and to know what you're getting into. Facebook development certainly has a lot of value, but it is not without its trials as well!

Hopefully, by sharing with you some of the travails I've been you won't repeat my mistakes. In this chapter, I discuss the things you should be prepared for as you start this journey. I think you'll find that these tips not only help prepare you to work with Facebook, but also to work with any social network — these same problems arise on every social network I have worked on.

Preparing for API Changes

It's inevitable. You build "the next big thing" and launch it with much fanfare, only to find out that Facebook is deprecating the very feature that your new app is based on.

I've had this happen time and time again. In fact, the last book I wrote is completely (well, mostly) deprecated as I write this. These things happen, and you have to be prepared. This is one reason why you see phrases like "at the time of this writing," "as I write this," or "refer to the Developer documentation" so frequently in this book. The fact is that Facebook's API is a living, breathing interface that will very likely change significantly at some point over the lifetime of your application or Web site.

You have to embrace change to get along with Facebook's API. This isn't hard to do — almost always it changes for the better.

Building an idea that withstands change

The first thing you need to do as you're preparing for such a volatile API is to prepare an idea that can withstand change. Building an idea around something that only Facebook provides isn't always the best approach, because if Facebook were to ever remove that functionality (which often happens), your entire product will be irrelevant. Your idea should be one that stands, regardless of change.

I like to use the example of a LEGO set when I explain how businesses building on "the building block Web" should consider their ideas. If you think about it, each LEGO set, as a whole, is an entirely different product (such as a car, a spaceship, a skyscraper).

However, when you examine these products piece by piece, you find that they are just made of LEGO blocks. Each set consists of the same LEGOs that other sets use. They're just different colors and combinations put together differently.

Some LEGO sets embrace other brands' ideas: *Star Wars* sets, *Harry Potter* sets, and so on. Some sets use chips to control motors. You can even buy LEGO magnets that you can put on your fridge.

Although each of these sets may use ideas and technologies from other brands and vendors, they all rely on one essential ingredient — the common LEGO block. Although you can combine LEGO blocks to integrate with things that others have made, LEGO has built upon its core to keep its brand and company going.

You need to make your own core. You have to come up with your own core building blocks that, no matter what you combine them with, never go away if one of those things you've combined them with goes away. That's how you deal with change on Facebook Platform. Always be thinking, "If this API or piece of the API goes away, can my business still exist?"

Designing and constructing for change

After you have your core idea and you're ready to integrate with Facebook, it is time to start designing and building your application. You should plan your servers, your code base, and more so that if Facebook's API changes (and again, it will), you will need to do minimal shuffling on your end to deal with the changes.

Ideally, you should only need to change one section of code if a specific piece of Facebook's API changes. If it goes away completely, you should only need to remove the references to that code.

Refer back to the LEGO example. I recently purchased a LEGO spaceship kit containing thousands of LEGO blocks. LEGO's instructions for the kit came in sections. First, you build the cockpit, then the perpendicular wings, then additional pieces of the wings, and so on. Each instruction module helped me create a piece, which, when assembled to the other modules, made the bigger spaceship.

Imagine that I lost one of the pieces or that LEGO went out of stock for that particular piece. Because I built the spaceship in modules, I can just replace the wing with a new one, one I created myself, and it still looks like a spaceship when I'm done.

You can do the same with your code. Here are some code-oriented ways of building in modules:

- ✔ **Use object-oriented code.** If you don't understand object-oriented code and you're building an app or Web site meant to last a lifetime, take the time to understand it. By placing your API-specific code in methods and objects, you can reduce the number of things that you have to change when specific methods go away. When a method is deleted, just kill the class or the accessor method within the class and all references to it, and you're on your way. You aren't stuck dealing with the repeated removal of similar code through the rest of your application.

- ✔ **Use an MVC or similar methodology.** MVC stands for *model view controller*. It's a way of writing your code so that it is divided by function: All the stuff that deals with the user is in one area of the code, which is separated from all the stuff that deals with business logic, which is separated from the areas that handle the database. I recommend getting a book on the topic if you aren't aware of this yet and you want to get into serious software development, because it can seriously eliminate a lot of headaches when Facebook removes or changes things in its API. For instance, if you just need to remove something from the parts of your Web site that the user sees, you have to edit just one section of code.

✔ **Put your Facebook-specific methods in their own individual modules (the more the better).** A number-one rule in computer programming is to never duplicate code. You always want to create methods that you can access when you need access to that same block of code later. You should find ways to make every call to Facebook and the common things you do with those calls in their own methods, and in their own sections within your code. Maybe they're all in one class, with multiple methods in that class. Whatever it is, you want to make it as easy as possible to change as little as possible if and when Facebook makes changes to its API.

Following Facebook's road map

Facebook is actually one of the better platforms at letting its users know when changes are about to occur. Facebook has a six-month road-map section on its Developers Web site that you can always (and should always) reference to see what's changing in the next month. This way, you're never caught by surprise.

To find out what is happening for the next six months on Facebook, go to `developers.facebook.com/roadmap`. If it isn't there, do a search for "road map" on the Facebook Developers Web site, and you're sure to find it.

Facebook makes all its planned updates to the API available on this page.

Enabling updates with migrations

Facebook usually allows developers to determine when changes go live on Facebook Platform. To do this, go to your application settings and click the Advanced section. You'll see a section on that page called Migrations.

In this section, you see features and bug fixes that Facebook has updated that you can enable and disable. You can choose when you want them to go live for you. Select the Enabled check box next to a feature, and it will go live for your application. At that point, you can test it and make sure that your application still works with those new changes.

Each of these features has an expiration date on which the new feature will become enabled by default. Always check when this happens so that you can prepare!

Dealing with Rate Limits

If an API change doesn't get you, rate limits will. You'll probably only notice them if you're getting or sending any sort of traffic to or from Facebook.

A *rate limit* is a cap on the number of requests you can make to an API within a given time frame. For instance, depending on how often your app hits Facebook's API, they might keep you from accessing it very often. As I write this, Facebook returns a 600-transactions-per-600-seconds limit. You can't post any more than 600 requests in a 600-second time frame, per this rate limit. Rate limits keep developers from causing too much strain on Facebook's servers, and avoid spam among the Facebook user base. Unfortunately, Facebook doesn't publish the exact method of how it limits API calls. This is something you have to detect by reading the errors Facebook sends back to your application and handling them accordingly. You may also want to do some logging, so you can log the various rate limits your application may be hitting in order to adapt your application to meet those limits.

It is best to set some hard limits on your own and ensure that you don't exceed those limits. You could set it so that your application only posts to Facebook Platform 500 times in every 600-second time frame, for instance. It will be up to you to detect how often your application makes API calls and throttle that to a reasonable limit you have set for yourself. Also, finding ways, such as storing the data so that you don't have to make API calls in the future, can also help you avoid rate limiting.

Rules! Rules! Rules! — Knowing Facebook's Terms of Service

Understanding Facebook's platform policy can take you a long way in planning your application. Facebook has many rules that you must understand and follow to prevent yourself from getting banned in the future. While legal jargon can appear scary at times, spend some time reading through Facebook Platform's policy and trying to understand it.

The following sections describe some current highlights of Facebook Platform's policy. To read these, go to Facebook's Developer Web site and click Platform Policies.

Understanding Facebook's principles

Facebook lists a few guiding principles by which all developers should abide. These principles center around having a good experience for your users and building trust with them, extending Facebook's core experience into your own. According to Facebook, these principles are as follows:

- ✔ **"Create a great user experience":** By this, Facebook means that you should build engaging applications that give users a degree of choice and control and that help users share opinions and content.

- ✔ **"Be trustworthy":** By this, Facebook means that you should respect users' privacy and that you should not spam, mislead, confuse, or surprise users. In other words, you should be respectful and encourage genuine, open communication with users.

I think it's safe to say that if you generally follow these core principles in your Web site or application, you'll be fine. More than anything, treat your users with respect and be smart.

Understanding core policies

You should adhere to some basic policies when writing your application or Web site. You can find more than these, but they are probably the most important ones:

- ✔ **Use Facebook's login functionality.** You never want to collect a user's username and password directly, and you especially don't want to store them in a database! You should use the OAuth methods and JavaScript options available to initiate a login for the user. (See Chapter 9 if you want to read more about this.)

- ✔ **Contact Facebook if your application is going to be *really* big.** This won't apply to most of you, but if you think that you're going to have tens of millions or more users, or exceed incredible pieces of bandwidth, you should contact Facebook before doing so. If you exceed reasonable limits, Facebook has a right to ban you from continuing. This actually happened to both Apple and Google due to the traffic they were putting on Facebook's servers.

- ✔ **If you log users in to Facebook, you must also give them an option to log out.** Some JavaScript methods make this very simple. I suggest that you use them and include a link on your site that allows users to log out of Facebook if they've logged in through your application.

- ✔ **Request only the data that you need.** You may be tempted to gather as many permissions as possible to be prepared should you need them down the road. You may also be tempted to gather a little more information about the user in case you need to use it in a future product update. Don't. Not only does that break trust between you and your users, but Facebook could also ban you if you get caught. Most importantly, your conversion rates will be affected, as applications that request all the permissions they need up front often see a higher rate of turn away than applications that only ask for permissions as they need them.

✔ **Keep any data that you store up to date.** In Chapter 11, I cover Facebook's real-time API, which was written mostly for this purpose. You should use Facebook's real-time API as much as you can so that you always keep your stored data as current as possible.

✔ **Get consent from the user if you're going to do anything but display his or her data.** If you're going to send the user an e-mail or if you're going to use his information later to compare his friends, make sure that you get the user's permission. It's always better to be safe than sorry, and it builds a much better experience for your users. Even though it may be tempting to do this behind the user's back, you'll find building that user's trust can be a much more rewarding and long-term opportunity for growth than breaking that trust would be.

✔ **Don't give any of your users' Facebook information to an ad network.** This should be obvious, but some are tempted. You should never give, either directly or indirectly (via URL parameters, for example), your users' information taken from Facebook to an ad provider.

✔ **Don't sell data gathered from Facebook.** This too should be obvious. This data isn't your data! Don't sell what isn't yours. The data that you collect should be for your Web site or application only.

✔ **For applications, you can't display alcohol-related content (to those outside the age limit), gambling content, hateful content, nudity, gratuitous violence, or anything illegal.** Facebook wants to keep Facebook.com clean and safe for all ages. Therefore, it has policies in place to ensure that's the case. No matter what your morals, you should always be respectful, especially when providing data on Facebook.com, to users of all ages and types.

✔ **Don't incentivize users to message their friends in any way (post to the wall, send invites, chat, and so on).** Don't say, "We'll give you $5 if you refer five friends to this app or Web site." You can't offer points for publishing something to a user's wall. The main exception to some of this is for promotions on pages. Read the policies for Facebook Pages and promotions carefully to find out what you can and can't do on a Facebook Page.

✔ **Don't prepopulate things like the user comment area of the** stream. publish **form (unless the user told you what to put there).** All fields provided by Facebook intended for a user to enter should not be prepopulated by you unless the user has told you what to put there. This includes the status box on the stream.publish dialog box, notes titles and content, photo captions, video captions, and more.

✔ **Don't publish stream stories without the user's permission.** Always make sure that the user has given you permission to publish to the stream (her news feed or wall). Not only do users hate getting surprised, but doing so could also get your application banned as well. Always either prompt the user beforehand (using the `stream.publish` dialog box is a good approach) or provide a check box of some sort that gives her this option to choose.

✔ **Only publish stream stories to one person's wall at a time.** Facebook doesn't want you to spam a whole bunch of users at once.

✔ **Don't abuse the user's @facebook.com e-mail address.** Facebook intends for `Facebook.com` e-mail addresses to be for user-to-user communication only. Sending updates to a user's `Facebook.com` e-mail address from an application or Web site could get your application banned. In addition, Facebook could prohibit your IP address from sending e-mail to Facebook as well.

✔ **Don't use Facebook trademarks.** This is simple legal policy — don't use the terms *Facebook, Face, FB,* or any other trademark of Facebook in your application or on your Web site unless it's been provided by Facebook. You also can't include these in the name of your applications.

The best advice I can offer beyond this is to read the terms, stay updated to the terms, and be wise! Don't be stupid and you'll be fine.

Improving Site Performance

Performance is an important thing to pay attention to in order to be successful on Facebook Platform. Especially for Canvas applications, it's important that your server responds quickly to provide the most efficient user experience. If your server takes too long, users get impatient and leave your application. In addition, too many API calls can result in rate-limit errors from Facebook (errors saying you made too many API calls), and can cost you extra money in server bandwidth.

A simple `Facebook.com` iFrame application must take a lot of steps before returning data to the user. It has to request the data from your application. Your application has to return that data to the user. Your application also has to make API calls in the meantime to get information about the user. This can all increase the amount of time it takes to return something to the user.

You can do some basic things to prevent this from happening. Especially, you want to provide as smooth an experience as possible for your users so that they aren't kept waiting. The longer users wait, the less money and the less traffic you see. Here are my suggestions for optimizing your code to provide the most efficient experience for the user on Facebook, while saving you in server bandwidth costs:

✔ **Combine API calls.** This is one of the most effective things you can do to your application to improve performance. Facebook hasn't yet ported this capability to Graph API. However, you can currently use Facebook's `batch.run` and `fql.multiquery` methods to send multiple API calls in one single transaction. Use these as much as you can. This significantly helps reduce the number of transaction limit errors you see, and it should lower your bandwidth costs at the same time.

There actually is one way of combining API calls with Graph API — sort of. You can do this by batching IDs of objects, by passing the `ids` parameter to your Graph API request. For example, `https://graph.facebook.com?ids=dummiesbook,jessestay,stay` would return just the `dummiesbook`, `jessestay`, and `stay` objects. That said, this is still only a limited form of batching calls, and you'll get much more out of using the `batch.run` and `fql.multiquery` calls.

✔ **Use FQL.** FQL can also help you to combine multiple API calls into a single one. Use subqueries where needed, and only retrieve the columns of data you need. This reduces the amount of data returned and speeds the entire request time.

✔ **Optimize your own code.** The cheapest thing that you can do is to make sure that you have optimized your own code. Look at how you're storing data in memory. Could you reduce the amount of memory used? Can you reduce the number of disk writes and reads? Can you bring more data from disk and put it into memory, which is faster to read? Can you compress some of the data? Will a hash table make retrieval faster for you? What is the fastest algorithm to solve the problem at hand? You should be asking yourself all of these questions as you write your code.

✔ **Optimize your hardware.** This tends to be the more expensive option, but sometimes throwing some additional memory or processor speed into a server can significantly speed your response times. If you can afford it, this is the easiest approach, but it only scales so far.

✔ **Optimize your database.** Sometimes just configuring your database a little differently can speed things up significantly. Make sure that you're optimizing your database so that your reads and writes to the database are as fast as possible. Look at the memory limits. Do they need to be increased? Decreased? Check out your queries and make sure that you're using the most optimized queries for your database as possible. Most importantly, make sure your tables are indexed, and the columns you're searching on are indexed columns.

✔ **Use an IP address instead of a domain for your callbacks.** This is one trick that I've found really helps a lot. DNS servers (the servers that map your domain to an IP address) add additional steps to the query process and can slow down the time it takes to load your app. If you specify an IP address for your callback URLs, Facebook tends to return data faster because it can find your servers faster. Try that and see whether it reduces response times.

✔ **Cache user data.** The best option is to bypass Facebook entirely! When you get user data, store it in your database and then start to access it from your own servers. (The caching software Memcached is also a great way to do this.) Always update your cache when you have new user updates, via Facebook's real-time API!

- **Preload your queries.** In your application settings, you can set some predefined FQL queries that you can reference later. This way, Facebook prepares these queries ahead of time, and Facebook isn't stuck reloading that data every time. Reference Facebook's performance guide in the Developer documentation for more information on how to do this.

- **Use JavaScript.** By using JavaScript, you can skip your servers entirely, ensuring that you're only using Facebook's servers to return data to the user. Try to use JavaScript as much as possible to offload some of your servers' load onto the user's browser, and not your servers.

- **Use** `api-read.facebook.com`. Facebook has a read-only API that you can use. To use it, replace the URL you're making the API calls to with `http://api-read.facebook.com`. You might have to get into your library of choice's files to edit this. Doing so will significantly speed response times, because this URL is fine-tuned not to worry about write requests.

If you can master these things, you'll be a pro at providing a very smooth and fast experience for your users. After all, the faster you can return this data, the more likely users are to stay and buy things from you!

Facebook has provided a great resource for learning about how to increase the performance of your app in its Developer documentation. You can get there by searching for "performance" in the Developer documentation, or by going to `https://developers.facebook.com/docs/guides/performance/`.

Part VI
The Part of Tens

The 5th Wave   By Rich Tennant

"Has the old media been delivered yet?"

In this part . . .

This may be the easiest, and perhaps most fun part of the book! The Part of Tens is a series of chapters in which I cover lists of ten items I think you might be interested in. In this section, you get to see all the miscellaneous stuff I couldn't fit into the other chapters.

In this Part, I show you some of my favorite companies and applications implementing Facebook API, and I show you what makes them successful. I explain how to get help, and define what resources are available to you.

Chapter 17

Ten Successful Facebook Applications

* *

Facebook is a force to be reckoned with. Integrating Facebook into your Web site or application keeps users on it longer, improves page views, increases engagement, and spreads knowledge about your brand.

Don't just take my word for it, though. As I've been working with various organizations over the years, I've come across many Web sites and applications that have seen success by integrating Facebook Platform into their marketing strategy. I've tried to take note of my favorites as I've gone along.

In this chapter, I compile ten different companies, Web sites, and applications that have found success by joining forces with Facebook. Some of these are current or former clients of mine, and with others, I just really like what they've done.

Each of these has implemented Facebook in a unique way and has seen successful results because of it. In this chapter, I highlight what makes these companies unique, discuss how they use Facebook, and describe how combining with Facebook proved successful.

JibJab

JibJab (www.jibjab.com), the animated, personalized electronic greeting card company, integrated the predecessor to Graph API, Facebook Connect, in 2008. (See Figure 17-1.) Before that implementation, JibJab used e-mail to share videos with its users, and encouraged users to share those videos via e-mail with their friends.

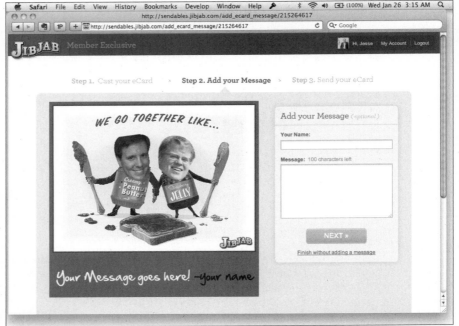

Figure 17-1:
JibJab uses
photos
from your
Facebook
friends list
to populate
its videos.

This was the way it was done prior to 2008. It was called viral marketing. Smart programmers would write their apps, Web sites, and programs so that users could share those experiences with their friends. At the time, the only way to do that was (a) through the phone, (b) by mail, or (c) by e-mail. E-mail was obviously the most effective means of spreading a message about an app or a Web site, so users were encouraged to type in e-mail addresses of those they knew might be interested in what the developer wanted to share.

JibJab got this, and it mastered it, so much so that JibJab's video "This Land" went viral soon after it was released as word spread about its videos.

However, one flaw existed with this approach — it was slow. Incredibly slow. To build a list worthy of getting word out quickly took time. Users were required to remember the e-mail addresses of their friends, and they were required to reenter those addresses each time they wanted to share a video.

When Facebook Connect came out, all this changed. In just five months, JibJab achieved the following:

✔ Gained 1.5 million new users — it took JibJab eight years to accomplish in the era of e-mail (five years of that only getting to 130,000)

✔ Got six to ten times the number of clicks back to the site from shared media on Facebook

✔ Reduced the friction of sign-on, making it easier for users to get in and start using the Web site

JibJab realized that by leveraging Facebook, it was able to connect with users and bring those users' friends back to the site. JibJab found that 80 percent of those users used Facebook Connect, meaning a broad reach and potential to spread its message even further.

JibJab uses Facebook in a number of ways:

✔ **JibJab leverages profile data, specifically images from your Facebook profile, so that users don't have to find and re-upload images from their hard drive to include in videos.** As a result, users are able to seamlessly create personalized videos with pictures of them, their family, and their friends to get people talking and sharing with each other.

✔ **JibJab provides an easy means for sharing to a user's Facebook profile.** Using `stream.publish`, JibJab is able to easily allow users to share their videos with friends on their Facebook news feed to let them view and reshare videos with their close friends and family. Each video links back to `JibJab.com`, where users can create more videos and share those with their friends as well.

✔ **JibJab integrates Like buttons on every video.** This allows users to like their favorite videos. Their friends can see that, can also like the video, and can discuss it with their friends.

✔ **Each video also integrates Facebook comments.** This provides a simple way to foster conversation about the video right on `JibJab.com`. Each comment prompts the user to also share that comment on Facebook, fostering even more conversation and bringing more users to the site.

JibJab was one of the pioneers in showing off what people can do with Facebook and integrating Facebook on one's own site. It is a prime example of "building a farm" using Facebook to bring Facebook users back to your own site.

HuffingtonPost

HuffingtonPost (`www.huffingtonpost.com`) is one of my favorite implementations of Facebook and Graph API. (See Figure 17-2.) First, some stats. According to a PaidContent article, HuffingtonPost

✔ Has millions of people interact with its "News Feed," a social experience showing what a user's friends are reading daily on the site

✔ Saw Facebook referral traffic up 48 percent from before it integrated Facebook on its site

✔ In less than one year, saw a 500 percent increase in visits on the site because of Facebook referrals

✔ Saw comments jump to 2.2 million from 1.2 million on the site in just one month

✔ Saw 15 percent of its comments come from Facebook.

The stats, I think, explain themselves, but if you try out the HuffingtonPost site, you'll see why its Facebook integration is so powerful. The social experience sucks you in. Immediately you're immersed with content shared from your friends and family, and soon you find that you're consuming content that you are more interested in — stuff your friends talk about, not just stuff that HuffingtonPost thinks you might like.

When you click the Social News section of HuffingtonPost, you are presented with a news feed of activity, somewhat similar to what you might see after logging in to Facebook. The news feed is populated by news articles that your friends on Facebook and Twitter are reading and sharing, and what they're commenting on. Click any article to read it, and your reading of the article will also be shared to your friends.

Figure 17-2:
Huffington Post's Social News Feed is a great way of looking at the news.

As more friends are added on Facebook, HuffingtonPost automatically adds their news items to the feed if they have logged in through Facebook on HuffingtonPost. If you first log in through Facebook, you're automatically presented with the news items that your friends have read. All this is done without the need of deciding who your friends are and whom you'd like to have participate. It all "just happens" — automatically! I think that's quite impressive.

On the side, a tally of stats is presented to you, showing you how many of your friends are commenting and how many news articles are being read. This creates a sense of competition or a sense of encouragement to ensure that your friends are also using the site. Straight from each article, one can share the article, quite simply, with his or her friends on Facebook, bringing more people back to the site.

Pandora

In 2010, Pandora (`www.pandora.com`) announced its own integration with Facebook's Graph API, as one of its initial launch partners for the new API. The idea of the integration was to allow Pandora's users to be able to listen to music that their friends and family like, integrating those elements into the already-brilliant music recommendation engine. (See Figure 17-3.)

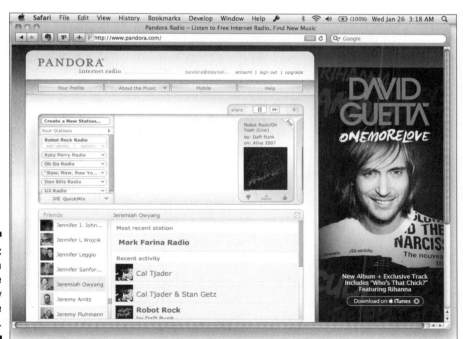

Figure 17-3: Pandora lets me see what my friends are listening to.

Pandora's integration is very simple:

- ✔ **Pandora allows you to see your "Friends' Music."** Clicking this gives you the option to authenticate with Facebook. When you do, you're immediately presented with a list of your friends on Facebook who use Pandora.

- ✔ **Pandora uses what your friends are listening to in order to suggest stations to you.** If you surf through your Facebook friends, you can see their recent music activity as well as other interests. It also appears that Pandora might pull in information from a user's likes and interests on his or her Facebook profile (but it's unclear whether that's the case).

- ✔ **As you're listening, you can also see which of your friends are listening.** A little bubble appears under each song that shows which of your friends like that song.

That's basically it, but it's very powerful to be able to see the music that your friends are listening to and listen to music that others close to you also like. It's a unique way to find new music.

To improve, Pandora could also include share links to share the songs you're listening to out to Facebook using `stream.publish`. In addition, it would be nice to see a live view of the stations your friends are listening to on the side so that you can switch stations and maybe even listen to music with your friends. Pandora could also integrate with Facebook Places to identify where you are and match music to the setting that you're currently in.

Digg.com

Digg (`www.digg.com`) is also one of my favorite Facebook integrations. (See Figure 17-4.) Digg doesn't boast much about it in public, but it really is one of the most brilliant uses of Facebook I've come across. Here are some of the things that Digg does with Facebook that impress me:

- ✔ **Offers one-click login and registration:** When you register or log in to Digg, you are given the option to just log in using your Facebook account. Clicking the "Login with Facebook" button takes you to your Facebook login page. Facebook authenticates you and takes you straight back to Digg, logged in if your Facebook authentication was successful.

- ✔ **Allows automatic friend addition:** The minute that you log in or register through Digg, you're immediately given the option to follow your friends on Facebook through Digg. You can also select a check box to automatically follow new friends who log in through Facebook on Digg. This means that any new friend you add on Facebook will automatically be added to Digg. In addition, every time you log in, you'll immediately be presented with a list of Diggs that your friends have posted instead of just the top news feed.

✔ **Shares to Facebook:** Digg has gone back and forth on this over the years. It used to be when you dug an article, you could set it to post that to Facebook. As I write this, I can't find that. However, you are presented with an option to share with your friends that you are on Facebook. When you click it, you are given the Facebook `stream.publish` dialog box, and users can post to Facebook that they are on Digg.

The very socialized experience that Digg provides makes it a powerful way of getting news from your friends and family. Not only does Digg present you with a list of news sorted by the top news stories from users on its site, but it also shows you a list of top news stories sorted by what your friends like, which can often be a much more relevant experience for each user.

In addition, as users see articles that their friends have dug, they are likely to comment and discuss those articles more. This means more time spent on the site, more people building interest in Digg's brand, and more people sharing Digg with their friends. Digg does this very well.

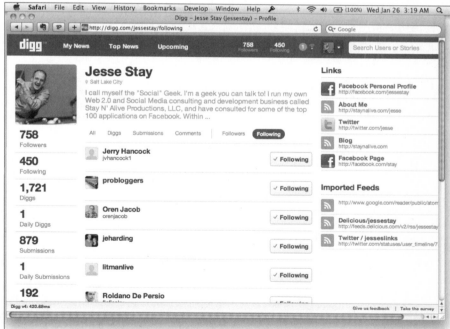

Figure 17-4:
Digg automatically adds my friends as they log in through Facebook.

FamilyLink

FamilyLink (www.familylink.com) started out as a Facebook application that existed on top of Facebook.com called "We're Related." The application worked to identify who your family members were on Facebook, and then sought to allow you to identify common ancestors between you and your friends.

In just a matter of days, FamilyLink went from just a few users to over 2 million users because of what Facebook offered, encouraging people to invite their friends and family to use the application. (See Figure 17-5.) The application used the following integration points, to name a few, to become popular:

- ✔ **The news feed:** FamilyLink posted updates to users' news feeds when new family members were connected. This got others aware of the connections being made, encouraging others to also want to try out the application.

- ✔ **Application invites:** This, I believe, was a key part to FamilyLink's success. Throughout each step of the process, users of the application were encouraged to invite their friends to become members of their family tree. An invitation from a family member is a lot of pressure to try out an application, and the invitations were worded such that it almost seemed necessary to join the family tree so that the family tree could be completed. Recipients were asked to "accept" the add, and when they did, they too were required to authorize the We're Related application, and they were encouraged to build their own family tree.

- ✔ **E-mail updates:** Later, FamilyLink was able to get permission from users to collect their e-mail addresses as they authenticated with the application. This allowed FamilyLink, following CAN-SPAM guidelines, to send regular e-mail updates to its users, keeping the users in the loop and aware of updates to their family tree. Before e-mail, FamilyLink did this with "updates," which were sent to users' Facebook Updates sections in their Facebook Inbox.

- ✔ **Profile information:** FamilyLink used the profile information of its users to collect names, images, and other information about family members. This made it so that users weren't stuck trying to find pictures and other information from all their family members repeatedly. The information was already in Facebook, so why not use it?

- ✔ **Custom tabs:** This is an early feature of Facebook that has since been deprecated. It used to be that on user profiles (you can still do this on Facebook Pages, remember), you could create custom tabs that users could add to their Facebook profile. FamilyLink had one; I think it was called "Family." The profile, being one of the most visited pieces of Facebook, would attract users to that Family tab, because users wanted to know what their friends' families were like. They would get curious and start using the application. At least that's how I envision it worked for FamilyLink, and I'm sure that it saw success from that.

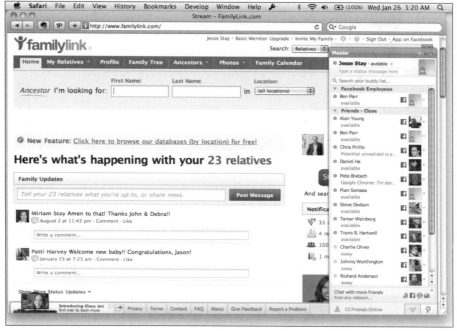

Figure 17-5:
FamilyLink
presents a
news feed
of my family
based on my
Facebook
contacts as
I log in.

As FamilyLink evolved, it created its own Web site for identifying and collaborating with family members around family history. The site itself integrates very well with Facebook, and it continues to grow.

To register for the site, all one has to do is click the big blue Connect with Facebook button, and that person is in. Users are immediately prompted to give permission to access some additional information about themselves, which FamilyLink can then use to build the experience for the users.

When you get into the site, you are greeted with a Facebook-like news feed, already populated with your family members on Facebook's latest updates. The site uses Meebo to integrate Facebook Chat and allow you to chat with family members. You can look up family events, birthdays, and other things that are happening within your family. You can also see which relatives are adding information to their family trees.

The site uses numerous Facebook integration points to build its experience through Facebook:

✔ **One-click login/registration:** To register, if you have a Facebook account, you can log in with one click. FamilyLink also gets permission to get additional information from you. (Beware, the site forces you to post on your friends' walls when you add friends to your family tree, something I don't recommend. This is borderline on Facebook's terms of service.)

- **Use of the news feed:** FamilyLink takes the entire news feed on Facebook and extracts the updates from people whom you have identified as family members. It then organizes just those family members into one feed on the site.

- **Access to family lists:** Facebook allows users to identify their family members and puts them into a list. Developers have access to this list and others that the user has created, with the user's permission. FamilyLink uses this to identify your family members, and it automatically populates the site with that information.

- **Facebook chat:** I don't cover it much in this book, but you can find out about it in Facebook's Developer documentation. Facebook provides an XMPP interface to chat that you can take advantage of. FamilyLink uses this, in coordination with Meebo, to allow you to chat with your family members, from FamilyLink, on Facebook.

- **Access to birthdays and other profile information:** For a family-oriented site, birthdays are critical! FamilyLink will remind you of your family members' birthdays when they are coming up. FamilyLink also integrates with your Facebook events to show a calendar of events that your family members are scheduled to attend.

Sometimes FamilyLink sends out too many updates and has at times tried tricking users into thinking they have to use the app to "accept" a relative request, so they can be a bit spammy. However, I really do like the extent that the site has gone toward integrating Facebook into its environment. With a few tweaks, I think it could remove the "spammy" stigma and really go far.

FamilyLink has since expanded even further, and it is now integrating with a new virtual gaming site called Family Village. This new site seeks to award people for connecting with family and collaborating around family history.

JumpStart

JumpStart (www.jumpstart.com) has an interesting challenge in front of it. It's a gaming site for kids, mostly under age 13. The problem is that Facebook is for people ages 13 and up. So what would a site like JumpStart be using Facebook for, you may ask?

JumpStart used Facebook to target the parents of children. With Facebook, parents can share what their kids are doing on the site with their friends, and find ways to interact better with other parents whose kids are using the site. (See Figure 17-6.)

Figure 17-6:
JumpStart
allows
adults to
register and
log in with
a single
click of the
Facebook
Login
button.

As a parent, it's powerful for me to meet the parents of whom my kids are interacting with. That's why it's fun to see other parents' updates in my stream, sharing what their kids have done in the game. It makes me want to discuss with them how our kids can meet.

JumpStart has a very simple Facebook integration. It has two basic integration points:

- ✔ **Single sign-on and registration:** It takes parents basically one click to identify that they're over 18, and they can autopopulate the information that JumpStart needs to register them. This speeds registration and makes it easier for them to get to the part of setting up their kids in the game. In addition, parents just need their Facebook login to log in to the site and get their kids playing the game.

- ✔ **Publish to Facebook:** As kids accomplish new things in the game, JumpStart updates the parents' feeds for their friends to see. This fosters conversation and gets parents talking with other parents about the game, bringing more kids to play JumpStart.

Although it is very simple, JumpStart uses Facebook in a very unique way to spread something targeted toward young kids through their parents.

Cinch

Cinch (www.cinchcast.com), owned by BlogTalk Radio, is a site devoted to allowing people to very simply share sound bites of information with their friends. Think of it as Twitter for audio. With Cinch, simplicity is key.

With Cinch, it starts with the premise that with a simple phone call and no account, you can start using the site to post audio. Then, when you associate your phone number with the site, your audio is automatically linked with the site.

When I worked with Cinch, it wanted to take this simple concept further into Facebook and Twitter. We took the basic, similar premise and made it so that with a simple click on the Facebook or Twitter Login button, you could immediately register for the site and start posting audio updates.

Cinch also created an iPhone app that integrates with Facebook (see Figure 17-7), and using your Facebook login there, you can also log in or register for the site, as well as publish back to Facebook when you post your audio update.

Cinch uses numerous integration points:

- **Single sign-on and registration:** As I mention earlier, it takes one click and you're in. Cinch then asks you for additional information along the way, but immediately you can get started posting updates to the site. This minimizes the barrier to entry and makes it much easier for users to get started and try out the site.

- **Access to friends:** Cinch also uses your Facebook friend list to find other Cinch users who are in your friend list. Cinch can then organize a news feed of audio updates from your friends that immediately appears after you log in the first time with that one click. With one click, you immediately see the audio updates of your friends on Cinch without having to do anything else — that's powerful!

- **Publishing to Facebook:** Cinch also allows users to select a check box when they post updates to Cinch that also posts those updates to Facebook. When the updates go to the user's Facebook news feed, other friends of that user can listen to the audio right on Facebook without ever having to leave the site. This promotes conversation and builds buzz about the product.

Cinch is a very effective use of Facebook Platform. I recommend that you play with it a bit and see how Cinch embraces Facebook. It's one that I think others should model after (and one that I helped design, so you know it has my stamp of approval!).

Figure 17-7:
Cinch's
iPhone
app allows
you to
post audio
updates to
Facebook by
selecting a
check box.

SocialToo

SocialToo (www.socialtoo.com) is my own Web site, so it should be the cream of the crop. (See Figure 17-8.) I started the site with a focus on Twitter, though, ironically. I do have some Facebook integration included right now that I think you can learn from, and a lot more is on the way, so stay tuned!

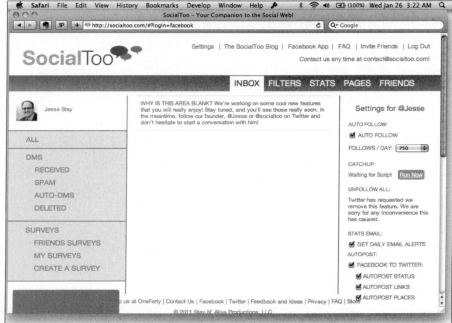

Figure 17-8:
You can
post
updates
from
Facebook
to Twitter
using
SocialToo.

SocialToo is a tool for managing your reputation as a brand online. It's built to help you build relationships on the social networks that you belong to and to track those relationships along the way.

Here are the ways that I embrace Facebook:

✔ **Single sign-on and registration:** SocialToo was one of the first sites I know that integrated a single sign-on solution for Facebook. I built it because I knew that all my users were either Twitter or Facebook users. I had no reason to integrate a traditional login system into the site. Therefore, I removed the traditional login completely and replaced it with two buttons on the home page: a Facebook Login button and a Twitter Login button. With one click, whether you're registered or not, you're into the site, and I immediately present you with things that you can do with your Facebook and Twitter relationships. Because signup is so simple, I saw great success in new users joining the site and trying out its features.

✔ **News feed use:** One of the site's most popular free features (many features are for a monthly fee) is the capability to publish status updates, links, and places check-ins to Twitter from your Facebook profile. I

detect new updates to Facebook and then publish those out to an associated Twitter account. I just use the feed Graph API calls to access this
data, and I poll it regularly. Of course, I could always improve it by integrating Facebook's real-time API on top of it all, something I hope to do
at some point if it makes sense.

✔ **Publishing to Facebook:** Another free product that I offer is the capability to share simple polls to your friends through Facebook. You
create the poll, and you can very simply share the poll on Twitter and
Facebook. I then prompt the user to share it with his or her friends.

✔ **Custom page tabs:** One lesser-known feature (it may be more known by
the time you read this, I hope!) is the capability that I provide to create
promotions for your Facebook Page. Users can click a simple Enter
button from a custom Facebook Page tab that I provide, and I can even
require them to like the page to enter. Then those users get entered into
a sweepstakes for a giveaway or discount of some sort that you provide
for them. I obtain permission to get their e-mail address, and you get
their name and e-mail address in a nice interface when they win so that
you can e-mail them. This is something that any of our users can contact
me to implement.

✔ **Facebook search:** One feature that is slated to launch shortly before this
book goes to print is a feature that allows businesses to track what is
being said about them on Facebook public status updates. This can be a
valuable way of finding out, on Facebook, what is being said about you
or your brand when users and Facebook Pages want to share that with
the world. This simply uses Facebook search to find relevant updates
from keywords that you specify.

I'm of course biased in promoting SocialToo, but if you're looking for a simple
tool to avoid building custom apps that do these sorts of things, SocialToo is
a great site to use for this kind of stuff.

Quora

As I write this, Quora (`www.quora.com`) is all the rage. Quora is a question-
and-answer site with a Wiki twist. (See Figure 17-9.) Users can post any question, assign and remove topics for those questions, and answer questions
from their friends and topics that they follow. They can then vote up the
answers from people who provide the most interesting and relevant answers
to those questions.

Figure 17-9:
Clicking the
Up button
next to an
answer
allows you
to like the
answer on
Facebook.

Quora, founded by one of the founders of Facebook, should have no excuse not to integrate Facebook. Indeed it does. In fact, it uses some undocumented features that I share in a bit. Quora's very simple Facebook integration just allows users to associate a Facebook account and post answers or questions to their friends on Facebook through the news feed.

However, Quora does a couple of more advanced things that I really like:

- **Quora pulls in your Facebook friends list and organizes your news feed through it.** You might notice after you associate a Facebook account on Quora that you start to get e-mail updates about all your Facebook friends following you on the site. This is because they're immediately being presented with a list of their Facebook friends to follow on the site when they do the same. You get regular e-mails, and you're constantly reminded that Quora is getting a lot of use by your friends. This is partly why Quora has become so popular so quickly.

✔ **Quora allows users to auto-assign the Vote Up button to answers to also like those answers on Facebook.** This is the undocumented feature I mention earlier. Developers can, with special permission from Facebook, be added to a whitelist on Facebook's servers that allows developers to automatically like a Facebook Page through Facebook's API. Quora uses this, and as a result, it can push likes, with the user's permission, to Facebook when the user clicks a simple Vote Up button on answers on the site. You'll find no Facebook Like buttons on the site. Whether you can get the whitelisted Like button like Quora has is still a question (no pun intended), but I do recommend trying to get in touch with Facebook and seeing what it can do for your Web site or application, especially if your company is paying Facebook advertising dollars.

Instagram

Instagram (www.instragram.com) is a mobile application that allows users to take photos, apply filters to those photos, and share them with their friends. (See Figure 17-10.) Instagram has a very simple Facebook integration. It has two basic integration points, which have made the application quite popular:

✔ **Auto-add Facebook friends:** On Instagram, users are prompted to add their friends through Facebook friends that Instagram has detected through Graph API are already using Instagram. These friends' updates then get shown in each user's news feed on the Instagram application.

✔ **Publish to Facebook:** When you publish a new photo, you can also post this to Facebook. This posts the photo in your news feed on Facebook, with a link back to Instagram to view the bigger version of the picture.

Although they are very simple, these two features have made Instagram a big hit, and it's one of the top iPhone applications in the iTunes App Store. As you can see, you can still integrate very simple Facebook features and be successful.

Figure 17-10: Instagram allows you to share any of your photos to Facebook.

Chapter 18

Top Ten Facebook Application Development Resources

* *

*T*he first things you need to know when developing your application are whom to ask, where to look, and how to find the information you need when you're in a bind. Facebook has a help section (available in the footer of Facebook via Help), but a help section isn't ever going to help you find out how to develop applications. A number of resources are available to get you through the difficulties you're experiencing. Facebook is known to frequently change its documentation, and it's known to have ambiguous documentation at times. For this reason, you probably need someone to help you when Facebook's documentation doesn't offer what you're looking for.

When Facebook doesn't answer your question, and this book doesn't get you where you need to go, consult with the following social resources to get those questions answered. Remember, you're not alone!

In this chapter, I compile resources that can help you to be a better Facebook developer and marketer. These are my ten favorites!

Facebook's Developer Forum

The Facebook Developer Forum (http://forum.developers.facebook.com) should always be one of your first resources for finding information. (See Figure 18-1.) Always search for your problem before asking someone else about it, because with thousands of answers, you're bound to find a thread that answers your question. Also, occasionally a Facebook employee may chime in, as they like to hang out and make sure questions are getting answered.

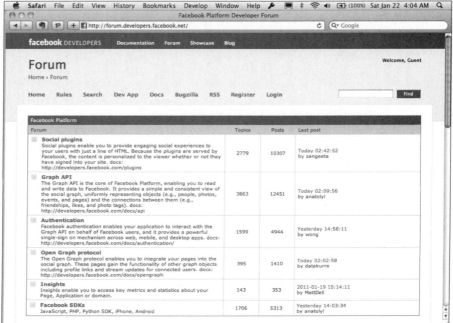

Figure 18-1:
Facebook's
Developer
Forum
should
be one of
the first
resources
you visit
when you
need help.

The search box for the forum is in the upper-right corner of the page. Use this to search for your question. Enter any keyword or phrase that you think might return the results that you need.

When you search, a list of all the items that match your search query will appear. They will be sorted by the most recent, first. Each will be in its own topic, showing the person's response that matches your keyword. Click the topic name to see the full thread (or click Go to Post).

As I write this, Developer Forum is organized into five basic sections:

- ✔ **Facebook Platform:** These are general questions about Facebook development and access to the API.

- ✔ **Basics:** Here you can find questions about getting started on Facebook Platform, updates from Facebook, and policies, and you can also leave feedback.

- ✔ **Technical:** This is more a miscellaneous discussion for platform topics, and it covers some of the older Facebook APIs and access points, but it also covers desktop, mobile, and handheld questions.

- ✔ **Business:** If you have any questions or want to start a discussion on a business-related topic, this is a great place to get your questions answered. If you have a job opening, you can post that here. Any advertising questions? This is also a great place to go.

🖊 **Archived Topics:** These are all the deprecated areas of Facebook, or areas that are announced to be deprecated. If your app still uses an old API, you can look here. This is also a fun place to discover more about the history of Facebook and see how Facebook Platform used to be.

To create your own topic for discussion, follow these steps:

1. **Go to** `forum.developers.facebook.com.`

2. **Log in.**

   Interestingly enough, Facebook still hasn't integrated your Facebook login into this experience. If you haven't registered on the Forum, you'll also need to register.

3. **Pick the topic that's applicable to the question or discussion point you have.**

4. **Click Post New Topic.**

   Enter a subject for your post and your message to start a discussion. If your post has punctuation sequences like ":)," ";)," or similar ones (that is, character sequences that aren't intended to be emoticons or smiley faces), select the Never Show Smileys as Icons for This Post check box. Also, if you want to be e-mailed when new people answer your post, click Subscribe to This Topic.

5. **Click Submit and wait for responses.**

Any new response to your post will be sent to the e-mail address that you specified in registration. To respond to the topic, click the link in the e-mail and fill out the form with your new comments.

Another secret I like to use to get help is to use the Comments sections for each of the topics on `developers.facebook.com`. If you go to many pages on the Developer documentation, you'll see a Facebook comments Discussion section. (See Figure 18-2.)

If you leave a comment there, someone will probably be able to help you with the issue related to the topic that you're reading. Often, the Facebook engineer or employee who is working on that particular feature monitors those comments, and you may even get a response from Facebook itself, so don't be afraid to try.

This can be a great approach to getting an "official" answer. Even if not, it's a great way to let Facebook know what the issues are or what problems the developers are having.

Figure 18-2:
Many
sections in
Facebook's
Developer
documenta-
tion have
Discussion
sections,
where you
can ask
questions
and get
answers.

Facebook Application Development For Dummies — the Facebook Group

I've created a Facebook group just for this book, so you can find help from me and other readers who have similar problems. (See Figure 18-3.) To join or post discussion topics, follow these steps:

1. **Send an e-mail to** dummiesgroup@facebook.com, **and your question will appear in the group.**

   You can go to http://stay.am/dummiesgroup and ask to join. I generally approve requests to join pretty quickly, so just wait and you'll be in the group in no time!

2. **Post your question or topic, or join in other conversations!**

Invite your friends! After you're in the group, don't hesitate to invite your friends whom you think could benefit from the group. You can do this by clicking the Add Friends to Group link in the right column and selecting the friends you'd like to add. They'll immediately be added and can start partici-pating with everyone else.

Figure 18-3:
This book's Facebook group can be an excellent place to collaborate with other readers and get the answers you need. Come join our community!

Facebook Groups offers you all sorts of great ways to collaborate with other Facebook users. In this case, you'll be collaborating and conversing with other readers of this book. Here are some things you can do with this book's Facebook group:

✓ **Post discussion points:** This is the default status area at the top. Feel free to introduce yourself. Ask a question. Share what you're working on, or whatever you feel like talking about. This is a great place to meet other people who are reading this book who are interested in Facebook development or marketing in general.

✓ **Share links:** Have an interesting link that you want to share? Post it here for other readers of the book and interested developers to read. This is a great way to share knowledge and get others' thoughts on the latest and greatest news of the day.

✓ **Ask questions:** At the moment, you can use the Post section at the top to do this. At some point in the future, you might also use Facebook Questions to post questions to a group. Use this to get the answers that you need to tough programming topics.

✓ **Share photos and videos:** I want to see your photos with the book! In fact, let's play "spot the book." If you post a Facebook Application Development For Dummies sighting in your place of work, I'll randomly pick offices that have the book in their library and send your place of work an additional copy that you can either keep in the office or give to a hard-working employee of your choice. I want to see photos, screen shots of your application, and video screen casts of what you're working on. Feel free to post whatever you like, and get people talking about it! (By the way, this same request applies to this book's Facebook Page as well.)

✔ **Share your Facebook development or marketing event:** Having a Facebook Developers Garage? Having a meet-up or conference some-where? Share these with the group, and maybe others in the area can also find out about the event.

✔ **Share documents about Facebook:** This is a great place to share white papers, studies, or maybe research papers you did in school. I'd love to see what you come up with!

✔ **Chat with other group members:** You can also initiate a group chat with other members in the group by clicking the Facebook Application Development For Dummies chat box in the lower-right corner of your browser window (next to Chat). You can turn this on and off in your group settings.

Facebook Application Development For Dummies — the Facebook Page

I'd be doing you a disservice if I didn't tell you about this book's Facebook Page as well, which I also mention in a few other places in the book. The book's Facebook Page (see Figure 18-4) is a great place to find these items:

✔ **Updates about the book:** If I have any corrections or new news sur-rounding items in this book, I'm going to try to list these here as they become available. Also, as new editions come out, this will be where you can subscribe to get updates.

✔ **The newest news about Facebook and Facebook development:** I'll fre-quently share links with the latest Facebook-related news as it develops.

✔ **Discounts and promotions on the book:** Hopefully, I'll provide several promotions, enabling you and your friends to get special deals on the book. It's also here that you can share the photos of book spottings in your office and other unique places. I may randomly pick some of these offices to send them free copies of the book.

✔ **Events surrounding the book:** As I speak, or travel, I may do book sign-ings, and you might have other opportunities to find out about Facebook development. I'll post these here.

✔ **The capability to sign up for my newsletter:** At some point in the near future after I write this, I hope to provide a newsletter that you can subscribe to in order to get more exclusive tips on Facebook development. Stay tuned to the Facebook Page for more information about this.

To subscribe to this book's Facebook Page, go to `http://facebook.com/dummiesbook` and click Like. Go do it now!

By default, Facebook doesn't send e-mail notifications when it has new updates on a Facebook Page. You can get updates on this book's Facebook Page in two ways:

✔ **Add the book's RSS feed to your RSS reader.** You can do this by adding `http://facebook.com/feeds/page.php?format=atom10 &amp;id=120809261289270` to your preferred RSS reader. Any new posts on the page will go to your RSS reader now.

✔ **Use HyperAlerts to notify you by e-mail when updates are available.** HyperAlerts is a free service that can send you e-mail alerts when new posts or comments on pages are available that you want to monitor. Go to `http://alerts.hyperinteraktiv.no` and add `facebook.com/dummiesbook` after registering, and you're set!

Figure 18-4:
If you haven't done so yet, now is a good time to like this book's Facebook Page so that you get important announcements and information.

Contacting Facebook

A little-known fact is that you can actually contact Facebook when you have a question about Facebook Platform. (See Figure 18-5.) You should keep these requests limited to only special requests that you need for your application. If you need to have whitelisting on anything in particular (such as the capability to like something via the API, as I mention in the Quora example in Chapter 17), for instance, or maybe have an exception to Facebook Platform's policy, this is the form to use. The form that you can use to contact Facebook is at

```
http://www.facebook.com/help/contact.php?show_form=dev_support
```

Again, use this sparingly. Facebook is also often fairly slow at responding to requests submitted through this form, so you may be better off using the other communication and contact channels I mention previously.

Figure 18-5:
As a last resort, you can try contacting Facebook to get your questions answered, but don't expect an answer immediately!

Facebook Developer Documentation

Facebook Developer documentation (see Figure 18-6) is the most thorough resource that you'll find on Facebook development. I cover this thoroughly in Chapter 1, so I encourage you to refer to that chapter for more details. Suffice to say, though, that anything you need to find out about Facebook development can be found somewhere at `developers.facebook.com`.

Figure 18-6: Become familiar with the Facebook Developer documentation — it will be your friend as you discover what you can and can't do on Facebook Platform.

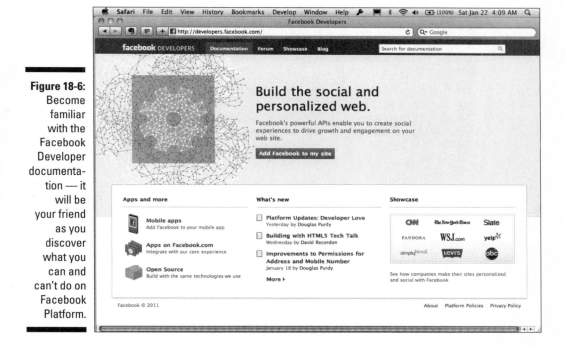

StayNAlive.com

StayNAlive.com is my blog. Look for a tab called Dummies. It's here that I provide a section devoted to educating you about Facebook development. Look for tutorials, Webinars, screen casts, and more to result from this section.

In addition, I blog semiregularly here, and when I do, I cover both Facebook-related news and information. I also cover things outside of Facebook related to social media and things you might have heard of in the news. I often cover misperceptions in the media and debunk myths. I'm certainly not shy to share opinions, and basically, anything I find that you might be interested in, I share it here.

Subscribe by adding it to your RSS feed through the URL `http://staynalive.com/feed`. You can also subscribe via e-mail via the appropriate links on the site.

MariSmith.com

If you're a developer looking to gain a better grasp of what you can do with Facebook and Facebook marketing, or if you're a marketer just trying to find out more in your field, Mari Smith doesn't disappoint. Her Web site is chock-full of how-tos and other information on how to use Facebook as a productive tool and how you can use it to grow your business and profit from Facebook. (See Figure 18-7.)

Figure 18-7:
Mari Smith's Web site is a great resource for discovering what you can do with Facebook and how you can get value out of it for yourself and your business.

InsideNetwork and InsideFacebook.com

Mari Smith will dazzle you with her happy personality and excite you about new features and new ways that you can use Facebook. If you have questions about anything regarding Facebook, you'll probably find something here to spark your interest. Subscribe and check back often!

`InsideFacebook.com` is a great blog, founded by Justin Smith, that focuses on Facebook news and information. (See Figure 18-8.) Part of the InsideNetwork, InsideFacebook is the general Facebook news piece of what the site offers.

InsideNetwork also provides several other, more specific, Facebook-related blogs. Specifically, it has the following sites:

- **InsideFacebook.com:** This site focuses on the more general Facebook-related articles. By subscribing to this site, if you were to pick only one source, you generally get all the updates you need about Facebook from this one. Go to the others, though, if you can't get enough about Facebook.

- **InsideSocialGames.com:** This site focuses on specific social games. Some of these aren't Facebook related, but any game, such as FarmVille, that has a social aspect to it will be covered on this blog.

- **InsideMobileApps.com:** If you're passionate about mobile, come here to get your mobile fix. You can find all kinds of news, tips, and secrets about the iPad, iPhone, Android, Windows Phone, and other types of mobile apps that are available.

- **InsideVirtualGoods.com:** Virtual goods and currency are the hot topics among Facebook developers these days. Using Facebook Credits and other online currencies, games can sell things that are completely virtual, and you can have a pretty successful business off of that income. This blog focuses on all the news surrounding virtual goods and discusses where this booming industry is going.

- **AppData.com:** This is another fascinating site. If you want to find out what the top apps on Facebook are at any given point in time, come here. AppData organizes all the latest apps and information currently available about Facebook.

- **InsideFacebook Gold:** If you're a social strategist like I am, you should consider this subscription-based service. InsideFacebook Gold is literally a gold mine of information about the progress of Facebook and where it stands in the world today. InsideFacebook Gold provides articles and statistics about the use of Facebook around the world and describes how brands are using this information for success.

Figure 18-8:
Inside
Facebook.
com is a
great news
resource
for getting
up-to-date
informa-
tion about
Facebook.

InsideFacebook Gold is somewhat expensive (depending on your budget), at $295 per month or $695 for three months. It's a service that's certainly worth its weight in gold though, and it can get you information that you need to stay competitive in your industry with other businesses that are on Facebook.

AllFacebook.com

AllFacebook.com, founded by Nic O'Neil, is a blog that is part of WebMediaBrands (owner of MediaBistro). AllFacebook.com is a great resource for news and information about Facebook. (See Figure 18-9.)

AllFacebook.com is the site's blog and news source for Facebook-related news and information. You can pretty much guarantee that by subscribing to both this blog and InsideFacebook.com, you'll get every piece of Facebook-related news that's available. The two are very thorough in their coverage of Facebook.

Similar to InsideFacebook's `AppData.com`, `AllFacebook.com` has a stats section for both application statistics and page statistics. The application statistics show just about every bit of information about the top developers and applications on Facebook. The page statistics are a great place to find out about what pages are trending on Facebook at any given point in time.

SocialTimes is AllFacebook's general social-related blog. If you don't want to just pick up on Facebook-related news, this site can give you more general social-related news.

Like InsideFacebook Gold, SocialTimes has a premium plan as well. For $149 monthly or $999 per year, you can subscribe to this premium content service, which provides all sorts of information about what other brands are doing socially on the Web and what demographic information you need to lead a successful social campaign.

Figure 18-9:
All
Facebook.
com is
another
great news
resource for
getting the
latest news
and updates
about
Facebook.

Facebook Blogs

If you want to go straight to the source, Facebook has several blogs that you'll want to subscribe to. From here, you can generate your own opinions, but you'll always have the news, as it's released by Facebook. Facebook's blogs include the following:

- ✔ **Facebook's Official Company Blog:** You can access this at `http://blog.facebook.com`. (See Figure 18-10.) Here you frequently see updates from Facebook's CEO, Mark Zuckerberg. This is where you can get any and all official updates from Facebook regarding its user interface and the general user experience. Don't go here if you just want to get updates about Facebook Platform, though.

- ✔ **Facebook's Developer Blog:** This is available at `http://developers.facebook.com/blog` (and also via the Blog link at `developers.facebook.com`). This is where Facebook posts all news surrounding Facebook's Developer platform. If there are ever any new updates, Developer events, or deprecations to code, Facebook will post those here. This is an important blog that you'll want to subscribe to as a developer.

- ✔ **Facebook's Engineering Blog:** If you want to really geek out, this is one of my favorites. This isn't really a blog, per se, but rather the Notes section of Facebook Engineering's Facebook Page. You can access it and the RSS feed via `www.facebook.com/notes.php?id=9445547199`.

  This blog is where Facebook's engineers all share what they are doing behind the scenes to build Facebook. Facebook has a massive infrastructure, and this is where the developers who are working on that infrastructure share their experiences working in that environment. If you're a coder geek like I am, a systems geek, or an infrastructure geek, you'll definitely want to check out this blog.

Figure 18-10:
Facebook's company blog is just one of several official Facebook blogs that you can access to get new updates about the site.

Index

• U •

until parameter of paging variable, 210
Update Notification E-mail setting, 64
Update requests (REST), 136
Update Settings IP Whitelist setting, 64
updates
  admin privileges for posting, 127
  avoiding spam, 109
  call to action for, 108
  callback URLs for, 233–234
  ease of, 211
  to Facebook APIs, enabling and
    disabling, 328
  to Facebook Page, notifying users of,
    108–109
  to Facebook Pages, regular, 106–107
  increment counter for notifying users
    of, 80–82
  POST requests for, 211
  posting a status update, 100
  posting to users' news feeds, 83–85
  prompting users before, 212–219
  real-time APIs for, 227–237
  sending through Applications and Games
    Dashboard, 92–93
  subscriptions for, 233–237
  targeting your audience, 109
URL Linter, 273–274
user object for subscriptions, 234
user search type, 241
user support address for application, 57
user_about_me pp, 172
user_activities permission, 172
user_birthday permission, 173
user_check-ins permission, 174
user_education_history
  permission, 173
user_events permission, 173
user_groups permission, 173
user_hometown permission, 173
user_interests permission, 173
user_likes permission, 173
user_location permission, 173
user_message_prompt parameter of
  FB.ui call, 85

user_notes permission, 173
user_online_presence permission, 173
user_photo_video_tags
  permission, 173
user_photos permission, 173
user_relationship_details
  permission, 173
user_relationships permission, 173
user_religion_politics
  permission, 173
user_status permission, 173
user_videos permission, 174
user_Web site permission, 174
user_work_history permission, 174
username selection page, 101–102
Users analytics from Insights
  for applications, 294–296
  for Facebook Pages, 290, 292
  for Web sites, 290

• V •

Vander Veer, Emily A. (*JavaScript For
  Dummies*), 43
verify_token parameter for POST
  requests, 235
vim text editor, 29
visibility, Like buttons for achieving,
  116–117

• W •

wap dialog box display type, 213
Warning! icon, 6
Web site insights
  accessing, 288–289
  Demographics section, 290
  illustrated, 291
  integrating into your Web site, 299–301
  Sharing section, 289–290
  Users section, 290
Web sites. *See also* Facebook Pages
  accessing Insights for, 288–289
  adding user's friends' profile pictures, 164
  analytics for, 177
  data flow for Facebook interaction, 20–21